Divine Vibrations

By
Prof. Anil Kumar

Publications Division

PRASANTHI NILAYAM

SRI SATHYA SAI SADHANA TRUST,
Publications Division

Prasanthi Nilayam - 515 134
Anantapur District, Andhra Pradesh, INDIA
STD: 08555 ISD: 91-8555 Phone: 287375 Fax: 287236
E-mail: orders@sssbpt.org

ISBN: 978-93-5069-022-2

First Edition: April 2013, Reprint: October 2013

Published by
The Convener,
Sri Sathya Sai Sadhana Trust, Publications Division
Prasanthi Nilayam, India, Pin Code - 515134
STD : 08555 ISD: 91-8555 Phone: 287375 Fax: 287236

Printed at
Createspace

Publisher's Note

Bhagawan Sri Sathya Sai Baba has declared, "I am within you, in front of you, behind you, above you, and around you; I am everywhere," "Why fear when I am here," "I am with you to guide and guard." These assurances of the Lord are really proven beyond any doubt at this juncture, when Bhagawan has transformed Himself from 'Form' to 'Formless'.

Prof. K. Anil Kumar, the chosen translator of Bhagawan's Divine Discourses into English, always echoes 'His Master's Voice', elaborates and explains in his own simple, straightforward, and humorous style the teaching and philosophy of Bhagawan. In this interesting volume, titled 'Divine Vibrations', the Professor has succinctly put Bhagawan's teachings, the significance and benefits of the Darshan of the 'Maha Samadhi' of Bhagawan and the future of Sai's Mission in the lectures, which he delivered in foreign countries and to foreigners in Prasanthi Nilayam, after Swami's Maha Samadhi. This also includes interesting and spiritually elevating Questions and Answers sessions.

The Publications Division of Sri Sathya Sai Sadhana Trust gladly presents this volume to the ardent spiritual readers for their spiritual elevation and carrying on Sai's Mission further, with added zeal. It is hoped that this volume is welcomed and better received by the readers.

Dated: 26th January, 2013
Prasanthi Nilayam

Convener
Publications Division

Editor's Note

SWAMI has shuffled off his mortal coil, but with the following emphatic Parthian Shot: "Know that I am within and without you. There is no difference. My Darsan will pour forth from ME to and through you. You may be unaware of this constant action. Be ever pure of heart and soul, and mankind in your life time will benefit from your unique qualities."

Many have experienced divine vibrations while bowing down to the Maha Divya Samadhi. The contents of this fine volume, echoing our Master's Voice, are also divine vibrations with a difference, which must needs now tingle in every drop of our blood. Personally, I even feel, hope, and pray to Bhagawan that our veteran orator – Professor, a veritable SAI Kumar, who has hitherto left no stone unturned in his magnificent speeches everywhere, to inject the noblest ideals into the various compartments of our brain, will hereafter boldly and enthusiastically embark on the noble and sacred mission of continuously exhorting, in his own unique way, in his multifarious discourses here and abroad, all the SAI devotees of this world, to try their best in their precious life's sojourn to get themselves so elevated as to become embodiments of the SAI message in action and be role models to posterity.

P.V. Vaidyanathan
Thiruvananthapuram

v

Contents

Questions And Answers Session
Part I

(Sunday Talk by Prof. Anil Kumar, October 9th, 2011)

Can We Do Abhishekam To His Statue?

Q: Now that Swami has left His body, can we do abhishekam (a ritual of ablutions and symbolic offerings) to His statue?

A: This question has taken for granted a point, with which I beg to differ. This point is that, "Swami has now left His body." But, Baba clearly says, "You are not the body." So, how can He be the body? After death, the body has to be left; nobody is exempt from this.

Now, if we say that Swami has left His body — that is only our observation. It is only a physical, superficial, external happening, an event. It is better to say, "Swami has dropped His body."

So, can we do abhishekam to His statue? Well, the statue is different from the physical body. Perhaps, most of you know the meaning of lingam. It is one sign or symbol of Divinity. We do abhishekam to the lingam. There is nothing wrong in doing that.

Similarly, we can do abhishekam to His statue. (I don't think anybody ever did abhishekam to His physical body.) When you do abhishekam to His statue, you identify Him with Siva and the Siva linga. You hold the awareness that it is only an idol, but this idol will take you to the ideal.

Travelling from idol to ideal is the purpose behind abhishekam and so, there is nothing wrong in doing abhishekam.

The 86th Birthday Celebration

Q: When we celebrate Swami's birthday, what should that programme be called? Should it be called 'The 86th Birthday Celebration', or something else?

A: It can only be the 86th Birthday. We celebrate the 60th anniversary of Independence Day, or the 70th anniversary of Independence Day, or the 100th birthday of the Father of the Nation, and so on.

Celebrations are in that mode, because they are celebrations of eternal, immortal souls, who had neither a beginning, nor an end. Their memories are cherished forever and ever. Their lives are a benediction, an example for humanity to emulate and follow, and so, we continue to celebrate their birthdays. You don't have to search for another name.

Erroneous Notions

There is another wish, which some people have when they say, "Swami, I want to serve You in my next life."

Our Bhagawan is very smart and He would reply, "It is enough, if you serve Me properly in this life and forget about the next life!"

Some people say, "Swami, we want to die for You."

Swami will immediately say, "Live for Me, but don't die." We have to live for God, not die for God.

Recently, there was another foolish wave of thought floating about everywhere. It seems that Swami appeared in a dream, telling He had left this place (Prasanthi Nilayam)! When Swami says, "I am everywhere," where is the question of leaving this place? This is a Himalayan blunder.

Also, Baba gave a promise to His mother as well, "I will not leave this place."

If we say, "He left this place," it is an act of cheating the public and a betrayal of His words. We should not do that. Do you want to hijack or kidnap Him from here, or what? It is foolishness.

I have had forty years of association with Swami and twenty of them were very intimate. So, this gives me some credence, when I say His feeling is this, **"There is no place equal to Prasanthi Nilayam. There are no greater devotees than My devotees. There is no university greater than My university. This planet has not seen better students than My students. If there is any place, where there is peace, harmony, and brotherhood, this is that place!"**

Prasanthi Nilayam
And Swami's Students Are 'Number One'

For Swami, with His message of 'God is only one', to appear in a dream and declare, "I left that place," is something that only a fool could say. And only double-fools could believe it!

I have some common sense and have studied His literature. In addition, I have mingled with Him very, very intimately. Therefore (within the limits of my intellect), I have some idea of His message in that regard. He is so possessive, so very possessive.

Swami was talking at the Madras Assembly, where there were four governors, six central cabinet ministers, and four chief ministers present there on the dais. He suddenly stopped mid-speech to say to some students (who were with Him), "Hey boys, stand up!"

He announced to everyone there, "These are the boys of our university (Sri Sathya Sai University at Prasanthi Nilayam). You won't find such boys anywhere else. This boy has a triple M.A., this one a triple M.Sc. These other boys have an M.B.A. or Ph.D, or B.A. or B.Sc!" And so, He continued speaking, fully praising His boys.

In the Assembly, before all the governors and ministers, He spoke in this manner about the boys. He was so possessive and so positive about them! They are 'Number One', that is all. Such is God!

Therefore, when a person says that, He told in a dream that He has left this place for somewhere else, I consider that person to be quite mad. And those, who believe it, are doubly mad! Swami will never say that. You can take it from me.

Swami Is Like An Innocent Child

Baba tells us, "God is One." But, He may express Himself in many different ways. This is just one way — the childlike play of innocence.

Sometimes, Swami is like a typical child, filled with all innocence. Innocence is Divine, while ignorance is foolishness.

Somebody had presented a new, red, Jaguar car from England to Swami and He was waiting for its delivery. We told Swami that it had been purchased, costing one *crore* (10 million *rupees*) in those days.

On the day the car was due to arrive, He was giving a talk at Brindavan. He kept on asking, "When is the car coming? When is the car coming?"

"Swami, in twenty minutes."

"Arrey! Is the car there?"

"Ten minutes, Swami."

"It must be at the gate."

"Another five minutes to go, Swami." Then, the car arrived. He stopped His discourse to go and see it.

The Jaguar was a convertible car, so that Swami could give darshan when the roof was down. He sat inside and then, asked the driver to put the top down.

Swami stood up, "Let Me have a ride!" He blessed everybody like that and then, He called, "Anil Kumar, come here."

"What?"

"Have you seen this car?"

"No Swami, not yet."

"I will show you, come on! Look, the fridge is just here, hah!"

"Oh Swami, very nice."

"You can stretch your legs, like that!"

"Ah so, Swami."

Then, He wanted to try out the different seats. "Arrey! You stand there. Okay, now you sit here and I will sit there."

Swami asked me, "Do you know the make of this car?"

I said, "No," because I wanted to enjoy His company for some more time!

Swami then had some fun with me, "The windows are closed, right?"

"Yes, Swami."

"Tell the windows to go down. Say it loudly!" I did this and there was a whirring noise as they went down.

"Aahh! Did you see them go down? Now, say, "Come up!"

And there was another whirring noise as the windows came up!

Then, Swami laughed and said, "Arrey, see here! I am pressing this button to make them go up and down!"

"Hah, Swami!"

He pointed out something else that drew His attention. "Look, there is a screen here, where you can see pictures. But, take care that no pictures of Swami ever go there!"

Oh, the Child Sai, so happy! Lord of our heart! Blissful Sai! Vatapathra, Ranganatha, Ananda Sai!

At that time, the Jaguar was quite new to India and Swami told me, "This is the only (Jaguar) car here (in India), do you know that?"

I replied, "Oh yes, Swami."

Then, He said, "What do you know about cars, Anil Kumar? You know nothing about them!"

"But Swami, I do know."

"Arreh, how can you know, when you have only a bicycle?"

"Swami, I have seen Your car, so I don't have to see other cars."

Swami, our Lord, had yet something else to say on the subject. "What do you think about this car?"

"It is excellent, Swami! I have not seen this type of car before."

Then, Baba said, "There is only one God. How can you see a second God?"

What Were Swami's Last Words To You?

Q: When was the last time you spoke with Swami and what did He say to you?

A: Some journalists and some TV channels also asked me, "What was the last message of Baba?" Zee TV or the NTV stations like to embarrass you, but with Baba's grace, I have become resistant to it over time.

I told them, "God has no first message and no last message. The last is the first, the first is the last — and it will last, until we last. It is the last message, until you are lost and it is the last message, until you practise. So, don't ask

---

about the first or last message. There is only one message — the message of Love."

Once, He was asked, "Swami, why do You speak on love every time?" He answered, "Because you have no love, I have to speak about it. If you have love, I don't have to speak about it."

Where Is Swami Now?

Q: *So many people, especially in recent times, are claiming that Swami has told them that He is residing at their places. Some are even inviting devotees to come and visit them, because He is there. This means Swami is no longer in Puttaparthi. Where is Swami now?*

A: Many people are now claiming His presence at their place. They are fools, not knowing that He is already there. They are only claiming it today, because they only noticed Him today, not before. Swami is already present in our residences. This is not a claim. It is fact, the reality and experience of omnipresence.

So, some are inviting devotees to come and visit their places, "Please visit Baba at my house." He is not a doll, a showpiece, or a showcase. This is like an invitation to view the flooring in a wonderfully built house. "Anil Kumar, see the flooring!" Why should I go and see the flooring?

Let us suppose that delicious food is ready at my house, including my favourite hot pickles. Now, suppose someone invites me to go to their place for a meal and I go. Who is the fool? Not the fellow, who invites me! I am, because I know those delicious items are at my own place. The other man may invite me, but why should I go?

Similarly, the implication is that, if someone invites you to see God here, it means that God is not there. You are asked to see the Divine at their residence. But, God cannot be only somewhere – some one place, while missing somewhere else. He is everywhere and anywhere. So, these are non-spiritual, irreligious, inexperienced, ignorant claims concerning the presence of God.

We can confidently answer, by saying, "God is equally present with me." His often-repeated quote is this, "God is in you, with you, above you, below you, around you." While translating for Him, whenever I forgot one phrase, He would immediately tell me to add it in, "Say that also!"

So, should any fool ask me to come and see God at his residence, my answer would be, "Close the doors and enjoy Him yourself."

What Are The Advantages Of Mahasamadhi Darshan?

Q: What are the advantages of Mahasamadhi Darshan (experiencing the spiritual blessings of Baba at His sacred tomb)?

A: What are the advantages? This is a commercial question, absolutely commercial, because we always want 'advantages'! Knowing our mentality and fully understanding our psychology, even the Bhagavad Gita (the holy Indian scripture) speaks of phala sruti (the advantages of reading this chapter), or sundarakanda parayana (the advantages of reading that particular story). But, we are forgetting about another advantage: the advantage of our life to others. There are disadvantages also!

However, there is no advantage, because of the way
we live. Somebody asked, "Anil Kumar, would you tell me
how you came to Swami?" Why are you interested in that,
since I have not done anything special? Somehow, you reach
Swami. It might be by the Godavari, Brindavan, or Krishna
Express trains. Why? How? What? Those details do not
matter. That is how I look at it.

Anyway, you want to know the advantages of
Mahasamadhi darshan. Well, do you know about the
Machkund power project, which supplies power or
electricity to the whole state? If anything goes wrong in
Machkund, there is a power-cut. We then live in total
darkness, as all power comes from there. Likewise, the
Mahasamadhi is a power project or thermal station, and the
current of Divine blessings flows continuously from there.
From this Mahasamadhi, grace, benediction, mercy, and
compassion flow. That is one benefit.

Another is *Kalpavrksha*, the wish-fulfilling tree. There
was such a tree here once. People went there, meanwhile
forgetting Baba Himself. We wanted to see the tree, but not
Baba, as we have so many wishes and they have to be
fulfilled there. That tree fell down recently and now, we have
no *Kalpavrksha* tree anymore. I look at it this way: from now
on, the Mahasamadhi is the *Kalpavrksha*. There, all our
desires and all our aspirations are fulfilled.

The Darshan Of Baba

We have yet another advantage or benefit from the
Mahasamadhi *darshan*. If you look at the Samadhi, you will
see it is made from white marble stone with a gold border

on all sides. On His birthday, Baba wears white and His dhoti has a gold border. The Mahasamadhi is an ever-vibrant birthday dress, because every day is the Birthday of Bhagawan.

When I see the golden border, Swami, I see Your robe with its golden border. When I see that white stone, Swami, I see You in Your white dress. You are resting here. You are resting in Your royal, beautiful, Birthday dress to give darshan to all of us.

You must have heard of these particular gods: Sri Ranganatha Swami, Mohana Ranganayaka Swami, Sri Mahavishnu, Anantha Padmanabha Murthi. They are always shown in the reclining posture.

So now, we also have Sai Ranga, Sri Sathya Sai Panduranga Bhagawan resting in Samadhi, giving blessings and darshan to everybody. That is how I look at it.

We Live In Tension

Today, our minds are full of problems, worries, anxieties, tensions, and stress. We are not able to manage our life. After the age of forty, we get blood pressure. In times past, people didn't get blood pressure, until they were eighty. Diabetes, hypertension, and cardiac arrest were words never heard of before. People lived until over eighty, eating thrice a day and doing farm work. My mother lived to the age of ninety-three and my mother-in-law until ninety. They ate plenty of ghee and pickles, whereas if we have one tablespoon of ghee, we get high cholesterol levels! Or one spoonful of mango pickle and it is blood pressure!

What is all this? When we can't eat food, what is the use of money? We have plenty of currency notes, but end up like Sultan Ghazni Mohammed (971-1030), who died watching over his golden currency. See what a shame it is! I don't blame the present generation, but it's true that we live in tension.

There is intense competition today. When I did my M.Sc, only two posts were advertised and there were only three applicants. They asked us to give an undertaking in writing that we would work throughout the year, without resigning during that period. Out of the three of us, one fellow said he had applied for jobs elsewhere and, therefore, could not write the undertaking. Then, only two of us were left for the two jobs. I told my prospective employers that I was prepared to give a lifelong work agreement!

I was so eager for that job, because I was an old student of Andhra Christian College. All my teachers, whom I adored and worshipped, were there and to sit, talk, and work with them would be a blessing. So, to work in an institution, where I had studied would be the highest blessing. The teachers were my heroes not only in the art of teaching, but in their style and dress. I used to imitate them — the ties, coloured suits, and all that. What more could I want than to work with them as their colleague? It was worth more than the whole world to me!

Bhagawan Is Everything For Us

Similarly, Bhagawan is our treasure. Bhagawan is everything for us. So, when we go closer and closer to Swami, closer and closer to the Samadhi, we find our identity, our true self.

If you see a friend in the distance and call out, "Hi, how are you?" the usual closeness is not there, as you are apart from each other. It is different from touching your friend and shaking hands warmly, "How are you?"

So, coming to the Samadhi has the warmth of love and friendship. It carries the warmth of linking with God, the warmth of the Divine presence. Being here, you become free from all worries, anxieties, and stress. If you are healthy, you can enjoy life. Nowadays, a person may earn two lakhs (two hundred thousand rupees), but if he lacks health, he also lacks the enjoyment of life.

Therefore, to be free from worries, anxieties, and stress, bow down and put your forehead on the Samadhi. Tell me later of your experience. It is an open challenge. Yes, once you touch the Samadhi, you are free from all the stress and burden.

If I am carrying a very heavy trunk on my head and I put it down on the ground, would I still feel heavy? No! Why? I have put it down. Similarly, once you touch the Samadhi, there is absolutely no more tension, heaviness, or giddiness, nothing whatsoever!

Questions And Answers Session
Part II

(Sunday Talk by Prof. Anil Kumar, October 16th, 2011)

Life Is Full Of Questions

Life is full of questions. While on this onward journey, we are really lucky if we reach a state, where all questions stand answered and all doubts come to an end, through His Grace. We are working towards that.

These question and answer sessions are like any other talk: they are all filmed, recorded, and put on the website saiwisdom.com. So, this information goes out every day to thousands of people, who visit this website. Thus, these talks are shared and spread all over the world. About 65 people are serving on this team. These talks are available in thirteen international languages. So, when you put any question, all of our listeners and readers will be benefited.

Is It Fair To Celebrate Deepavali This Year?

Q: As Swami has left His body, is it fair on our part to celebrate Diwali (Deepavali, the Festival of Lights) this year?

A: As far as Indian tradition goes, as per our Hindu tradition, normally, the family members will not celebrate any function for one year after the demise of a member of the family. No celebrations will take place, until the first anniversary. They do not celebrate any function and even some don't visit temples or do any rituals, during that period. This has been a tradition or convention, which is practised amongst Hindus.

Left to me individually, with ill will to none and goodwill to all, I personally have no faith in this and I don't observe any rituals. So, that's my own individual life. But, let me come back to the question. Our tradition is that for one year, we don't celebrate anything, because of the demise of a member of the family. So, in Swami's case, shall we celebrate Deepavali or not?

It's a genuine question and I really appreciate the questioner for having taken Swami as a family member. In that sense, the traditions of the family will not permit him to celebrate any grand function. I appreciate him for having taken Swami as a family member with all the attachment, love, affection, and concern. But, my answer is this:

First of all, Bhagawan Baba is not comparable to any family member. When a family member is gone — out of sight and out of mind — we don't see him any more. But, Bhagawan Sri Sathya Sai Baba, though no doubt a family member — even closer than a family member — He is you and you are Swami. You and Swami are one. So, I cannot say that He has left me, because I have not left myself. So long as I am alive, my God is in me. So, my God is with me, because He is in me. Therefore, I cannot accept the concept that He has left.

Secondly, we know that Swami is manifesting all over the world today. Somebody told me that Swami appeared to him, while somebody else sent me an e-mail, saying, "I experienced Swami." People are talking to us from all over the world about vibhuti and amrita (Divine honey) flowing from their pictures. Bhagawan Baba is manifesting and showing His Divinity all over the world, more than ever before. In that case, how can I say that He has left us? No!

Moreover, Rama is not here amongst us, yet don't we celebrate Sri Rama Navami, the birth of Rama? Krishna is not physically available, but don't we celebrate Krishnashtami, His birthday, too? Christ is not physically available, but we still celebrate Christmas. Why? Because, Avatars don't leave us! They drop the body, that's all; but, they are still with us. They may resume the body and give individual appearances, depending upon the intensity of our feeling and the seriousness of our devotion. They can appear when they want to.

Also, life with an Avatar is a celebration. We don't even have to wait for Diwali. Every moment of life is a festival; every day is a celebration with Swami. So, don't have any other feeling. Celebrate Diwali even more prayerfully, in constant remembrance of the light of Diwali, that lamp of Diwali which truly represents us. The Light of lights is the delightful Bhagawan Baba. That light represents our centre of concentration and represents the knowledge that takes us out of ignorance. So, the observance of Diwali is the fittest celebration! It is not something to abstain from. Please carry on.

Pooja According To Vedic Scripture

Q: What kind of poojas can we do for Swami now? Is there any guideline according to Vedic scripture?

A: This question is also from a person, who is highly traditional and orthodox, someone who follows the rituals and family tradition scrupulously. They are asking, because we Hindus have special poojas marking the demise of our people and we have special rituals that mark the first anniversary of those, who have left us. All these are applicable to mortal human beings only.

Why? Because, God has no beginning and no ending. The One without beginning and ending is God. So, there is no question of special poojas for His 'end'. On the other hand, pooja means 'worship'. There cannot be ordinary worship, super worship, and special worship. No! Worship is worship. In fact, true worship is emulation or copying, imitating the noble qualities of the one, whom you worship.

When you worship Christ, there is no point in saying, "Oh! Lord, You are compassionate." Yes, the Lord is compassionate. You are not giving any certificate of conduct. He is not especially compassionate this morning, on Sunday only, no! Christ is compassion and compassion is Christ. Sacrifice is Christ and Christ is sacrifice. Love is Christ and Christ is love. Forgiveness is Christ and Christ is forgiveness.

So, when I say, "Oh Lord Jesus, You are really forgiving, Lord." He will laugh. Is it a discovery? Is it an invention or anything new? Are you telling me anything that I was not aware of until now? True worship is emulating and copying the noble qualities of those, whom we worship.

If you worship Baba, but hate everybody else, then your worship is just a ritual. When you love everybody, it is true worship. **So, worshipfulness is strictly following the essential teachings and principles of those, whom we worship.**

To Serve Swami,
Is It Important To Be A Member?

Q: Is it important to be a member of the Sai Organisation to serve Swami?

A: This question may be from a brother, who is feeling uncomfortable in the organisation, or it may be from a brother, who finds it difficult to serve in the organisation, or from the one, who could not proceed with service, because of the organisation. I will tell my views on this.

Baba is not a member of the organisation, but He is serving everybody. There cannot be anybody, who can serve more than Sai Baba and Sai Baba is not a convenor of any Sai centre or president of any Sai centre, nor even a bhajan mandali convenor. He has no position, poor Swami! But, He does service a lot! So, taking Swami as an illustrious example, I can say: service first, organisation next.

And secondly, why an organisation? Any organisation is an association of like-minded people. On Sundays, when all of our friends in the organisation go for service, we are also tempted to go. When all our friends do selfless service, we are attracted to join them. So, an organisation is a fellowship, a friendship, the company of like-minded people.

Then, when we work together, we can complete work within a stipulated time. When we work together, we can certainly undertake bigger projects, larger projects, over a wider area and thereby, serve more people. So, you can serve more people as well as undertake wider areas of service. Thus, an organisation will help you serve more people, reach the unreached, extend the frontiers of your service by widening and expanding your service projects.

In short, an organisation helps you and promotes you. It serves as a catalyst. So, service first, organisation next. An organisation will help you to serve better and to serve more. Therefore, organisation and service are complementary, not contradictory. One is the corollary of the other. Therefore, we are not confronting; we are supporting.

Leaders Should Be Role Models

Q: Is it important for the leaders to change themselves first? As per Swami's message of love and selfless service, leaders must change themselves and then judge others.

A: There are two parts here. The first part asserts that leaders themselves should follow the message of love, service, and whatever Bhagawan stands for. What a leader should follow, everybody should follow. This implies that you are keeping the leader above you.

A leader is not above anybody; he is also a human being. He has not fallen from heaven, so he is not an angel. He is also as weak as anybody, or as strong as anybody. So, in respect to devotion, in respect to self-purification via selfless service, love, fraternity, and all that, we cannot expect only leaders to follow these things. In fact, many leaders don't follow these principles.

As we look into things, we understand that if we also stop following, one day, we too may become leaders. Since we are following, today we are still not able to become leaders. No promotion, nothing! We continue in the same position—not elevated to the district level, not promoted to the state level, rotting at the same old level. If I stop following, I get a promotion.

Let's not bother about leaders. I have not come to the organisation, because of the leader. The leader is not the centre of attraction. **All of us should know one thing. There is only one true leader: Bhagawan Sri Sathya Sai Baba! He is the only leader. Why? He does what He says. He speaks and then, He does. What He feels, He says. What He says, He does. This is Trinity or Tripti or three-in-one harmony, or unity of thought, word, and deed. He is the only one!**

Somebody said, "There is only one Christian, by the name of Jesus Christ, Who died on the cross. Because He followed, He could not continue His life."

So, leaders are just communicators. Leaders are communicators and facilitators. They need not be role models or champions of human values. We need not worship our leaders themselves. Every centre president is not Baba. So, kindly do not expect any extraordinary qualities in them. It is enough, if they are not negative. It is enough, if they do not block our way. It is enough, if they do not discourage us. It is enough, if they do not bring a bad name to the organisation. That is enough leadership. Our true leader is Baba Himself!

Leaders Have To Follow Sai's Message And Not Judge Others

The second part of this question is to follow Sai's message and not judge others. To this, I also have an objection. The one, who follows, will never judge and the one, who does not follow, always judges. Why?

Jesus Christ saw an incident while passing by. In those days, where there was a breach of discipline or a breach of conduct, one was stoned to death. There was no hanging, shooting, or electric chair used then, in order to be conveniently transported to the 'other planet'. It was not like that. They were stoned to death. That was the punishment in those days.

So, Jesus was passing by and saw a woman, who had disobeyed the norms of society, being stoned by the people. She was to die. He saw that cruel thing. He stood there and said (paraphrased), "Look here! You are punishing her, okay. But, now tell me who has not committed any sin. Let that person throw the stone. The one, who has not committed any sin, can stone her to death. Come on!" But, nobody came forward, because no one was above board. Humans are making mistakes.

So, everybody left that place. Then, Jesus said, "Oh woman, you are forgiven. Go forth woman, but sin no more. You are forgiven." And then, Jesus told her, "Look here, I have not committed any sin. Those, who committed sins, have left. I don't judge you, I don't punish you." Therefore, no one has any right to judge anybody. Who are you to judge anyway?

I will give my own example. Long back, say 40 years ago, I was in the Purnachandra Auditorium. At that time, all devotees were clapping whenever Swami said something, or when He made an important declaration. I asked loudly to my friends, "Why are these people clapping like that? Is it a cinema hall or what? What is all this? Can't they observe silence?"

Then, after fifteen minutes, Swami made another statement. I was the first fellow to clap! I had just said, "Don't clap," but I was the first fellow to clap then! What does it mean? What you judge today will come back to you. Because, the Holy Bible says, "Judge not, lest thou shalt be judged." So, if you judge, you will be judged tomorrow. Therefore, we have no right or authority to judge anybody, as you could be guilty of the same thing tomorrow. Who knows? Therefore, let us not judge. Let us not be leaders, but only facilitators or communicators.

Normal Worker

Q: *If you are a normal worker, if a senior objects to you, what should you do? If I oppose, is it wrong?*

A: This must be a question from a victim, who is dominated by somebody else, who is not allowed to express his opinion. He feels forced to protest, but the norms of the organisation and love for Swami keep him silent. Now, he feels, "What is wrong if I object?" In the interest of the organisation, what does Baba say about it?

Baba said that, we cannot argue and counter-argue. You cannot protest or raise slogans, or see to it that one is out of power by taking up a no-confidence motion, as in a parliament or democratic society. There should not be protests like that. So, what shall I do? I can meet these seniors privately, when they are alone, and talk to them convincingly, softly, and sweetly, so that they understand my position. Then, they will sympathetically understand your view. If the other man is convinced that you are interested in the organisation, he will listen patiently. If the other man feels that you are there only to oppose — that you are making Sai centre a House of Parliament — he may still oppose you.

Therefore, we can protest and we can oppose. But, these two words are negative. They have negative connotations. It is better to say, "Let me share my view with you," or, "Let us share our views with others." Then, if you choose to oppose the other's view, talk convincingly and separately. That is the way, rather than taking it up on a platform in some kind of a forum. That is not advisable.

Where There Is Love, The Problem Will Not Arise

Q: As a worker, what should I do when office bearers are wrong or biased?

A: Naturally, this question can only be from a member of the organisation also. One possibility is to point out that he is wrong and biased. Then, there is a second possibility. If I keep quiet, knowing that he is wrong and committing some mistake, does it mean that I am not doing the work of Swami? Should I say 'yes' to everybody? Should I like all the 'likes' of the office bearers? Should I dance to the tunes of 'likes and dislikes' of the office bearers? What should I do? Really, these are all very sensitive questions. But, where there is love, these problems will not arise.

In our family, do you mean to say that we are open and free? The eldest son says, "Mother, you love the youngest." The youngest son will say, "Father, you love the eldest." Both the sons come and say, "No, no! She being the only daughter, you love her the most." So, even our children feel we are prejudiced. Our children will feel we are biased. So, even in the family, we are not free from criticism or attack. In fact, most probably, it begins within the family!

So, this question is: Shall I dance to the likes and dislikes of my seniors?

The husband may ask, "Should I dance to the likes and dislikes of my wife?"

The wife may say, "Why should I dance to your likes and dislikes? This is the age of women's liberation. Do you understand me? You can dance, but I don't dance any more! We have danced enough for centuries. It is time for husbands to dance. Why not? Why not?"

This is just a game of 'give and take'. When I just accept what you say, though I do not like it, then next time, you may ask and get to know my opinion. Try it once. Instead of saying, "I don't like it. No, no, no, stop it," just follow. Next time, this person in charge will ask you, will consult you. The problem only arises, if we are not patient enough and if we only want whatever we say to prevail. In that case, where we want whatever we say to happen, if there is any contradiction from others, we protest loudly, "No!"

In a family, are we not moving together, even with all our likes and dislikes? Take TV for example. Kids want to see 'Pogo' or other children's programmes, while ladies want to see TV serials, where there is a lot of opportunity to cry. They go on crying and we, too, have to cry in chorus.

Meanwhile, gents want to follow the news for 24 hours. I am no exception. I always have to follow news — regional, national, and international.

So, there are three sets of people: the *Pogo* gang, the serial gang, and the news gang. Together, all the three make a nuisance in the hallway. So, what happens is, the children will change the channel and then, the wife/mother will change it back with the remote, while the husband/father is shouting, "Silence!" to both sides. Such is the nature of likes and dislikes.

Out of two sons, one likes his food sweet, while the other son likes it hot. Or she wants this to be made for lunch, while he wants that to be made for lunch. Is not the mother an excellent manager? Mother should be given Ph.D in Business Administration. Every woman is a Master of Man Management (MMM). Any woman can manage man in an excellent way. Yes! If the man goes on saying, "Nothing doing, nothing doing," she won't oppose him. She will simply wait.

First, he will wash his feet, change his clothes, have a glass of cold water, and then, sit relaxed at the dining table. She will start serving item after item, very interesting items. Then, she will say, "Shall we do that?" He will say, "Yes, why not?" (Though earlier, the useless fellow had said, "No!") Now, the same fellow says, "Come on, do it right now!" It means that she knows when and where to ask, finding the right mood of the husband. (Husbands also know the techniques of how to treat their counterparts, how to cool her down, and all that!)

So, are we not managing our home and family successfully? If we were not doing this successfully, we would not have continued on as a family unit. We would have been separated already. But, we are still together, though our views have not changed. When one wants money, the other does not want money. One may want a fully furnished, grand and gala house, while the other one says, "A hut is enough for me." What to do? But, are we not living together? We are! How and why? It is all due to love.

Polarities And Opposites

Out of the two, one is talkative, while the other is silent. One is active, while the other is passive. So, to maintain balance, God created couples with a paradoxical (opposite) nature. Ironically, couples often have paradoxical natures, being quite the opposite of each other. He did this intentionally.

There are two wires: one is positive (+) and the other is negative (-), allowing the electrical current to flow. Why not use two plus (+) wires? If you do, then forget about getting electricity! So, even with electricity, opposites work together.

Another example: In some places, they have two tap fittings in the restrooms. Two taps are there, with both hot and cold running water. Again, opposites! Then, there's chilli powder and salt, again opposites. Or coffee decoction, sugar, and milk. Opposites! Try to find and tell me where two are completely identical. You won't find, no.

Parvathi stays in the Himalayan range of mountains, on a mountain called Kailash. Meanwhile, her husband Siva is moving around the burial grounds. What to do? Also, Parvathi loves all the jewels and silk saris, "Ah! What a wonderful border!" Meanwhile, husband Siva is a naked man, wearing no dress at all — no jewels, only ash or vibhuti. That is all. No jewels, nothing. While she has got a crown and all that, Lord Siva is having snakes around His neck! She has status with a tiger as her chariot, while husband Siva is having an ordinary bull as His vehicle. But, are they not ideal gods, an ideal couple? They are an ideal couple, even though they are just opposites!

So Let Us Not Worry That We Differ

So, let us not worry that we differ from each other at the family level. No! We belong to Siva's family, being the progeny of Lord Siva. So, this has to be like that described above. Therefore, we can accommodate our likes and dislikes. We can support each other and we can understand the areas, where we differ.

There is a beautiful phrase. You can say politely, "Let us agree to disagree." Then, there's no fight! Therefore, even in the organisation, the more you love Swami, the more you will be able to accommodate differences. But, when there is ego, there is a clash. When there is pride, there is a rift. When there is selfishness, there is a quarrel. So, quarrels and fights are all due to selfishness, ego, and pride.

A simple example is how Baba is able to tolerate all of us! If you want to pity anybody at all, first pity Baba. Please sympathise with Him, because He is tolerating all of us. None of us follow Him. Baba has completely failed in making us follow His teachings successfully. In short, most of us are successful in not following His teachings. But, He still loves us.

A child may play on the ground with the sand. The child may even throw some sand on its head, spoiling his clothes, and making his body dirty. But still, the mother loves her child, lifting him into her arms. Why? Because of love! Mother's love does not depend upon ironed clothes. If the child sits still like that in its ironed clothes, not spoiling them, the mother will take the child to a child specialist!

Some people come and tell me, "Mr. Anil Kumar, my children are mischievous."

Then, I always tell them, "If your child is mischievous now, then in adulthood, he will be disciplined. If the child is disciplined now, the problem starts later on, as an adult." If you are undisciplined in adulthood, it is horrible, terrible. So, it is better we complete our mischief in our childhood. Don't worry if the child goes on jumping around; we may shout at him!

When the grandson or granddaughter leaves the family home, the whole house suddenly feels empty. You are left with nobody to shout at! Whom do you shout at? Then, you will complain, "I am not able to spend time without my grandchildren. When the grandchildren are around, I am shouting and I lose my energy. But, when they are not here, I am not able to enjoy my time." That is the paradox in life.

Those, who live in cities like Washington, Chicago, or San Francisco — the very, very busy cities in the United States — or in London, in the United Kingdom, they feel like staying in a hamlet or a village, so very, very peaceful. If you ask a villager, he wants to go to the city to enjoy city life.

So, the mind always moves towards the opposite. When you have money, you will feel, "What is this money giving me? Let me have peace of mind." The fellow with peace of mind will ask, "When will I have money?" That is the mischief of the mind; it is not our fault. Therefore, likes and dislikes are mind-oriented, or mind-based, so never mind!

Control Of The Mind

It is not easy to control the mind. Can you control the waves of the ocean? Can you prevent leaves from fluttering? No! Leaves naturally flutter. Waves upsurge. You cannot stop them. It is natural! Mind thinks, mind is full of thoughts. One thought will make you very happy, while the next thought can make you very unhappy. One thought is of an enemy and then, the next one is of your nearest and dearest friend. One thought is about your success, followed by the next thought about your failure. In the meantime, the sun rises. During the whole night, there are thoughts – counter thoughts. If you are unable to control the thoughts and counter thoughts, what shall I do?

The Ringmaster, Bhagawan Sri Sathya Sai Baba

Baba gave the answer, because He knows! What He said is this: "Circus!"

What happens in a circus? All the wild animals will be there, like lions and tigers. The ringmaster of the circus will be able to control these wild animals. If the ringmaster is not there, if the fence is not there, we become their lunch and dinner! But, the ringmaster is there, so the animals are highly disciplined.

Similarly, our mind is a circus, full of wild thoughts, full of cruel, harmful, animalistic views and thoughts. How to control them? **Bring the Ringmaster Bhagawan Sri Sathya Sai Baba here. He will control your thoughts. Once the Ringmaster Bhagawan Sri Sathya Sai Baba is here, He will control your thoughts.**

That is why we sing, *"Manmohana, Madhusudana, Brindavana Nandalal, Manmohana Nandalal Manmohana."* You sing smilingly, Manmohana, the One, Who enchants the mind, the Ringmaster. Therefore, when you sing like that, when you pray to Him, the Divine Ringmaster will take charge of all these 'wild animals' of thoughts. That is the way to control. There is no other way.

"I Am Your Servant, Waiting At The Door"

During bhajans, if we are very sincere and sing loudly, there is no possibility of thoughts coming into the mind. During bhajans, if you do get thoughts, then stop bhajans. If you are really active in bhajans, these thoughts have no place. How is that? While I am talking, I cannot have any other thoughts. If I have got thoughts relating to food and eating, I will say, "It's time, let us wind up." If I have thoughts relating to my class, I will start speaking about botany, not about satsang.

So, while speaking, there is no other thought, because I am in constant concentration while speaking, with completely focused attention. That's what bhajan is! It is not that God is interested in listening to your melodious voice. Even the neighbours are not able to bear it! Even nearby house owners and landlords have given you notice to leave, as they are not able to bear your hoarse voice. But still, we sing. Why? It is for the mind to be fresh, to eliminate all our thoughts.

Those, who sing Baba's bhajans, Christian hymns, or any songs in praise of God will be very healthy, always smiling, with no reason to cry. They will have the support of God. When I call you by name, you will be there immediately, isn't it? I call your name. "Yes sir!" Don't you say that?

Similarly, during bhajans, we call God by name, so He will respond, "Yes, sir, I am here." Baba is at your doorstep, waiting for your call. **Phone calls always fail and may never reach Him, but with bhajans, Baba is waiting at the doorstep.** He Himself said, "I am your Servant, waiting at the door. You may call Me any moment. I am ready to serve you." Therefore, to develop this equanimity, which is a steady and balanced state of mind, go on singing devotional songs.

Suppose we fought with each other. You may have directed bad words towards me. How can I swallow all that insult, shame, blasphemy, and character assassination? How can I take it? Shall I fight with you? Or bring some lorry-load of rowdies to beat you? Or sharpen my knife to finish you tonight or fetch some guns?

God Is Non-Dualistic

Those, who feel very happy in praise, feel unhappy with blame. When you blame me, I feel so badly. Why? I feel very happy, when I am praised. But, in respect to Baba, praise Him, that's all. Even if you criticise Him, He is not at all bothered by it.

So many newspapers have written against Him and so many people have spoken against Him, while millions of people worship Him. But, He is not disturbed by either their worship, or their blame. Those, who worship Him today, may change their political party tomorrow, thereby joining a group, where interviews are not given, where results are not seen and dreams not fulfilled. So, we don't know. Those, who worship Him today, may condemn Him tomorrow.

And those, who condemn Him today, may change their tune tomorrow and join the believers. When the doctors give up all hope that he can survive, only then someone comes and tells him about Sathya Sai Baba, "Pray to Him and you will be all right!" So, he changes his political party and joins the devoted side.

So, praise and blame are just based on an opportunistic mentality. It is just a bargain, commercial and business-like. But, God is beyond all praise and blame. God is non-dualistic. Therefore, when I sing in praise of Him, what happens? Just like God, Who is above praise and blame, my mind also gets lifted above praise and blame. My mind is elevated above pain and pleasure. So, when I sing praises to Him, my mind becomes non-dualistic and then, I am happy.

'Bhajans' Should Be
Our 'Bhojan' Or Main Food

Therefore, Baba has given us a very easy key, but we don't use it. Come on, sing Baba bhajans and your blood pressure will never increase! But, we don't sing, because we prefer to go on fighting with everybody. Hence, there are so many doctors. In those (olden) days, there were not many doctors. Do you know that? There were very few of them. But today, every street has a doctor and every locality has a super-speciality hospital, all because we are fighting at a super level!

Once we stop fighting, once we stop quarrelling with each other, once we sing His praises, nothing, no enemy can disturb you. Failure cannot disturb you, nor can birth and death disturb you, because bhajans make us equanimous. Bhajans are sacred. **Bhajans should be our bhojan or our main food.**

Is God The Doer Or The Witness?

Q: Is God the Doer (as many people say) or is He the Witness?

A: My answer is this: God is not the doer, He is the Witness. Then, who is the doer? Are there two? When you turn inward, you are the witness. When you turn outward you are the doer.

When the sun rises, it is day time. When the sun sets, it is night time. It's the same sun. Do we have one sun for the day and one sun for the night? No. I may have two sons-in-law, but not two suns. The same one sun exists during both day and night.

Similarly, when the mind is outward, it is the doer. The outward, extrovert, externalised, worldly mind interacts with the senses; then, this is ego. There are some people, who say, "I have done that, I have done this, I have done that," "I, I, I, I." This 'I' is the doer.

Some people ask, "What is your son doing?"

"Well, I got him educated."

"Shut up! You got him educated, when you yourself are not sufficiently educated? So, how do you take the credit for your children? Nonsense!"

But, because of courtesy, we simply say to ourselves, "Father, forgive them. They know not what they do."

So, this doership is ego. Doership is due to the extrovert mind. Doership is body identity, feeling like a separate entity. Doership arises in the present life due to the consequences of actions taken in the past life, karma phala.

All this is recorded in the mind, which is like our software programming. This DVD of mind carries the software full of the samskaras or consequences of our past life. Our current body is the hardware. So, the hardware is our present body's life, while the software in the mind carries the past life. Hence, we act according to that software.

So, what do I have to do? It's called 'wear and tear'. I have to 'wear' (or experience) my past; I can't help it. But, also I have to 'tear' (or detach) from those samskaras, so that I am free from all past actions (karmas). That is what we call karma kshaya or annihilation of the past, withdrawal from the past. So, this is all one aspect of doership.

The same mind, when turned inward, is functionless. It is silent, passive, and thought-free (thoughtless). It is a non-entity in fact! So, mind turned outward creates an apparent entity, while mind turned inward becomes a non-entity. Turned within, passive; turned without, active. This mind, turned within, gets absorbed into the Self. In fact, mind is a product of the Self. Mind comes out of Self or Atma.

Baba says, "It is like the relationship between father and son." So, the mind (the son) withdraws itself into the father, its source, sinking back into its origin — something like a pen being retracted or closed. Like that, the mind sinks into the Self. Then, there is only the witness.

Samadhi Is The Place For Contemplation

Q: In each and every ashram, it is common that the living area of a deceased guru is freely available for everyone to enjoy. But here, it is guarded by the police. What went wrong?

A: A "deceased guru" you said. But, I beg to differ. Guru is never deceased. Body is deceased, but guru is not the body and the body is not the guru. So, the place, where the body is laid to rest, is a place of contemplation, not enjoyment. Here, the questioner mentions that the guru's place is available for everyone 'to enjoy'. But, the place, where the body is laid to rest, is not meant for enjoyment. It is meant for contemplation and meditation.

When you look at the holy cross, you do not 'enjoy' the cross. This cross is the symbol, upon which Jesus Christ was crucified. Do you enjoy the cross? No! But looking at it, you may contemplate upon Him. You think of His sacrifice, His love, and His life, which He shed for the love of mankind. You reflect on His shedding His blood, in order to cleanse all the sins of the vast humanity, then, now, and forever. So, all these objects or places are centres for contemplation, not enjoyment.

Yes, this ashram is guarded by police, but not for that particular place. There are guards to guard and protect us. It is for the visitors. This policing, this protection, is for the pilgrims, for the visitors here, so that nothing would ever happen to them. But, for the Samadhi, police are not required. They can visit the Samadhi, if they wish. Otherwise, they are only here for our protection, not for the Samadhi.

Satsang With Brazil Group

(Special Talk by Mrs. Vijaya Lakshmi Kamaraju,
October 22nd, 2011)

A Miracle In Mrs.Vijaya Lakshmi's Life

So many people come to Swami, because of some illness, accident, or shock. They usually seek solace from their visit, seeking it from Swami's speeches and discourses.

Illness brought us to Swami. I had undergone a major operation and even after many days had not fully recovered. All my children were small, so I was continuously worried, "If my health is so delicate, what will happen to my children? How can I manage them?" I asked myself as I went on worrying.

I visited many doctors, who said there was no medical problem. "It is a psychological problem. She is perfectly alright," they told my husband.

But, I was not at all comfortable with their explanations. I continued worrying, telling myself, "These doctors are not able to diagnose what disease I have."

Every evening, my husband used to take me to temples in our home town, to help me get my mind off my worries. I felt so happy with that. We used to go to the temples of Rama, Krishna, Shirdi Baba, and others.

One day, when we were going, we heard some *bhajans*. The singing was so close by, so we decided to attend. Inside, we saw an altar, where Swami's photo and Ganesh's photo were kept. They were singing about the glory of Swami and Ganesha. That was the first *bhajan* session we attended. Afterwards, I felt so happy and energetic that we continued to go to *bhajans* wherever they were performed.

Then, I began to think about Puttaparthi. "Why shouldn't we go to Puttaparthi and see Baba? So many people are saying, 'Baba is God.' Why not go to Parthi and see Baba ourselves?" I began to ask myself. Then, I asked my husband. He agreed, because he was also worried about my ill health.

First Bhajan
Heard In Prasanthi Nilayam

We came to Parthi by bus, along with a Punjabi family. We arrived early in the evening, at 4'o'clock and then, went for *darshan* and attended the *bhajans*. The first *bhajan* we heard was *"Deva Devottama Deena Samrakshaka."* (It means, "God in His highest Divinity protects all the needy and helpless.")

Raja Reddy was singing that *bhajan* about God being the protector of all people, who suffer. Immediately, Swami called the Punjabi family for an interview.

We stayed in Parthi for one week, but Swami never talked to us. He never even looked at us. Yet, somehow, I was so happy here. The peaceful atmosphere, the *bhajans*, and the natural scenery — everything made me feel so happy and healthy.

Our trip came to a close. My husband was worried about getting back to the college the next day, so we prepared to return to our native place. As we left, I felt some disappointment.

In my heart of hearts, I thought, "Swami never looked at me. He never talked to me. He never gave me an interview. What will happen to me? What is the use of coming to Parthi?"

Somebody came to my husband and advised him to write a letter to Swami, but he was reluctant. He thought, "If Swami is God, He knows everything. Why should I write a letter to Him?"

After we went back home, unexpectedly, a miracle happened. Swami appeared in my dream. He created *vibhuti* and then, said, "Hereafter, no complaints, no complaints."

After that, I recovered completely and perfectly. Because of my recovery, my husband developed much faith in Swami and started going to many villages, giving speeches. I became silent and he became very active! All this came about after our first trip to Parthi.

Darshan Of Swami
Varies From Person To Person

The feeling, which we get after the *darshan* of Swami, varies from person to person. Some may see their lost mother in Him. Some may see Him as their father. Some see Him as their son. Some may observe Him as God and *guru*. It all depends on your understanding, your mental comprehension. If you feel Swami is like a small boy, He appears like a small boy in front of you.

Wherever You Go, Swami Is There

One day, my granddaughter came to me. She had eaten a sweet and came to me to wash her hands. I took her to the sink and as I washed her hands, I somehow felt as if I was cleaning the hands of Swami. I got that feeling. Similarly, whenever I go around Ganesha, when the branches of a coconut tree touch me, I feel the touch of Swami.

Through experiences like this, He makes us realise that He is everywhere. He is in the delicate touch of branches. He is in the delicate, tender hands of children, and the beautiful singing of the birds. That's how He reveals His omnipresence.

Swami plays many tricks on us. Sometimes, He shows His presence in the *Samadhi* there, in Sai Kulwant Hall. At other times, He shows His presence in Easwaramma Samadhi and sometimes in the altar in our home. It means He is showing us that He is everywhere.

Swami has said, "I am wherever you go. I am everywhere, I am everywhere."

It is your mistake, if you are not able to perceive this. He will be observing everyone, everywhere, throughout the world, whether you are in Russia or in the USA, or Puttaparthi or Andhra Pradesh. Everywhere, He will be observing His devotees and protecting them.

Amrutananda Swami Performed
Forty Homas Of Ganesha

Perhaps, you have heard of the great saint named Amrutananda. For a long time, this swami stayed near Ramana Maharshi, the sage of the famous *Ramana Ashram* at the base of Arunachala Hill.

Swami Amrutananda not only followed all the teachings of Ramana Maharshi, but was also a great devotee of Ganesha. At the age of seven, he started doing forty *homas* of Ganesha. (*Homa* is a fire ritual or *pooja*). However, after doing forty *homas*, he felt he didn't get any results. So, he was always worried about this.

Some people will get a good result immediately after some *pooja* or some good work, God's work. But, for a long time, he felt he was not getting anything. Much later, at the age of 80, he went to see Swami, Bhagawan Sri Sathya Sai Baba, Who was only thirty then.

At that time, Swami told him, "You were feeling that you did so many *homas*, but you didn't get any benefit. That's how you were thinking. But, where are you now?"

Amrutananda: "I am with you, Swami."

Swami: "If you are with Swami, is it not a great benefit to you? Because you did so many *homas*, you could come to Me."

Amrutananda realised his mistake. Then, Swami gave him Ganesha *darshan*, appearing in front of him as Lord Ganesha with ten hands. "Because you did Ganesh *homams* and you love Ganesha, I have given you Ganesha *darshan*," Swami said.

Swami Cures Amrutananda's Asthma

At a later time, Amrutananda fell ill with asthma. Swami wanted to cure him. For three continuous days, Swami gave him some *theertham* or holy water. After that, Swami created some powder to rub on Amrutananda's chest for the asthma. Then, Swami brought red bananas for him to eat. So, step-by-step Swami cured his illness.

After that, Swami brought some leaves for Amrutananda to eat. Amrutananda saw that the leaves on the plate had thorns. "These leaves have thorns! How can I eat them?" he asked.

"Oh! Do you see thorns there? Give me the leaves," Swami replied. As soon as Swami touched the leaves, the thorns disappeared. "Now eat the leaves."

Amrutananda took one leaf and started eating it, but it was too bitter. "Swami, it is so bitter that I can't eat it!" he exclaimed.

Again, Swami touched the leaves and asked Amrutananda to eat them. Now, the leaves were sweet!

Do you see all these steps? First, the leaves were with thorns, then they were bitter, and finally, they were sweet and without thorns!

Life Is Not Full Of Roses,
But Contains Thorns Too

Similarly, when you want your life to be sweet, you have to go through all these steps. You have to face the thorns. You have to experience bitter things, which can be transformed and become sweet. When we want blessings from Swami, we have to go through all these steps.

When we go into Sai Kulwant Hall, we get permission to go inside and then, we have to sit wherever we are told to sit. We have to pass through all these steps. Only then can we have Swami's *darshan.*

Whatever Swami does is for our good, our benefit, our progress. He protects us as His children. We have to undergo everything with the grace of Bhagawan. As we face challenges or even shocks, Swami protects us at all times, especially during the most difficult times of our lives.

God And His Devotee

One day, God and His devotee were walking on the street. They used to have a good stroll every day and they talked a lot as they walked. One day, when he was suffering from some disease, this devotee could not find God beside him.

"See, God was with me all these days, when I was okay. But, now that I am suffering, He is not there next to me. God has done an injustice to me! He is not fair!" he complained to himself.

"Oh fool, why are you thinking that?" God instantly asked. "I am keeping you on my shoulders. I am protecting you now. I am taking extra care, so that you will be okay in a few days."

Whenever we have depression or disease, or face some challenge or illness, we should remember that Swami has given us the strength to deal with everything. He is our ultimate protector.

This may be your first visit to Puttaparthi, but don't think that this is the end of it. You should repeat your visits as often as possible. In one day or even during one trip, you cannot understand Swami. He is beyond comprehension, beyond language, beyond everything. He is limitless. Have faith in Swami and love Swami. Wherever you go, practice whatever *sadhana* you are guided to do. Always take the guidance of Swami. He will definitely respond to you, if you pray from the bottom of your heart.

When you attend *bhajans* and *satsangs*, you will be so happy. Swami will start talking to you. If you do some *sadhana*, His inner voice will guide you. When you come to that stage of hearing or listening to His inner voice, the voice of the Indweller, you will reach a stage of understanding.

The Inner Meaning Of Deepavali

(Sunday Talk by Prof. Anil Kumar October 23rd, 2011)

The Purpose Of Deepavali

On the 26th of October, we are going to celebrate the festival of lights, the festival we call 'Deepavali'. Celebrations during this festival are very important for children in particular, because they love to burst crackers and enjoy the display of fireworks. In North India, it is a more important festival, because Deepavali represents the festival of the Goddess of Wealth, Dhanalakshmi. In big shops, they keep coins and start worshipping them—a grand function indeed—and then, start distributing sweets.

When all is said and done, the meaning behind the celebration is to make our minds think of God in some way or other. That is the purpose of celebrating this festival. It may appear rather peculiar and strange to many people to see us celebrating one or two festivals every month. For those, who follow Hinduism, it may look as if they are celebrated simply to create more holidays or vacations. But, the intention of these festivals is to turn our minds towards God. The festival of lights, also known as Deepavali, has a special significance, as interpreted by Bhagawan.

The Light Of Knowledge Dispels The Darkness Of Ignorance

Deepavali is the festival of lights. Light dispels darkness; where there is light, there is no scope for darkness to exist. Therefore, Deepavali, the festival of lights, has this significance. Usually, darkness symbolises ignorance, while light represents wisdom, as in 'the light of knowledge'. Where there is this light of knowledge, there is no darkness of ignorance. We cannot continue to live in ignorance for a lifetime. We need light. Long ago, one biologist stated that, if one were to continue to live in darkness forever and ever, one would not be able to see light later, even if he is brought out of his cave. It is the same, if we continue to grope in the darkness of ignorance till the last moment of our lives: there is no chance of any wisdom at all! No chance of recognising awareness. Therefore, Deepavali is important in that it signifies the development of this light of awareness. This festival is significant, because it helps us to have the light of Self-knowledge or the knowledge of the Self.

The Sharing Of Knowledge Is Important

We see lamps being lit during Deepavali. People come here, light their lamps, and go. Say there is a candle that is burning here. Many people will come to light their candles from this candle. Thus, one candle helps light up many. Likewise, the sharing of knowledge, the sharing of experiences, and the sharing of bliss is equally important. We shouldn't allow this knowledge to die down.

If true knowledge were to die down without any sharing, what would happen? You would be at a loss and no one (who otherwise might have listened to you) would have been benefited. At least you, if not the others, would have benefited! This kind of sharing is absolutely necessary to help everybody and also, to benefit one's own self. That's the reason why satsang or study circle is an important wing in the Sathya Sai Organisation, where everyone contributes his own thoughts.

The Guru Holds The Light Of Wisdom

There are three important points regarding Deepavali: the light of Self-knowledge, the light of Self-enquiry, and the light of wisdom. These are the three goals or objectives behind the celebration of Deepavali. Were this not the case, Deepavali would be meaningless.

Who holds the light? Who brings the light? If I am in the dark, somebody should help me by bringing a torch (flashlight) and switching it on, so that I will be able to see and continue on my way. Because I am in darkness, somebody should show me the light. So, when we are in the dark, somebody should show us the light and take us out of this darkness. The torch symbolises wisdom and the torch-bearer is the guru or the Divine Master. He is the one, who switches on the torch, so that we will be able to see the light and come out of the darkness.

And what is this darkness? It is the illusion, ignorance, and duality of this world. This ephemeral, momentary, sensual world, which is full of attachment, represents darkness. However vast or attractive it is, it is darkness.

How Long Should We Be In Darkness?

The next question is: how long should we be in this darkness? How long? When we are happy in the darkness, nobody can help us. *King Dhritharashtra* of the *Mahabharata* was born blind and when he was later promised vision, he refused the offer. This gentleman was later promised eyesight, but he said, "I am happy in the darkness!"

Similarly, some are happy in the darkness of ignorance. Narrow-mindedness, pride, and the feeling of ego—"I am right and the other man is wrong"—all this is darkness. The light that will dispel all this darkness is the light of wisdom.

So, how long should I remain in darkness? Baba gives a beautiful example. It seems a person was passing by a cave and he asked a local resident, "Is that a cave?"

"Yes sir."

"Ah... ah... How big is it?"

"I don't know."

"How dark is it?"

"Sir, it is pitch dark."

"Eh...?"

"Pitch dark."

"How much darkness is there?"

"Sir, I cannot say. It's very dark."

"How long has it been dark?"

"I don't know. My father told me that it was dark enough. My grandfather told me not to go there, because it is very dark. All these people have been telling me this, so it's been dark a long time. But, for exactly how long, I don't know."

Then, this same man adds, "Arre! Don't worry. How long has it been there? How dark is it? Just light a match! The age-old darkness will immediately go. The age-old darkness, which has been prevailing for generations, will be gone the moment you light a match!"

Self Awareness Helps Us To Know The Divinity Within

Similarly, when Swami says, "You are God," many people say it is very difficult to reach that level. The same question was put to Bhagawan, "Swami, it's very difficult to reach that level."

He said, "It's no level at all, no level at all! You don't have to reach anywhere, because there is no distance whatsoever."

If you want to reach the canteen, you will have to go some distance; it takes time. So, the two factors involved in order to reach the canteen are time and space. But, to know that you are God, there is no time and no space involved.

How do you reach that level? For this, He tells us, "You don't have to reach."

"Why?"

"The 'you', who wants to reach, IS God. You want to reach - but you ARE God! Where is the question of 'reaching' God?"

Also, Bhagawan gives an example: If my name is Rao and I go on asking everybody, "Where is Rao? Where is Rao?" the answer is, "Arre! YOU are Rao! Why are you asking for him? Why are you searching for him? You are Rao."

Therefore, Deepavali's message is that you are God. The light will show you this! The light, while dispelling darkness, will make you aware of the fact that you are God. Because of darkness, we are not able to understand this. We are not able to visualise or experience it. Therefore, awareness will help us know the Divinity within, so that we don't consider ourselves just a human, much less an animal. In fact, the only purpose of life is to experience the Divinity within, as Baba says.

Self-enquiry

Many people ask me, "What is the purpose of life?" Yesterday, someone asked, "Mr. Anil Kumar, everyone in the family is settled. All the children are married. I also distributed the property. So, I have nothing else to do."

I said, "Now, the real thing starts! To get your children married and have your family settled, and also to have property matters settled, is not the end. It is the beginning of the next chapter!"

What is the next chapter? The chapter on Self-enquiry, the chapter on awareness! From now on, we live for our Self. Until now, we lived for our families, we lived for our children. Until now, we lived for our jobs and our bank accounts — the bullion market, interest rates, chit funds, and so on. That's all. Chapter one is now finished!

Now, chapter two begins: "Why am I here? How long will I be here? What am I here for? Am I in the light or darkness? Who cares for me? Who wants me? What is it that I want?" These are the questions we are confronted with in the second chapter of life, the life after retirement.

But, Baba said, "Start early!" If you start early, yes, you will have all the knowledge from the beginning itself, without having to wait that long. Start early, because by the time you boys reach our age, you will pick up some spiritual book, but immediately fall asleep. All old-timers want to repeat God's name, but instead they sleep! We don't need chloroform, we don't need morphine, and we don't need any sleeping tablets! If we start reading Bhagavad Gita, we will go to sleep. Or, we start saying "Sai Ram, Sai Ram..." But, by the fifth time, we will be in samadhi (sleeping)! These things happen as we age, because we haven't practised from the beginning. So, it is a question of practice.

Somebody said to Ramana Maharshi, "Swami, that man is in deep meditation!" Then, Ramana Maharshi joked and told him, "He is also snoring, go close to him!" Ramana Maharshi is known for his jokes, though very few people know that. If we complicate the spiritual facts, if we complicate the dissemination of spiritual knowledge and make it serious, life becomes a torture. Life is already torturous enough; we don't need to complicate it with the addition of philosophy.

Baba does not complicate. It is so simple, Baba says. It is so simple — softer than a rose petal, softer than butter. Why? Baba is the torch-bearer, holding the torch of knowledge, the torch of Self-knowledge and wisdom. Everything is easy for Him.

Deepavali Signifies Slaying
The Demonic Qualities Within

There is a story associated with this festival of Deepavali, where a demon is killed by God, Who is assisted by His consort. To repeat again, the demon that is killed is named Naraka, the Narakasura! What does it mean, Narakasura? Naraka means 'hell' and asura means 'demonic'. Narakasura means 'spending life in a hell of demonic qualities'. That's what Narakasura means and that Narakasura was killed. By whom? By Lord Krishna Himself! Good! So assisted by His consort Sathyabhama, Krishna killed Narakasura.

The question is, why can't Krishna kill Narakasura by Himself? Is He running short of power? Does He need Sathyabhama to inspire Him? Why can't He manage this Himself? Swami gives the answer: Sathyabhama represents Sathya or Truth. Assisted by truth, Krishna, Who is the God of Truth ("Truth is God, God is Truth"), kills Narakasura, the one who spends his life in the hell of demonic qualities. That is the celebration behind Deepavali. So, Deepavali represents killing or slaying the demonic qualities, as the demonic or inhuman qualities constitute Naraka or hell.

We don't have to go to some particular place to be in Naraka. We don't need any special visa or any transport. This life that we consider permanent, this ego with which we identify ourselves, this body identification — the feelings of 'I', 'mine', 'thine', 'thou' — are all enough of Naraka or hell. Hell is nothing, but the feeling of division. Division is always hell. Wholeness is full and so, wholeness is heaven.

Poornamada poornamidam… That totality is Divinity. What is fragmented and cut up is what we call hell. So, Narakasura-Naraka-hell is nothing but cruelty and violence.

Knowledge Is Demonic,
While Wisdom Is Transformative

Most of the asuras or demons in these mythological episodes all convey one thing. What is it? These demons are highly qualified fellows! Take for example the boss, *Ravanasura* – *Ravana* is the top man. Well, he has ten degrees, did you know that? He is an expert in the four Vedas – four PhD's! He's an expert in the *shad shastras*, (the six shastras): so he has six Masters' degrees! So, four PhD's and six Masters' degrees means a very, very intelligent fellow! If we consider knowledge as important, if we consider an almirah (cupboard) of books as important, if we consider bookish knowledge, the ability to quote, the ability to articulate as important, then our boss is Ravanasura himself. But, all this is merely knowledge. What did he do with that knowledge? He became an enemy to pious people; he became an enemy to those ancient saints, those spiritual people, who were doing penance at that time. So, knowledge is a demonic quality.

You may then well ask me, "Why do you have a degree? Why did you go to university?"

The point is that knowledge misused is demonic, but knowledge properly used — put to use for the welfare of everybody — turns into wisdom. Wisdom is beneficial, universal, discriminating, and judicious. Wisdom means proper decision-making.

Knowledge is only a collection of facts. It is merely informative. Knowledge is just information, while wisdom encourages transformation. Ravanasura had all knowledge. He had a lot of information, but completely misused it all to kill any good man that he came across, while protecting every idiot and cruel fellow, all of whom became his colleagues. Every fool will have foolish colleagues; every fool will have foolish followers. Ravanasura also had a big gang behind him. So, knowledge that is not put into proper practice is demonic.

Physical Strength
Without Intelligence Is Demonic

Now, consider the power of so many demons: these fellows can go on fighting. Then, what happens? Every drop of blood that falls on the ground gives birth to another warrior, another fighter. It is a mighty power, a demonic power, more powerful than atom bombs, hydrogen bombs, and nitrogen bombs, like Kartavirya Arjuna (a legendary king of an ancient kingdom during the Ramayana period; an invincible warrior, having a thousand hands).

Why is this? This physical power has given an ego the confidence that it can handle any situation. Baba gives the example of an elephant. An elephant is a large creature, but he is controlled by a small mahout. A short fellow sits on the back of the elephant, with an iron rod and he can make the elephant sit and dance. Who is more powerful, the elephant or the mahout? The mahout. It is the same in the case of physical strength: intelligence is more important than physical power. Physical power, is merely demonic.

Intuitive And Psychological Intelligence

What is meant by 'intelligence'? From a worldly point of view, intelligence is cunning. People may say, "He is a very intelligent man, so be careful of him!" This means that his intelligence is manipulative, political, and commercial. It is business-mindedness. His intelligence is nothing but manoeuvring and managing others to his benefit. The intelligence I am talking about is something more. The intelligence that we often refer to is not of our mind, but beyond our mind.

To give Baba's example, in a bag of sand mixed with sugar, the ant knows where to go. The grains of sand and sugar may be mixed, but the ant is intelligent enough to pick up only the sugar particles, not the sand particles. That is intelligence!

A new born calf rushes to the udder of the mother cow to find the milk. Nobody teaches it that. The calf will never go to the tail; it goes straight to the udder to drink milk. That is intelligence. The newborn offspring of the monkey is able to catch hold of the mother. There are no training classes or gymnastics exercises. It is natural and intuitive.

So, intelligence is natural. It is only when that intelligence is perverted that it becomes political and business-oriented. This kind of intelligence is harmful and abhorrent; it must be condemned. The intelligence I am referring to now is intuitive. Intelligence comes from the mind, while intuition arises out of the intellect. Hence, we come to intuitive intelligence versus psychological intelligence.

Deepavali Kindles The Light Of Intuition

Psychological intelligence is from the mind, while intuitive intelligence is from the intellect. So, this kind of intuitive intelligence always tells us that this world is not the be-all and end-all. It tells us that there is something more, something essential, deeper than what we have been thinking.

In this way, the intellect continually warns us, whereas intuition always guards us. Intuitive intelligence directs us. It is non-dual, whereas psychological intelligence is dualistic. Intelligence of the mind is divisive, fragmented, worldly, and physical, whereas intuitive intelligence is non-dualistic, spiritual, and whole.

Therefore, Deepavali should help us awaken this intuitive intelligence that discriminates what is right and what is wrong, what is ephemeral and what is eternal, what is momentary and what is immortal, what is awareness and what is inert. Deepavali kindles this light of intuition and out of this intuition, the intelligence functions at a higher level. So, Deepavali is not merely a performance or the observance of a festival. **Deepavali is a festival, where there is an occasion to go inward.**

Three Layers That Conceal The Light Within

There is so much darkness inside, which we do not know about. We are able to see the darkness outside, but what about the darkness within? The darkness within signifies the absence of awareness of Self. So, absence of Self awareness is the darkness within.

In the material world, there is light and darkness; this is dual. But that, which is dark within, is illusion. The darkness within is delusion, because it is mistaken identity. In fact, there is no darkness within. That is the truth, because the Self within is effulgent. The Self within is brilliant and ever vibrant. The Self within illuminates and brightens. So, why is there darkness? There is no chance for any darkness within, whereas in the world, we have night time and day time.

There should always be light within, but what happens? Baba gives us this example: we have a lamp here, but over it we put a silk cloth, a thick shirt, or a blanket. Can you see the light then? No, it's impossible! But, can you say that there is no light? No. There is light. Why don't you see it? It's because of the cloth, a cloth so thick that the light appears to be extinguished.

The knowledge of the Self is Atma vidya. The perception of inner light is known as Atma sakshatkara. The experience of inner light is called Atma anubhava. So, to repeat, there is awareness of light (*Atma Vidya*), perception of light (*Atma sakshatkara*), and experience of light (*Atma Anubhava*). That light is within us.

Body Identification Is The Thickest Layer

We have three types of cloth or layers covering the brightness of the inner light of Self. What happens? A thin cloth, a thicker cloth, and a very thick cloth are covering the light. What are they? One is the body — the body is a thick cloth. Body identification is a thick cloth, a very thick one!

Baba gives an example. If we take a stick and beat a buffalo, it will go on saying, "Hmmm... Ahmmmm... Mmmm..." Now, Swami says, "Come on! After the death of this buffalo, take out those nerves and make them into the strings of a violin." And when you touch the strings of the violin, you will hear a melodious "Thum...thum...thum..."

So, a buffalo, which is full of arrogance, says, "Hmmm... Ahmmmm... Aiiii... Aiiii... Aiiii..." When all jealousy, other unnecessary bad qualities, and body identification are removed, the nerves will say, "Thum...thum...thum..." which means, "You... You... You..." So long as you say, "I," one is a buffalo; when you say, "He," you are a man. That is the difference between a man and a buffalo. We are now buffaloes; we still have to become 'fellows'!

Mind, The Extrovert, Is The Next Thick Layer

Underneath the body identification, there is a thicker cloth. That thicker cloth is the mind. The mind always wants to be an extrovert: it never tries to look within; it never goes into the light. It is something like this: though there are many delicious sweets at home, some feel like going to a hotel (restaurant) and eating outside. Why? No reason other than to go out. That's all! While so much good stuff is at home — delicious items prepared by mother with all love and purity — we want to eat some other stuff outside, because that probably goes well into our stomach.

Similarly, though there is light inside, though there is brilliance inside, the mind does not want to look at it. No!

'Let me go outside, let me go outside! There are tube lights, not inner light!' This is the nature of the mind.

So, the mind is always extrovert; it doesn't want to be introvert. It doesn't want to turn inward. The mind is very powerful, when it is outward, because it feels, "I am so-and-so, I can command you. You are only that and this, and this and that!"

When the mind is inward, who are you? There's nobody to answer this, because the mind is inward. Mind that is inward cannot answer. Mind turned inward has no status, no dignity, nothing whatsoever. Why? Because it gets lost! Mind turned inward is lost. It becomes a non-entity. So, mind turned outward is mighty, while mind turned inward is a non-entity!

We want to be mighty, so we are extroverts. If you turn within, you are nobody: 'you' is gone. In other words, 'I'-ness is gone, when we turn inward. Therefore, the second cloth that covers the light is identification with the mind.

Intellect Or Individual Discrimination Is The Thinnest Layer

The third cloth covering the lamp is the thinnest one. It is the intellect. The intellect also covers the light, because the intellect is not-intuitive. The intellect is an aspect, which is so convenient.

Suppose our boys give an answer to, "Arre! Why do you get such low marks? Why low marks now?"

"Sir, our teacher did not teach." Very good! That's the intellect!

If you ask some thief, "Arre, why have you stolen the money that was there?" he answers, "Why not, sir? When ministers are taking away crores and crores, what's wrong if I steal one hundred rupees? What's wrong with that?"

This kind of intellect follows the extrovert, outward-turned mind. This bloody intellect also goes in that extrovert direction. It goes on supporting the mind.

"Arre! Why do you copy in the examination?"

"Everybody is copying!" That statement implies that nothing is wrong in doing this!

Deepavali Is The Experience Of Inner Light

It is only Bhagawan Sri Sathya Sai Baba, Who makes things so very simple. When we are used to Sai's gospel, Sai's message, and Sai's thought, when we are on the wavelength of the Sai style of communication, we don't feel like listening to anything else! You don't need anybody's assistance. You will understand the truth.

What does Baba mean by 'individual discrimination'? Individual discrimination is the positive, discriminating quality of the intellect. When we use our discrimination, the extroverted mind will have a supportive intellect, always discriminating to the advantage of the individual. That is what Baba calls 'individual discrimination'.

Now, when the mind turns inward, the intellect also turns inward. When the intellect is inward, what happens? To use Baba's phrase, fundamental discrimination arises. All over the world, Baba is noted for these expressions.

'Fundamental discrimination' is that, which is applicable to everybody at all times and not specifically to anyone's advantage. In contrast, anything that is applicable to your advantage only, anything that is set for your convenience only, is called 'individual discrimination'. But, when it is applicable to everybody, it is known as 'fundamental discrimination'.

Therefore, Deepavali is the experience of inner light. Deepavali is the experience of inner wisdom. Deepavali is the experience of the brilliance of inward-turned intellect, which is based on fundamental discrimination. Deepavali is an occasion to make the mind turn inward, leading to what we call 'intuitive intelligence'.

Preparation Is Sadhana, While Celebration Is Ananda

According to Bhagawan Baba, Deepavali is not simply a festival, where we wear new dresses and eat delicious food items. We don't have to wait for Deepavali for that. We can walk into any cafeteria or hotel any day and find a number of preparations there. Thus, making special preparations does not constitute a celebration. So, preparation is different from celebration.

In spirituality, we have both preparation and celebration. Preparation is our sadhana or spiritual practice, while celebration is the fruit, the result, or consequence of our preparation. So let's make our life a preparation and a celebration! What constitutes preparation? Preparation means reading Sai literature, thinking of Him, singing His bhajans, being humble and simple, prostrating in front of the *Mahasamadhi* — all this is preparation! These take you to the next stage, the stage of celebration.

What does the celebration mean? Celebration is the experience of bliss. Other forms of experience are only temporary. Baba tells us that in Sanskrit the word for happiness is *santosha*. But, this refers only to some temporary happiness, not total happiness. Santosha or happiness is limited, whereas *ananda* or bliss is much more.

'Aa' means Atma, the Self, while 'nanda' means 'the child of eternity' or 'son of immortality'. It means that you are essentially a spark of the Divine. So, ananda means that you are the nanda or child of Atma, the child of bliss! Santosha is only limited and temporary.

Deepavali is an occasion, where we celebrate this ananda. That is true celebration. It is a celebration, when we look at Bhagawan. It is a celebration, when we sing His glory or listen to Him. It is a celebration, whatever we do in His holy, matchless, sacred name. That becomes celebration!

Preparation Is Time-bound, While Celebration Is Eternal

In preparation, you are conscious of the time. Suppose I ask you to do something. You would ask, "Sir, how long should I take?"

Suppose I say, "Shirdi Sai Satcharitra — read it within a week!"

"Ah! Ah!"

"You will become a millionaire."

"Very good!"

Or, read Aditya Hrudayam! You will become a good wrestler. Guaranteed!

Then, read Sundara Kanda! You will cross all the obstacles in life. Lord Hanuman did.

So, there is a period, a time stipulated for preparation. But, for celebration, how long do you want to be in ananda? An hour? Half an hour? No, eternally! So, celebration is eternal, while preparation is based on time and space. Therefore, here, we pass through the first phase of preparation and then, we come to the celebration of Deepavali.

Getting Rid Of Bestial Qualities Is Deepavali

I was talking to you earlier about Narakasura. Naraka means 'hell' and asura means the 'demon'. Narakasura is a hell, where there are demonic qualities. Narakasura was killed by Krishna, God Himself, assisted by His consort Sathyabhama, or Truth. So, Truth is God, God is Truth!

The demon in everybody — selfishness, self-centeredness, the arrogance of power, the ego of the physique, and what not — are all sources of ego. They are all excellent qualities of Narakasura. Therefore, God thought he was the right man to be killed.

Narakasura was killed and in parallel, on this day of Deepavali, we have to get rid of all these animal qualities and bestial temperaments — the demonic nature — by following the path of truth, *Sathyabhama*, by the grace of Krishna. That is the *Narakasura-vadha* of Deepavali.

Pragjyotishapura — Light That Existed Before Is Forgotten

This Narakasura served as the king of a country, the capital of which was called *Pragjyotishapura*. What does *Pragjyotishapura* mean? Baba explains this. (Really, the whole world is running after Baba, because of these interpretations. We don't get this stuff anywhere. It is only He, Who can tell these things.)

Pragjyotishapura — as pundits tell in temples — is referred to in the *Kartika Purana* also. But, Baba tells us what *Pragjyotishapura* means. *Prag* means 'earlier' or 'before'. *Jyoti* means 'the light'. *Sha* means 'forgotten'. *Pura* means 'the place we live in'. All these together mean 'the place, where the light that existed before is forgotten'. That is *Pragjyotishapura*.

Pura has another meaning. It is not necessarily the city, where we live; it can also mean the body. So, who is our king now? *Narakasura!* Yes, because *prag jyoti*, the light that existed within before — the light of awareness, the light of Self, the knowledge of Self, the all-pervasive, all-powerful, blemishless, nectarine, unpolluted, immortal, eternal, Divine, spiritual light within, which has been in existence all through — is now *sha*, forgotten, *pura*, in this life. So, what has *Krishna*, done? He has killed him!

The Purpose Of Sathya Sai Avatar Is To Transform People

This Avatar has decided not to kill. Because if He decided to kill, the world population problem would have been solved long back! He decided not to kill. And He gave justification for that also. Why not kill? "Because earlier I killed, so now, I don't."

Why? In earlier times, during *Rama*'s time, what happened? Bad fellows stayed at one place, in *Lanka*. Good fellows stayed at another place. So, it was nice to go there and finish them off! An easy job! *Krishna*'s job became a little more difficult, because both the wicked *Kauravas* and the pious *Pandavas* lived in the same place, *Hastinapura*, the capital. Also, they were very closely related. So, He had to separate them and then, kill the wicked ones. So, it took a little more time and became more complicated!

But, Sathya Sai Baba's problem is most complicated. In the morning, one man is a pious *Pandava*; but, from six o'clock in the evening, he becomes a wicked *Kaurava*! The same person! The same person has both the Pandava nature and the Kaurava expression in him. Twelve hours that side and then, twelve hours this side! The same man!

So Baba said, "It is not wise to kill anybody anymore! So, what I have decided is to transform people."

Durgunambulu Savarinchi Thodarutakuno

Sadhu Samrakshanammu Salupu Koraku.

Bliss Of Self
Is The True Celebration Of Deepavali

To protect the pious quality, the saintly quality within you, that intuitive intellect that is value-based has to be nurtured, guarded, fenced, fostered, and developed. So, like that, the bad qualities are converted, changed, and transformed. Sathya Sai Baba is not a surgeon, but a physician. He won't cut you; but by His pills, by His capsules of Divine messages, He brings about a transformation and that's what is happening all over the world. It may not be apparent, it may not be conspicuous, or clear. But, how do you account for so many changes?

Ninety percent, even ninety-five percent of Sai devotees are vegetarians. Those, who until then were strong, staunch non-vegetarians, are all vegetarians today. Baba did not tell them, "You be vegetarian from today." No! That is part of our inner transformation. Many have become non-smokers, many are non-alcoholic, teetotallers. Many people all over the world! Why? Transformation! Therefore, Deepavali brings about inner transformation, a silent, spiritual revolution.

This silent, spiritual revolution is not conspicuous and it does not take you to death. Rather, it takes you to eternity! It takes you to great heights. That is the true celebration. The true celebration of Deepavali is this *ananda* experience — *Atma anubhava*. The experience of Self comes after getting rid of all the devilish characteristics. Then, one experiences and knows the light is already there within.

The Only Sadhana: Be Good, Do Good, See Good

Many people ask, "What is it that Baba has given us?" Well, what is it that you need? Many people ask, "Did Baba give you anything?" My answer is, "He has given me something: not to ask for anything!" Some people ask, "Are your desires fulfilled?" What is your answer? "He made me desire-less!" Some people ask, "What sadhana did Baba give you?" You can tell him, "The only sadhana is, be good, do good, and see good."

You don't have to get up at two o'clock in the morning or keep vigil throughout the night, observing *jagarana*. If we do that, we will be successful as watchmen, but not as spiritual seekers! We must be ever-vigilant towards the Self, rather than observing vigil or *jagarana*.

Excitement Is Physical, While Ecstasy Is Intuitive

May this Deepavali bring you all joy and the thrill of ecstasy! Ecstasy is different from excitement. Excitement is physical, whereas ecstasy is intuitive. Excitement is worldly, while ecstasy is spiritual.

Therefore, let Deepavali bring bliss, which is above happiness. Let it take us to the heights of ecstasy, not excitement. Let it dispel the darkness of illusion and delusion by exposing us to the light, which is already in existence.

Baba gives a wonderful example: Suddenly, because of darkness, somebody said, "There is a snake, there is a snake! Keep away!" One wise man came there. He put on the torch. It wasn't a snake, it was only a rope!

This wise man said, "The snake has gone."

Baba asks this question, "There was no snake to go! Why do you say the snake has left? It was not there from the beginning."

So, now we say, "Oh! The rope has come!"

"No! The rope hasn't come. It is a rope. It was there all along. The snake did not go, nor did the rope come. The rope was there all along."

Similarly, with the light: *Jyotisam Api Taj Jyotis Tamasah Param Ucyate*. That's what the *Gita* says:

Jyotishaam Api Taj Jyotis Tamasah Param Ucyate Jnanam Jneyam Jnana Gamyam Hrdi Sarvasya Dhishtitham.

Jyotishaam Api... Tamaso Maa Jyotir Gamaya.

This means, "From darkness to light, that which you are already." *Tat Tvam Asi*. You are That.

It is only masi, the darkness around, which is responsible for this delusion.

Your Life Is My Message

(Special Talk by Prof. Anil Kumar,
Jakarta, Indonesia October, 2011)

Do Not Confine Bhagawan
To The Physical Frame

So long as we lived under the protection of our Divine Father in physical form, we received lots of name and fame, because He was in the physical frame. We also had many opportunities to talk to Him, whenever we were privileged to have interviews. It was possible to pass on our letters to Him. There were many occasions to personally hand over wedding invitations and such on special occasions.

We would wait for Him there, every day. As we saw Him, we forgot our problems. We did not know where we were! All our tiresomeness and our burdens of life were gone. Now, that powerful *darshan* is no longer available. So, questions come to our mind: "Why should I go to Prasanthi Nilayam? Who am I going to meet there? Who is there to talk to me? Who is there to comfort me? Who is there to bless me?" These questions naturally arise in the minds of everyone. We were used to His physical form and we got used to private conversations.

Unfortunately, some of us have developed a spirit of ego, because of that closeness. Some even proudly say, "I am close to Bhagawan!" Some even egoistically declare, "Swami gave me an interview every time!" People of publicity show the rings and chains gifted to them by Swami.

Therefore, this category of egoists, this class of exhibitionists, and this group of proud people feel the absence of physical Baba. But, there are millions of devotees, who have never spoken to Him. There are millions of devotees, who were never close to Him. There are many, many, who never even saw Him.

If you calculate those, who were close to Him physically, it would be less than one percent. Most of them continue to be devotees. The problem is with these egoists or proud people, the people of publicity. Those, who have never met Him from the American states, like Mexico, Brazil, and Argentina, still come to have the *darshan* of Swami and pray to Him. Last week, a group of about fifty came from Brazil. They say they feel Bhagawan every day, there. About two thousand devotees came from Canada. They tell me they experience Bhagawan each day.

Now, it is clear that there are those, who experience Him in the absence of His physical form, as well as those, who find it difficult to experience Him in the absence of His physical form. Then, we can conclude that those, who restrict or confine Bhagawan to the physical frame, are certainly inferior or immature. Those, who experience Him in His physical absence, are more mature, experienced, and spiritual.

God Is To Be Experienced, Not Expressed

God is to be experienced and not expressed. We are used to expression. We go on saying, "There is only one seat in the flight and I got it! There is only one room left and I got it! Only one Baba and He gave me *padanamaskar*!" We are used to those kinds of stories.

That cannot continue hereafter. There are some, who say, "I was coming in a lorry. There was another lorry that hit this lorry and Swami saved my life!" or, "My grandmother was about to die, but Swami saved her life!" This is how we have spoken of Baba, till now.

There are some people, who go on speaking about their family matters: "Swami performed my first son's marriage!" He will go on explaining that for one full hour! Then, Swami performed his second son's marriage — another hour full! "And my wife is very close to Swami!" For half an hour! "There is *vibhuti* flowing in our house." At least fifteen minutes! This 'family business' should discontinue hereafter. Nobody is prepared to hear your family story. Those days are gone.

Devotion Cannot Be Merely Restricted To Experiences

I heard that a particular speaker was about to be invited to some of the places I visited recently. I know that speaker. I know what that speaker talks about: only grandfather experiences, father experiences, grandmother experiences, family experiences — like a repeating DVD, continuously playing wherever that speaker goes! People know the whole speech by heart already! They have learnt it by heart! They are very much tired of this speaker. I told them, "Why do you invite a headache like that?"

There are many, many people, who can speak. So, we should find that today, the scenario is different from the past. Your devotion cannot be a family narration. Your devotion cannot be merely restricted to experiences. From the year

2003, the number of interviews was far less, very, very few, almost nil! From the year 2003, except for some handful of administrators, not many people could be close to Swami. They could not see Him in close quarters. They had no chance to talk.

So, we have one large section of devotees, who have never been close to Swami, who never experienced His physical closeness, who never had any interviews with Him. Then, we have a second category: those, who heard of Swami, but never saw Him; and a third category: those, who neither saw Him, nor experienced Him. That is the largest group today. If you talk to them about your family experiences, you have to distribute Anacin tablets as *prasadam!* So, we should stop that. In household *bhajans*, in private groups, at a family gathering, at the dining table, you can go on bragging or blowing your own trumpet to your heart's content — or at least until the other gentlemen decide not to visit your house again!

Baba Wants Us To Evolve Spiritually

Baba is much more than what you think. He is much more than what you estimate. Baba is personal and impersonal, Baba is individual and universal, Baba is general and unique, Baba is form-full and formless, Baba has attributes and is beyond attributes, He is time and beyond time. We have not seen the other side of Bhagawan. We have seen only the form-full Baba with a name.

Now, hereafter, we have to experience the nameless, formless, time-less, attribute-less Baba. This is a process of spiritual growth; this is a process of spiritual development.

Swami never wants us to remain immature and inexperienced. One's education does not begin and end with kindergarten study. It is from school to college, from college to university, and from university to doctoral degree. We have to continue our spiritual journey; we have to evolve higher and higher. If water flows on and on, it remains fresh. If water does not flow, it becomes stagnate; it stinks and is unfit for consumption. So, today, we have to evolve and understand the reason to evolve.

Baba spent about seventy years teaching about spirituality. The seventy years of teaching will go wasted, if we do not evolve. Father has given me property; so, if I don't know how to use it, I am a useless fellow. Father will be happy, if I inherit the property and improve it. Similarly, Baba has given us this spiritual treasure, this spiritual property that we have to use and improve upon.

In our younger days, when we started learning, there was a picture of a cat. Underneath was written 'C-A-T'. Under a picture of a dog, 'D-O-G' was written. In the next class, only 'cat' and 'dog' were written, with no pictures! In the next stage, we have to frame the sentences and read the books ourselves. You cannot stay at the elementary school level. "Where is the dog picture? Where is the cat picture?" You are not a dog to say that! Learning is a continuous process. So, Baba wants us to evolve spiritually.

Baba Is
Omniscient, Omnipresent, And Omnipotent

Somebody asked Him, "Baba, we heard that you saved the life of a boy, who fell from the third floor. When did

You go and save him?" Swami told him, "I did not go. I was already there!" So, though Swami is here, He saves somebody elsewhere. This only means that He is here, there, and everywhere!

One evening in Bangalore, when Swami was to receive a car from a devotee, Swami was talking to some boys and teachers. He said, "Car is there at the airport, now!" Then, He talked about some other things. Then, He said, "Now, the car is at the railway junction." And then, He talked some other things. "Hmm boys, the car is here now, right over there. Go and see!" While conversing there, He gave the running commentary on the car's whereabouts. It means that He is here and there.

To be here and there is the quality of Divinity. He knows everything. We cannot bluff Him! When I say something, He will add many other things that you did not tell. Therefore, Baba is omniscient, omnipresent, and omnipotent. There is nothing He cannot do.

There was a TV artist from California, who visited Prasanthi Nilayam and then, went back. For lack of leave, this lady had to go to the TV station straight from the airport, without preparation, and she was to make some announcements, plus a short commentary, which she didn't have time to prepare. While she was talking, Baba started whispering into her ear what she was supposed to speak. She listened and then spoke. **This is Sathya Sai Baba! He is there in Bangalore, but at the same time coaches a TV artist far away in California. That is Sathya Sai Baba! So, if anyone says, "I don't see Sai Baba, I miss Him, I cry for Him," it is no doubt true. It is natural, but we cannot remain at that stage. That cannot be the be-all and end-all.**

Spirituality Is The Awareness Of His Presence Within Us

Our God expects a higher expression in our lives. Our God expects an evolution in our spiritual path. He will be very happy, if we feel Him right now! Baba said so clearly at one time, "I know many of you are very attentive to My talk right now." Do not forget this statement of Baba. What did He say? "I am always here, right now by your side!"

So, when He is here right now by our side, where is the question of missing Him? Why do you cry? Shall I cry, because I like to cry? There are some, who either cry, or make others cry. Crying is not spirituality! Laughter is spirituality, bliss is spirituality. So, let us be blissful, let us laugh, and let us smile with the feeling of His presence, with the experience of His presence, with the assurance of His presence within us, in full awareness of His presence within us. That is spirituality.

Let the whole world feel that here are Sai devotees, who feel Him even in His physical absence. Let the whole world know that here are Sai devotees, who are highly devoted, more devoted than ever before, because Sai devotees have spiritually evolved.

"How is it that Sai *bhajans* are full of Sai devotees? How is it that such a number of service activities are undertaken by Sai devotees? How is it that they feel His presence?" That should be the comment from society.

Changing to some other *guru* would be the worst thing of our life: it would be the worst tragedy that could happen in our lives! To quote Baba, "It is a living death!" **To change** a *guru*, to change our God, is a living death. God is not a dress to be changed every day. Your relationship to God is not political. So, it is unfortunate that some are feeling Baba is not amongst us.

Samadhi Is Vibrant, Radiant, Wish-fulfilling, And Energetic

Devotee numbers are increasing day-by-day to Mecca, though Allah is not there in the physical form. Devotees are increasing day-by-day in Shirdi, but Shirdi Baba is not there in His physical form! *Dargah* (a Sufi shrine built over the grave of a revered religious figure, often a Sufi saint) is only a *Samadhi*, but people go on visiting there. Jerusalem and Bethlehem, which are the main holy pilgrim centres for Christians, are full of devotees, though Jesus is not there in His physical form. People go to Bodh Gaya, Sanchi, and Sarnath, where there are well-known temples of Buddha. But, Buddha is not there in physical form. Then, why would you not visit Prasanthi Nilayam, though He is not there in His physical form?

As Buddha is electrically vibrant in Bodh Gaya, as Jesus is very much alive in Jerusalem, as the Kaaba of Mecca is ever vibrant, as Shirdi's Samadhi is wish-fulfilling, Sathya Sai's Samadhi is vibrant, radiant, wish-fulfilling, and ever energetic! Submit your prayers there, surrender to the Samadhi, touch that Samadhi, or let your forehead touch that Samadhi. You will experience what Baba is!

An electricity socket is hanging there; touch it with your fingers and you will know what electricity is! You will get an electric shock! Go to the Samadhi, touch the Samadhi, or merely think of the Samadhi, and you will experience Sathya Sai Baba's vibrations entering into your body. When you think of your father, you begin to imagine him. When you think of your mother, you begin to feel her presence. Similarly, when you think of the Samadhi, when you pray to the Samadhi, it is the same as Bhagawan Sri Sathya Sai Baba. It is Bhagawan Sri Sathya Sai Baba, no doubt about it!

Every Atom Of Prasanthi Nilayam Is Baba

Sai Baba is waiting there: Prasanthi Nilayam is His place. Puttaparthi is the place, where He was born and where He spent eighty-five years. He never moved out of Puttaparthi, except for occasional, sporadic, incidental visits to Bombay, Chennai, Delhi, and a few other places, that's all! Most of the time He spent in Puttaparthi as Puttaparthi was so dear to Him.

When you say '*Ayodhya*', you think of *Sri Ram*. When you say '*Mathura*', *Bhagawan Krishna* is there in our mind. It is the same thing when you say 'Prasanthi Nilayam': Bhagawan Sri Sathya Sai Baba comes to our mind. Not only that: when you walk on the sands of Puttaparthi, it is the same sand that our Lord walked upon. When you breathe the air of Puttaparthi, it is the same air breathed by our Lord. If you sit in the hall, it is the same place, where He moved about. When you look at His chair, it's the same chair upon which He sat. **Every inch, every speck, every atom of Puttaparthi, Prasanthi Nilayam, is Baba, Baba, Baba only!**

Swami Loves Prasanthi Nilayam Very Much

There are some people, who say that He shifted from Puttaparthi. It is impossible! Baba is not the type to shift from anywhere. A simple example: once, Swami said to a group of devotees, "I will come to Sri Lanka." It was Buddha Poornima. He said, "I will visit Sri Lanka."

I am also a selfish man. If He goes to Sri Lanka, I can also follow Him, because I will have a chance to translate His talks. Next day, I asked, "Swami, when are they taking You to Sri Lanka?"

Baba said, "Taking Me? Nobody on Earth can take Me! All have to come under the umbrella, under the shade of Sathya Sai in Prasanthi Nilayam. Nobody can take Me! The whole world must come here. I am not that type of a *guru* to go around everywhere. Here is jaggery or sugar. All ants come to jaggery or sugar, but sugar won't go to the ants! All My devotees come to Me: I am the sugar, this is Prasanthi Nilayam."

Therefore, Baba attracted devotees from all over the world, while being in Prasanthi Nilayam only. *Krishna*, when He went to *Brindavan*, was jubilant. *Rama*, while going back to *Ayodhya*, was exuberant. Swami returning from Bangalore to Puttaparthi, oh, He would be so joyful, blissful, and playful. He loved that place very much. He made a promise to His mother that He would never leave that place.

Dreams Are Individual And Personal

There are others, who say that they had a dream that Swami left Puttaparthi. Let us remember that life is not a dream. Though Swami says, "Life is a dream, realise it," He is speaking from a very high spiritual level. For mundane fellows like us, daily life is not a dream, but a very practical affair. So, dreams come and go. The dreamer may feel that his dreams are correct. But, these dreams are personal and individualised.

You cannot tell a government clerk, (even the President cannot say) "I dreamt that Indonesia should be vacant!" He cannot say that it should be vacant and that people should go away. Who are you to dream about me? Please dream about yourself! And then, keep it to yourself. **Don't be so shameless as to share your dreams with everybody, which is nothing but nonsense.**

Do Not Believe False Propaganda

There are some, who say that money should be donated for their cause: "I am starting a college in the name of Baba," "I am starting a hospital in the name of Baba," "I am starting a new Trust in the name of Baba."

Please tell them, "You may start the Trust, but I don't have trust in you, nor in the trustees."

There is only one God, Whom we have seen, Whom we have experienced, and Who has given us plenty. He is Sathya Sai Baba. There is only one Trust that He started, the Sri Sathya Sai Central Trust. He was the President of the Central Trust till recently — the President! That is the only authoritative, legal body.

Let us be sensible and logical, and let us behave properly in not believing others' words. Go anywhere, listen to all those words said against Swami's statements, but don't believe them!

Someone asks a question: "How is it that there are gold bars in the cupboard of Baba's room?"

My answer is, "I have not seen those cupboards. I have not seen those gold bars. I was there physically for the last twenty-two years. How could you see His room? How could you see His cupboards? How could you see these gold bars? Your eyes must be like X-rays to see them, not ordinary eyes."

That's all bogus, that's all false. So, don't believe this false propaganda. There was a lack of communication. People did not talk to the reporters at the right time, in the right way. Therefore, journalists have written in their own way, whatever little they know.

Sathya Sai Baba
Is The Only Champion Of Poor People

The whole world can agree on one thing. Sathya Sai Baba is the only Champion of poor people! Sathya Sai Baba is the only Divine Personality, Who achieved, within seventy years, a maximum number of welfare programmes. For humans, it would require five hundred years to complete that much. Yet within seventy years, He could do it all.

Puttaparthi was a village with a population of only one hundred — a village that had no roads, no power supply, filled with illiterate people, who were totally poor, cut off from the madding crowd, uncivilised — such a remote village was transformed by Him and today, attracts the whole world. The whole world may not know where Bombay is, may not know where Hyderabad is, but the whole world knows where Prasanthi Nilayam is! That is Sathya Sai Baba! He made it globally important. He made it the centre of the universe and He made it a place of spirituality.

Bhagawan Baba
Is Inter-continental, Universal God

Here is a Boy, Who, in seventh class, discontinued schooling. With no college studies or degrees, He reached such a position. He could talk to doctors, engineers, politicians, and scientists — that seventh class Boy would later even challenge scientists, doctors, and professionals! That Boy is Sathya Sai Baba, the Divine! When the doctors were confused, Sathya Sai Baba told them what to do and what medicines to give.

You all know the Hanuman statue above the Hill View Stadium. There, Hanuman is in a standing posture, carrying a mountain, but with one leg up in the air. Such a large statue is not found anywhere else in India! It was taken up to the mountain top to be erected there. All the engineers said to Swami that, it was impossible to erect it, because the mountain is too pointed on the top, like a cone.

Baba went up there. "Come on! I will be up here, so bring the statue. Don't worry!" Today, Hanuman is installed, because Sai Rama was there at that moment! That is Sathya Sai Baba.

You must have heard of L&T Company. L&T stands for Larsen & Toubro: they are well-known construction engineers. They came to Baba, showing maps and plans.

"Swami, we do it here like this and then, like that and finally, like this." He will appreciate them and thank them.

Finally, He will say, "Why not do it this way? Is it not cheaper, if you do it this way? Will it not be completed earlier, if you do it this way?" Engineers have only one way — to fall at His Feet helplessly. L&T is an international company. But, they have to fall at the Feet of Baba. Why? It is an international company, but Bhagawan Baba is inter-continental, a universal God!

Bhagawan Baba Is The Super Surgeon

There is a man from Chittoor, who is a business magnate. He served as a Member of Parliament and as the TTD chairman (*Tirumala Tirupati Devasthanams*). He came for Swami's darshan. Swami spoke to him and said, "Just go to the hospital and see how nice it is!"

This man went to the hospital and walked around the hospital. It was very nice. He saw his classmate, who was there on a visit, a cardiologist by the name of Dr. Choudhary. He said, "Hey, doctor! How are you? We are classmates, right?" and this man added, "Check my BP, let's just see what it is!" (Just as a matter of fun.)

Upon checking the BP, the doctor said, "You cannot go out now; you have to go into the hospital. Such high BP! You will not survive. Come on inside. Fast! Treatment should start now!"

He was alright till then. He spoke to Swami and Swami just asked him to go to the hospital, on a visit. He never thought that he was to be admitted to the hospital. He was in bed, when Baba came to see him at 10 o'clock in the morning. "How are you, boy? Is the hospital nice? Is the bed comfortable for you? Don't worry. You don't need to inform your children and don't inform your wife. Treatment will start and you will be perfect. Don't worry." Baba gave him *prasadam* and He left.

Doctors did all tests and investigations: sugar was high, BP was also high. (Wherever money is high, these complaints will also be higher!) The doctors said, "We cannot operate on you now: BP and sugar should be under control before we can operate."

This man lost control of himself. Doctors went and reported to Swami, "Swami! We cannot operate."

Swami said, "You are operating tomorrow. I am coming to the theatre." Swami sat there in the theatre, while the doctors' hands were shaking, performing a heart surgery with high BP levels!

Baba said, "I am here, so no BP! You should be happy, no BP!" Naturally, the operation was successful! The doctors could not believe it. Normally, it is impossible to conduct surgery on such a patient. How was it possible? That patient, although totally in a bad condition, was in the hands of a super-surgeon, Dr. Sathya Sai Baba! So, he was saved!

Sathya Sai Baba Cannot Be Known, Only Experienced

He did not study any medicine, nor did He study engineering. So, how can He advise engineers? How can He advise doctors? A few cosmonauts, who made air travel to the moon, came on a visit to Puttaparthi. Swami went on talking about stars and the galaxy of stars, the lunar system and the solar system in such a way that even they did not know. He has shown them what the moon is, right there in the interview room and then, He told the cosmonauts (please follow this statement), "Man going to the moon is not important. Man travelling in space is not important. God taking life in the Form and with the Name of Sathya Sai Baba is most important!" Man going to the moon is less important, while God walking on Earth is most important! That is Sathya Sai Baba!

When He moves and talks to us, we think we know. First thing we should know is that we do not know. To think that I know is the beginning of foolishness. To think that I only know is madness. To know that you do not know is wisdom! Why? God cannot be known.

Can you see the air? So, how do you know God? He cannot be known and He is not supposed to be known. He is not meant to be known. He is not a subject to be studied, nor is He material to be experimented with in a laboratory. Simply, He has to be experienced. **Sathya Sai Baba has to be experienced, but He cannot be explained or expressed!** Please understand that! Sathya Sai Baba cannot be known; Sathya Sai Baba can only be experienced. Sathya Sai Baba represents all values.

Swami Is Not The Physical Body

He says, "You are not the body, you are not the mind!" So, how can Baba be the body? How can Baba be the mind? When you are not the body, how can He be the body? Baba was there in the hospital for twenty-seven days. Please believe me: I touched His Feet thousands of times, so I know His body. I pressed His Feet upto knees. His body is softer than a rose petal, softer than butter, softer than cotton! How could He bear all the injections and the pain? How could He bear the pinches of the needles? How could that body bear that suffering? How is it possible to be on dialysis for twenty-seven days? How is it possible with a liver problem, a lung problem, a heart problem, and asthma to continue to live for twenty-seven days? Thirty-six doctors both from India and abroad treated Him.

I can openly say this with confidence: In the hospital, He allowed His body to remain on the bed, but Baba was not there in the hospital. The body was there in the hospital, but He was not there in the body. Then, where was He? He was on a holiday trip — Malaysia, Indonesia, Tanzania, America — an inter-continental traveller, our Bhagawan Sri Sathya Sai Baba!

He started visiting devotees. He started talking to them, while leaving the body there in Puttaparthi. "So, doctors, do whatever you want to do with this body. I am not there! Come on, do it! Any number of tests, but I am not there! I know how long to be here and I know when to get out. You doctors cannot say that I should go now. You doctors cannot extend My stay. I decided when to come and I decide when to go! From the worldly point of view, come on, do your tests!"

Swami Took 27 Days To Prepare People

Then, why did Baba stay there in the hospital for twenty seven days? Why? He stayed there to prepare all of us, to meet that ultimate departure from His beautiful form! **If the end of His life had happened right at the beginning of His hospitalisation, thousands would have died throughout the world. It would have been a terrific shock!**

Many old people continue to live, because of Swami. Single parents continue to live, because of Baba. Many widows and widowers live in hope, with the support of Baba. Many, many people with so many health issues live, because of Baba's blessings. Even broken families are also hopeful with Swami there. There are so many people — vegetable and fruit vendors, many casual labourers, electricians and carpenters — thousands depend upon Him there in Puttaparthi! If that departure had been sudden, the whole of Puttaparthi would have been a burial ground!

Therefore, He delayed His physical departure. He took twenty seven days to prepare people. We are not that strong to receive such a shock. Even now, some people are still crying. What would have happened to them, if He had left His body immediately after entering the hospital?

Swami Has Given His Life For His Devotees

Look at Baba! From 2003, with all His health problems, He continued to shower His Grace, He continued to smile, to protect, to bless. Twice, He had a hip fracture, plus a fracture near the elbow, so that He could not extend His hand, or get up, and could not eat sometimes with all these health problems, particularly from 2003. But, the smile on His face, His Grace and Divinity never failed!

If anyone asked, "Swami, how are You?" He told them, "I am fine!"

"Swami, really how are You?"

"I am fine!"

"Swami, how ARE You?"

"If you ask again, I will send you out! I am fine!"

How can He be fine? With a fracture anywhere, can you be fine? How about us? A simple cold will create hell in our families. A slight rise in temperature will create havoc in our homes. A 98.4 degree temperature is enough to ask for casual leave. Did Baba apply for casual leave? Did He cancel any *darshan*? Did He stop blessing people? Did He put on a long face? Is there any expression of pain? Is there any expression of grief? Any word of ill health? Any complaint? No, never, never!

He went on smiling, blessing, talking, advising, encouraging, and curing the diseases of everybody, while neglecting His own health. He neglected all His problems; He never cared for His health issues.

Doctors said, "Take rest!"

He said, "Nothing doing!"

Doctors said, "We should examine You!"

He said, "Nothing doing! I don't want My devotees to cry for Me. I don't want My devotees to miss My *darshan*." So, He neglected His health. He has given His life for the devotees. That is Sathya Sai Baba! He was in bed, so that we can be on Earth. He was sick, so that we can be healthy; yet, with all the pain, He could smile.

Message Of Baba: Make Everybody Happy, Even In Sickness

The *Avatar* gave us all a message. His life itself is a message. In active life, Baba gave us the message: while you are active, serve poor people. Do everything that helps poor people, fulfil their needs; sacrifice and take up welfare projects. While you are young, think of God, meditate on Him, and make use of your active young life. The *Avatar* has this message for youth.

Baba in the hospital also had a message to convey. The hospital was never closed for one day: all the patients came and went, even while Swami was there in the hospital. His actions gave this message: "This body may be in pain, but all should be happy. This body may be sick, but all should be healthy!" That is the message of Sathya Sai Baba: to make everybody happy, even while His body is suffering.

His Life Is His Message

His life is His message! Many people have got a message, but it is not in harmony with their life. Their life is a divergence from their message. But, here is our God, Sathya Sai Baba, Whose life and message are in perfect, 100-unity and harmony. It is not a simple message.

A *guru* gives a message, while God lives according to His message. So, Baba is not a *guru*. He is God, Who lives His message! So, you may change your *gurus,* but you cannot change your God. Why? *Gurus* are many, but God is one! There are not two Gods, like Indonesian God and Malaysian

God. Impossible! Therefore, you cannot change your God. Sathya Sai Baba is the only One!

A *guru* shows the way and a *guru* will show you the goal. Baba shows you the way and He is the goal, because He is God. He is the way and the goal as well. He is the student and teacher as well. He is a bachelor and the *samsari* (householder) as well. Baba is like a departmental store, meaning the whole universe is in Him.

Let Us All Live His Message

Therefore, "Never give up Baba!" If you are to give up Baba and forget His name, it is the worst tragedy that can happen in one's own life. You cannot forget your parents. Impossible! More so, you cannot forget your God. If you follow His message, if you follow His life, our Father will be very happy. He taught us for seventy years. If we follow His principles, if we follow His values, He will be very happy. Therefore, from today, do service more than ever before, sing *bhajans* more than ever before, be devoted more than ever before; smile, laugh, and do Sai activities more than ever before!

All Sai devotees should set an example to the whole world: we represent unity. We are strong in our devotion and unity, and we devotees are pillars of values for this nation. A Sai devotee is a role model to follow and emulate. We have heard only about Baba till now. Now, the whole world should see, observe, and learn from us. The whole world saw Him earlier; from now on, they will see Him in us.

The whole world heard His messages; now, the whole world will see us practising His message. They have seen

Him as an Embodiment of sacrifice; now, the world should see us as men of sacrifice. They know Baba is kindness itself; now, everybody should feel our kindness. He is compassion, so everybody around us should feel our compassion. He is love; hence, everybody should experience that lovingness, that love, from within us.

Therefore, hereafter, His message should be our life. People should see His message in practice, in the lives of His devotees. Society will see His Form, while looking upon us. Where is Baba now? He is in everyone, in all these forms! Everyone is Baba: Sathya Sai Baba is in your hearts. That should be our feeling. Nobody should shed a tear; nobody should cry, because Baba is life and not death. Baba is eternal life, Baba is immortal life. So, Baba is ever active and dynamic.

Wife Is A Remote Control At Home And In Spiritual Field

When the husband is a devotee, the wife is not a devotee. When the wife is devotee, the husband is not a devotee. If both are devotees, their children are not devotees. This balance is there in nature. You cannot have only chilli powder. There should be some salt also!

There is something wrong with ladies. First, they go on complaining, "My husband is not a devotee, my husband is not a devotee!" They go on crying, until the husband becomes a devotee. So, the poor fellow becomes a devotee. He goes deep into the organisation. Now, the wife cries again, "He has no time for me!"

So, you cried then and you cry now. This is the law of nature. But, I can tell you this: Ninety percent of Sai Baba devotees are devotees, because of their wives only! So, a wife is the remote control at home and in the spiritual field also! Therefore, I compliment ladies, because they are the engine, while we are the compartments.

Questions And Answers

Q: How to purify our heart from jealousy and anger? Sometimes, it is difficult to do that even when we have already striven to do sadhana. So, how to purify our heart?

A: You don't have to purify your heart. The heart is already pure. You are born pure. So, just don't pollute it. The heart is not impure; you are making it impure. Your selfishness, self-interest, and narrow-mindedness have made the heart impure.

What should you do? You have to make the heart as pure as it was, when it was originally given to you. How to do that? Sai *bhajans* will clean your heart, Sai service will remove all impurities, and Sai meditation will extend your life. So, to be healthy, wealthy, and wise, follow Sai. That is the solution.

Q: Uncle Anil, my question is how to reduce our ego?

A: Not reduce it, but let it go! Go ego, you go! After all, why should you be egoistic? Baba gives us this example: in the whole of the universe, there are so many stars and planets and Earth is just like an ant. It means Earth is only the size of an ant! So, Indonesia is the size of one eye of that ant, while Jakarta is a mere speck in the eye of an ant. So, what is there for you to feel proud of?

What are you at home? Children don't listen to you! You are not sure of your wife, whether she will say 'yes' or 'no'. As you are not sure of your wife, what is there to be egoistic about? You can be egoistic for one thing: "I am fool number one," "I am crack number one," or "I am cheat number one." You can feel proud of those things, but not any other thing in this world.

Spiritually speaking, ego means I-ness, I-ness, I-ness! People say, "I built it. I did it. I educated my children. I bought the house!" This is all ego. But really, where is the chance to be egoistic? You may be very beautiful, but you are not beautiful because of yourself. Your parents are beautiful, so therefore you are beautiful! You cannot say, "I am very tall!" It is not your achievement. Your parents and grandparents are tall; therefore, you are tall.

This is all a weakness of the mind. The mind wants everything. The desire of the mind is endless and the imagination of the mind is endless. Mind never gets satisfied: it wants more and more. It wants you to be a singer. It wants you to be everything, which is impossible! All are His children, so He gives each one a gift. So, make this monkey mind turn to Baba. Mind then becomes a diamond. "Oh mind, never mind! Oh mind, follow Him! Oh mind, think of Him!" That is the only way you can be happy.

Sab Ko Sanmati de Bhagawan.

(Oh God, give all a good mind)

Q: *Just a little inquisitiveness: Did your faith in Baba grow with experience? If so, can you narrate a few experiences?*

A: When water is flowing, if you block it, there is a terrific speed out of which electricity is generated. Similarly, when you want to do good work, when there are obstacles, your speed will increase. You will be more determined; you will take it as a challenge. An ant is moving forward and there may be some obstacles. What will it do? It will take a diversion — that way and this way — but still proceed.

So, there may be obstacles, there may be negative-minded people, there may be people, who discourage, but none can stop me from doing! I may be lying low-key, but still, I will be continuing my work. Nobody can stop me.

In my personal life, there were so many obstacles. Many people wanted to stop me. There were none to encourage me. There were many people, who acted against me, but I never gave up my ambition, because my ambition is more important than my promotion. My ambition is more important than pleasing any bosses. My God is more important than all these people! That determination will allow you to go ahead.

Q: *Oh, non-devotees often ask me when Swami's replacement will come.*

A: Swami's replacement! How to replace Swami? If you replace your mother, I will tell you how to replace God! Very easy, please try. Replace your mother immediately and then, I will replace Swami! Impossible! If there are many, one can be replaced by the other. But, there is only one God. How can you replace Him? Impossible!

Q: Dearest Brother Anil, you may think that this is a unique question. Can you please throw light on an explanation as to why Baba left us at the age of 86 years, when we thought that He would be here until 96 years? Please clarify.

A: Why did you not put that question to Swami, when He said that He will be here till ninety six years? "Swami, why not one hundred and six?" Why did you not ask that question? When He said ninety six, why not for one hundred and six? But, we didn't say that. So, from ninety six, He has reduced it to eighty five. Why not? It is His privilege. He can extend or withdraw.

He said ninety six as per what calculation? That He did not tell us. There are two systems of calendars: one is the solar system, the other is the lunar system. According to the lunar system, He had completed ninety six years.

Should He follow your command? Should He wait for your instructions? Lunar and solar equally belong to Him. He can choose either of the two, or neither of the two. So, He followed the lunar system to keep His word of ninety six years. Thereafter, He has withdrawn from the body.

Baba will never utter a lie. What He says will happen and that has happened! Please keep it in your mind. When we have a problem, we pray and surrender. We feel at times that the world is upside down. We expect Swami to give a solution; but till then, what should we do? The world will never turn upside down; only we turn upside down! It's a simple thing: we think we are stable and steady, but we are not!

Earth is revolving at a high speed. In addition, it revolves around the sun. But, we think we are stable! We are not! We think this is day and that is night. We say 'sunrise' and 'sunset'. Actually, the sun never rises nor sets. We have named Earth-turned-towards-the-sun as day, and away-from-the-sun as night. So, the world will never really turn upside down. You only will turn upside down!

Coming by flight from Brunei, I may say, "Jakarta is coming, Jakarta is coming, Jakarta is coming!" As I leave Jakarta tomorrow to Medan, I will say that Jakarta left, Jakarta left! Jakarta has not come and Jakarta has not left; it is where it is! It is only I, who come and I who leave! That's all it is!

Q: In your closeness with Bhagawan, did Baba ever mention about life on other planets? Is there any planet beside Earth with life?

A: We are already bored with this life here on this planet! Why another planet? We are not interested. We have enough troubles and sufferings here, on this planet. If we are not able to get off of this one, why worry about the extra burden of another one? So don't worry yourself!

Q: Brother, is it okay to give our organs for others, after we leave this body?

A: After you leave this body, how do you say, "Okay, take my organs?" How do you say, "Don't take my organs?" If you are not there, nobody is there to take your permission. It's just left to the family people, not to you! You've already said, "Good bye!"

Q: Many times, I do suprabhatam at 2:30 or 3'o clock in the morning and then, do my meditation. Is it correct or not?

A: If you start your meditation at 2:00 am to 3:00 am (in the middle of the night), it is alright if you are a bachelor.

If you are married with a family, if you get up at 2:00 am for meditation, people will mistake you for the devil, not a human being! If you get up at 2:00 am to 3:00 am to meditate, you will sleep later, in your office. Then, you will be removed from service. Therefore, stop that!

Q: When someone puts you down, how does it affect your life?

A: No one can put you down! Baba gives this example: Dig a deep pit here and place a lamp inside. The flame is upward and the light is upward, though it is in a deep pit. You may put me down, but my light will be up! My delight will be up! So, nobody can put you down. If you hit the ball down with double speed, those, who put you down, are helping you to come up higher and higher.

Q: Where do souls go after they die? Do they automatically attain moksha or do they just go into another birth cycle?

A: Where do they go? Same place we go. There, we meet and say, "Hi, how are you?" We will have common *bhajans* there! My friends, do not bother about life after death!

There are some people, who are interested to know, "What will happen to me?" Nothing will happen to you! There are some people, who forecast what is going to happen. I tell you, you are losing money going there, nothing else will happen! There are some people, who go to *Nadi* books for readings. Those *Nadis* are correct so far as your past is concerned. The future predictions are never correct.

Why should you know your past? A Nadi fellow tells me, "Anil Kumar, you have four children!" Why should I give him five *rupees*? I have four children already! That fellow need not tell me. If the fellow tells me, "Anil Kumar, you are a Sai Baba devotee," I will say, "Shut up, I know!" Why should I pay him for that?

So, don't be interested to know the past, because it is already over. Don't be interested to know the future, because knowing it won't help you. Suppose some fellow said, "Anil Kumar, you are going to be a gold-mine owner, next year," then I might start spending money now, because the gold mine is waiting tomorrow. But, I may not gain the gold mine, so instead I will just lose my present money.

In short, it may not help you to know about a future, which might be better. How will this help you? Suppose someone is saying, "Next year, you will die!" This fellow may die tomorrow. No use in knowing the future! Future is mystery, past is history, so live in the present. Present is God, this moment is God. God is present, not past or future. Present is God! You are in the present, Baba is in the present. Baba is ever-present, omnipresent.

Q: Why did Baba cry on His 85th Birthday?

A: How do you know that He cried? How do you know that He cried on his eighty fifth Birthday? It is not crying! Suppose your mother sees you after ten years: You have gone to some foreign country and return home after ten years. First thing she does is cry. Shall I say she is crying? These are tears of joy, tears shed when she is finally meeting her son again! Similarly, on the eighty fifth Birthday, so many thousands of Sai devotees came to Puttaparthi. The Divine Mother Sai may have shed tears of joy. So, that is not crying.

Swami doesn't know what crying is right from His childhood. He always laughs and He makes you laugh. His life is full of jokes. Time flies in front of Him. Why do you expect Him to cry? Never, never! God is bliss, bliss is God. Baba is bliss, bliss is Baba. It is nothing short of that!

Questions And Answers Session

(Special Talk by Prof. Anil Kumar
in Kuala Lumpur, Malaysia, October 30th, 2011)

Q: I am curious to find out why Vedas are chanted on a daily basis. What do we really hear?

A: Many of the foreigners ask me, "Anil Kumar, we don't know Sanskrit. So, how can we chant the *Vedas*?"

My answer to them is, "God knows English also." Even true *pundit*s (priests) themselves don't know the meaning of *Vedas*. Ninety-nine percent of them don't know the meaning and only chant it, because it's their profession; that's all.

Q: One of our youth was recently diagnosed with cancer. His condition is deteriorating rapidly and he is fighting for his life. What would Swami want us to do?

A: Swami wants you to pray for him. We can pray. We are free to pray. Prayer heals and prayer cures. That's what we can do.

Q: Swami is always with us. In fact, He is Antharyami. We all know that through our personal experiences. So, why, at times, do we miss His physical form? We really miss Him and cry. Why?

A: It's because so far in our life, we have been used to talking to Him and we have been used to passing letters to Him, and having interviews. We've been used to presenting flowers to Him. Now that the physical proximity has gone,

we feel sorry; but, we will very soon overcome that by His
Divine grace.

*Q: Should we celebrate Swami's birthday, if those, who
want to do the celebration, call it, 'A Tribute to Sai'?*

A: 'A Tribute to Sai' is not a celebration. You cannot
'pay tribute' to Swami. You can praise the Lord and sing
His glory, but you cannot pay Him tributes. We are nobody
to estimate Him. So, sing His praise.

*Q: What can we do, when Mother Earth is suffering so
much? Oh, I am thinking of the Thailand floods!*

A: Mother Earth is already suffering, so don't add to
her suffering. A simple example: I never wrote a letter to
Swami about my family problems or about my children.
Never! People asked me, "How is it that Swami talks to you?
Why?"

I reply, "Because I don't talk about myself."

"How it is that Swami stops there and looks at you?"

"Because I have no petition, I have no complaint."

Therefore, don't add to the suffering of Mother Earth.

*Q: Why are some centres in Malaysia doing rituals and
not Sai's mission?*

A: Rituals are also part of a spiritual mission, but only
if the rituals take you to spirituality. Spirituality is the fruit
of all rituals. So, rituals are the root, while spirituality is the
fruit. Ritual is the foundation, whereas spirituality is the
mansion. Ritual and spirituality should go together. If I only

do rituals, it means that I stopped constructing my house — that I stopped at the foundation level.

Q: Swami says, "I am That. I am God." Does that mean I have no free will to decide my life?

A: The question is about free will. What has Swami said? You have free will. It seems God has said, "Do anything." Hah! The fellow is very happy. You want to smoke? Yes. Drink? Yes! Vagabonding? Yes! I want to do that and this. Okay, yes, please do!

But, there is one condition: you cannot escape from the results or consequences of your actions. You may do as you like, but you will reap the fruit. As you sow, so you shall reap. So, you should be prepared for the results. You can do anything — you have the free will to do anything, but you will get the results.

Q: What was Swami's final message to you, Professor?

A: Swami, Who is God, has no 'first' or 'last' message. The last message is the first, the first message is the last, and the last and the first are eternal. The last message comes, when you have to face the results of not having followed His command. The first message is to warn you.

The *Bhagavad Gita* is not the last message of Krishna; rather, it is the first message for every day. The *Bible* is not the last message; it is every day's message. So, Baba's message has nothing to do with any specific time. It applies to existence; it applies to the moment, the here and now.

Q: What is the difference between devotion and surrender? What has Swami said about devotion and surrender?

A: Once, it happened that a fellow came — a boy. You know that boys sometimes overreact out of immaturity. The boy said, "Swami, I am ready to die for You. I am ready to die for You! My life is for You." That boy thought that he was speaking with good sense. But, Baba knows everything.

"Oh! You don't have to give your life and you don't have to die. You have to *live* for Swami, not die for Swami." That's what Baba said. So, live for Swami, don't die for Swami!

Second, you say, "Swami, I surrender my property, I surrender my hands, feet, and eyes." But, they are not yours to surrender. They are not your property in the first place. The body is not your property. The eyes are not your property, because eyes start to look at what they are not supposed to look at. Ears start to listen to what they are not supposed to listen to.

If you are not the owner of your body, how can you surrender it to the Lord? You cannot donate someone else's property. Be the owner first.

Third, when it comes to devotion and surrender, remember that in devotion, there are two, the devotee and God. The devotee is devoted to God.

That is devotion — dual, duality, *dwaita*. Whereas, when the devotee totally forgets himself, when 'I' does not exist, when He only exists, that is surrender.

There are some people, who say, "*I* have surrendered." First, surrender that 'I'! Surrender is non-dualism. Devotion is dualism.

Take the simple example of water and sugar. If you take the two things separately, it is devotion. When sugar is totally mixed with water, it is neither sugar, nor water, but becomes syrup and that is surrender. In surrender, there is total identification with the Divine, with no exercise of choice and preferences.

Q: I have travelled to a number of countries in the past and noticed that many centres in these countries follow the Prasanthi model for bhajans. Every country has it's own language, so why don't they sing bhajans in their own language?

A: It is their fate. It is their bad luck to have such leadership. Follow the Malaysian model, when you are in Malaysia — love Malaysia! Be Malaysian and encourage the local language. Encourage the local culture and don't dictate something alien to this land. That is what Swami expects.

Why? For the Convocation, there is no *arathi;* instead, we have the national anthem. For medical conferences, there is no *arathi;* instead, the national anthem. So, respect every country, respect every culture, and respect every language. That is Baba's message.

Sai Mission And Its Continuity
Part I

(Special Talk by Prof. Anil Kumar,
in Kuala Lumpur, Malaysia, October 30th, 2011)

Life Is A Journey Of Continuity To Eternity

All of us have our own professional life, whether a professor, an engineer, a doctor, or a housewife. We each are engaged in our own way. Thus, life is a journey from womb to the tomb, from birth to death. This journey is the physical one, from birth to death. But, the life journey is one of continuity to eternity. This spiritual journey has no beginning or end. In this journey, we experience neither birth nor death.

This is the true life journey, for it is continuous, like the flowing of a river which goes on incessantly. This spiritual life journey is persistent and continuous, going on forever and ever forward and onward. Taking this journey along with God makes life worth living. So, life is a journey really worth living in the company of God.

When we are in Prasanthi Nilayam, we forget the day, the date, and the time, because we are with God. A journey with God makes you forget what you are and where you are.

On the normal physical level of our life's journey, we are conscious of our position and our scholarship, displaying vanity, ego, pride, publicity, pomp, aggrandisement, and self-glorification. Such a journey is a useless journey and not worth living.

On the other hand, life with God is the true journey. You just forget your status, your dignity, and your scholarship, because you become lost like a bubble in the ocean. The moment a bubble gets submerged in the ocean, it loses its identity and becomes one with the ocean. So, this spiritual life journey is the journey with God.

The 'I' Is Lost

You can come across people on their physical journey, who are boastful, proud of their own achievements and their simple little mushroom-like accomplishments. But, on a spiritual journey with God, you do not know who you are. The 'I' is lost.

"I meditate," somebody told Swami.

"Continue to meditate," Swami said.

"Yes, Swami. For how long?"

"Continue, until you forget 'I'-ness: 'I' do it, 'I' am doing it. Continue. Continue for 100 lives to come!" Swami answered.

Life is a spiritual journey with God. When the 'I' is lost, when the 'I' is no more, then only He is there. That is the spiritual journey. The spiritual journey of continuity to eternity is a profound experience, a real experience.

Who Is In The Delhi Darshan Queue?

There was a long queue waiting for His darshan, a very long queue at Golf Links in Delhi. Before darshan, Swami came out and saw a short man in the queue.

He came close to the man and asked, "Why are you here?"

"Swami, why not?" the man responded.

Then, Swami said, "Oh, you're the Governor of Uttar Pradesh, Dr. Burgula Ramakrishna Rao. You also stand in the queue to come for darshan?"

"I may be a governor outside," he answered. "I may also be a scholar in thirty international languages. But, in front of You, I am a humble, simple devotee. I am no longer a governor." That is the effect of the spiritual journey!

Some may go on saying things like, "I am this," or "I am that." "I am a VIP! Don't you know?" So long you say, "I am this...," my answer to you is that you are not this, for the spiritual journey knows no name and fame.

Swami Does Not Want Thanks

Somebody came to Swami and said, "Bhagawan, You have done this for me. Thank You, Swami. Now, the family problem is resolved. Thank You, Bhagawan. The business problem is gone too. Thank You, Swami."

Swami answered, "No 'thanks', *Bangaru* (a term of endearment used by Swami, meaning "golden one"). Thanks go only to a third person. I am not a third person. You and I are one. Do you say, 'Oh Daddy, thank you for the beautiful trousers?' Do you say that? 'Oh Mummy, thanks for the nice curry!' Do you say that? No. You are my children. You and I are one." That is the spiritual journey.

A true and correct spiritual journey is the one, where we do not crave for recognition, nor strive for fame. This is the journey we are supposed to undertake. Such a spiritual journey is a great experience. Experience what this life really is!

You Have Given Yourself To Me

One example of this occurred when Swami started introducing some VIPs to me.

"Anil Kumar, this man gave 100 crores of rupees to our hospital," He said. "Another gave 50 crores to our hospital. This one gave 25 crores to our hospital and he brings medicines worth crores and crores, every time he comes." As Swami was introducing everybody to me, I felt shy. I felt very much humbled and belittled.

Then, I said, "Swami, I feel very embarrassed! I feel very guilty. I have not given You any crores, as I don't have any, nor wish to acquire any. I have not given You anything, Swami. So when You introduced these people, I felt embarrassed."

Do you know what Baba said? "Those, who gave 100 crores or 50 crores, are staying in a hotel outside. You have given yourself to Me. What more can I want? You are here with Me! They have given what they have, but you have given yourself. That's why you are staying with Me."

That's the experience of a spiritual journey with God. A spiritual journey with God is an experience that can put you in a state of bliss!

Swami's Jaguar Car Incident

You know, Swami has a number of cars, many cars, all presented as gifts. He even has a Jaguar car! When this brand new Jaguar first arrived, Swami said, "Anil Kumar, let us have a photograph. You stand on that side and I will stand on this side."

Well, how to stand? So, I stood erect.

Swami said, "No, not like that! You are standing like a car driver. That's not the way. Put your head like that!"

So, I stood like that, as shown by Swami. That photo is still with us.

At the end, Swami said, "Would you buy this car? Are you ready to buy this car?"

I said, "Car? Swami, I cannot. I can't afford to buy Your car!"

This statement is important: "Are you not ashamed to say that?" He asked.

Swami repeated, "Are you not ashamed to say that? Is that the reply I expect from you? I'd appreciate it, if you'd say, 'Bhagawan, with You, I can buy the whole world. If I can buy the whole world, what is this car?'"

Such an experience with God is a spiritual journey. Moving with God is a spiritual journey. These experiences living with God are an education. Always observing God is an experience sufficient unto itself!

Proof That Swami Is Lord Krishna Himself

Dining with Swami was an experience, which we can never forget in a lifetime! There are many, many delicious items served, when eating with Swami. However, our God eats only one spoon of *ragi* (Indian millet), that's all. But, we are served many, many items.

In fact, all those, who follow Swami to Kodaikanal, are always eating all the time. But, there's no exercise. So, if they check their weight on the final day, the day of their return, they can see they have gained much weight.

First class curd (yogurt) is served at the dining table, at each and every meal. You need a crow bar to cut the thick curd! Well, we were all enjoying ourselves.

I said, "Swami, the curd is very nice, very tasty. Swami, why don't You take some curd?"

I asked that, because I wanted to eat some more. But, how can I eat that, if He doesn't eat it any?

I said, "Swami, how am I to eat? So, please . . ."

Swami's response is important: "Curds! Anil Kumar, I had enough curds and milk in a previous Avatar. I am tired of curd and milk. Therefore, I am not eating them anymore."

This was an indirect suggestion, an indirect declaration, an indirect affirmation that He is Lord *Krishna* Himself. That is living with God! A journey with God is such an experience!

Experience Of
His Omniscience And Omnipotence

One day, in the morning, Swami called one cook named Sai Krishna. He was a cook from the Anantapur campus, who followed Swami every year to Kodaikanal.

"Sai Krishna, come here!" That fellow came.

"You are stupid, you are an idiot, you are a donkey, and you are a dog." He went on scolding him. That fellow was shivering. We were all watching.

Suddenly, Swami said, "Arre (Hey) fellow, what's our breakfast time?"

He answered, "Swami, 7:30."

Swami said, "Right. But, you are giving coffee to a fellow at 5 o'clock, every day, without My notice. Is this your grandfather's property? Why do you do that? I'll kick you out!"

That fellow was shivering. The cat was out of the bag!

Then, he said, "Swami, only I drink coffee at 5 o'clock in the morning!"

Swami replied, "I said all this to let you know, that I know you're having coffee at 5 o'clock in the morning!"

Living with God and journeying with God is an experience of His omniscience and omnipotence. He knows everything. In a book about Swami, I may read something, quote it, or repeat it verbatim; but, to experience Swami directly, journeying along with Him, is really unique.

It's His infinite grace that made me stay with Him for 22 long years, and follow Him to Kodaikanal each and every time. Such an experience! Such a journey is a real experience with God.

Ice Cream From Divine Hands

At one time, it so happened that Swami acquired some additional land around a building. The whole land was cleaned up, the weeds removed, and the ground made ready by *seva dals*. I, too, joined the seva dals, doing some work. I know I am unfit for work, but yet I went there.

Swami came, stopped His car, and said, "Ah ha! What an actor you are, eh? How nicely you are acting! But, you are not doing anything. Just standing there acting. Acting!"

I said, "Swami, I know I am an actor. But, I knew that You would come to this spot. For You, I am acting. That's all. Not for anybody else. All this acting is meant for You only, Swami!"

He laughed and He left that place.

And then, *seva dal* people started distributing ice creams, very nice ice creams! I, too, had my share outside. And at the end of the work, calmly, coolly, I walked into Swami's building. Swami was also distributing ice creams to everybody there. I stretched out my hand.

Then, He said, "Ah, you had one cup already, outside. You already ate one cup."

"Swami, did I say that I did not eat?" I did not bluff.

"Then, why are you asking now?"

I said, "Since You are giving it, it is prasad. I want it!"

Such a journey is an experience — an unforgettable experience — that leaves an indelible impression on both our minds and our hearts. So touching!

Bottles Of Pickles

I can also tell you about another incident. One day, when Swami was very busy, I noticed that some new bottles of pickles had arrived there, at the Kodai house, half an hour earlier. I ate some and wanted more.

'It would be indecent, if I go on eating pickles while sitting with others,' I said to myself. So I went to sit near the next batch (of boys), avoiding sitting near the others (guests). Thus, I stood behind.

Swami looked around and asked, "Where is Anil Kumar?"

Somebody said, "Swami, there are so many guests that there is no seat here. Therefore, he is waiting behind."

Swami said, "Arre (Hey), to whom are you telling this? He wants a separate pickle session! That's why he moved there!"

Such an experience was ecstatic. Such a non-dual experience is really worth having, during one's lifetime. Journeying with God is this real experience.

Swami Always Gives Clues

I also remember how nicely Swami acts! It was Chinese day in Prasanthi Nilayam. For some reason, He gave heavy doses of scolding to the teachers there.

"You are not teaching properly. I will send you out! You are not behaving properly!"

Lots of scolding! All teachers felt very unhappy and I was no exception.

In the evening, He came into the auditorium. He wanted to divert our attention. He said to me, "Come here!"

'Is Swami going to speak now?' I asked myself. 'Is He going to speak again?' That was the question. 'What does this mean?' I asked.

"I am going to speak. Be ready." So, I got the clue.

Swami sat there. Immediately, we arranged the mikes. He was acting there and making a pantomime to me, cutting a finger across His nose (jokingly meaning, "Anil Kumar, I may cut off your nose!").

Then, I said loudly, "Bhagawan, our thirst is not quenched. Our appetite is not satiated. We are still hungering for Your talking! This morning, we had 'hots' (i.e. scolding). Swami, this evening, we pray only sweets will be distributed!"

Immediately, He gave a discourse! In any experience with Swami, we should take some clue out of what He says and then, dramatise the situation.

Somebody Should Bear The Cross

The MBA boys in Business Management presented a silver plate to Swami. But, He doesn't accept such things. So, He came out and shouted at everybody, "Idiots! Stupid! You present Me a plate like that?"

The fellows were shivering. I am a professor of bio-science, but he was scolding MBA boys! I noticed all this.

'Somebody should bear the cross,' I thought.

Then, I said, "Swami, the boys are nice (implying it is not their fault). We teachers have not advised them properly. Therefore, they bought it and gave it to Swami. It is their love. But, we have not explained things to them properly."

Then, He turned to me and said, "You fool, you donkey! You have not properly directed them!"

The boys knew that I am a bio-science man. And of course, Swami knows that I am a bio-science man. The mistake was committed by MBA boys, but I had taken it upon myself. "Swami, they did not know."

Swami interrupted and blasted me. Yet, while leaving, He waved and gave a beautiful smile.

The Spiritual Journey
Is A Challenging Experience

Such an experience! The spiritual journey is such an experience. It is challenging. The spiritual journey is not that comfortable. After all, in this physical world, you get some kind of immediate results. But, the spiritual journey is full of challenges, full of troubles, full of turmoil, insults and blame, and people who envy you. It's a challenging task.

So, the journey with God is challenging. But, He gives you a lifebelt so you don't sink; that way you can still float, keeping your head above water. At one time or another, we might feel like running away from that campus/ashram; but, He won't allow us to go.

Sometimes, you might decide that you want Him to let you go. But, He won't let you go. In the evening, when He comes for darshan, He gives you a nice smile. You then forget all those problems. All problems are instantly gone.

That's the spiritual journey, a sufficient experience unto itself. All other paths, all other areas are just ordinary journeys. But, journeying with God is the real journey. Let us walk with Him. Let us go along with Him, facing all problems.

The Divine Romance

Some of my colleagues at my native place have repeatedly asked me, "Anil, what have you got there? You left your family here, you left your parents here, and you left your lucrative job just to go there. What do you get there? What do you get by speaking all the time?" That's the question my colleagues ask me every time!

My answer is this, "If you ask a drunkard why he drinks, he will say, 'Have a bottle and then tell me! You have a bottle and then you let me know.'"

Living with God is similar. Though it is troublesome, once you are in the Divine romance, once you enjoy the experience of it, you cannot come out of it. Impossible! Life with God is not pompous. Life is not a luxury, when staying with Bhagawan; but still, journey with God!

Some Of Those Who Have Sacrificed

You must have heard of Mr. Lal, who is in charge of the stores there, in Prasanthi Nilayam. Mr. Lal hails from Colombo, Sri Lanka. He has got a big palace there, with 50 or 60 rooms. There is a big fort around his palace. He left it all and is staying with Swami in just one room! So, journeying with God is a test. When you journey with God, the path is narrow and tough. It is not like getting a ride in a limousine — impossible! Yet, many people accept that challenging path.

You may have also heard of another gentleman, who is no more, named Mr. Kundra from London. He was in charge of the North Indian Canteen. He, too, was a very rich man, a strikingly rich man. He left it all and stayed in a one-room flat also. So, life's journey with God is a matter of sacrifice.

Journeying with God is challenging and involves sacrifice, sometimes inviting troubles. For example, your own people may disown you. Your own relations may disown you, because you cannot come out without His permission. (There was a time, when Swami would let people leave only after getting His physical permission.)

Swami is such a Master. He avoids you, when you feel you are most in need for Him. Then, He will ask you, "How are you?" when you have nothing to ask Him.

He Will Hold On To You

So, this journey is not that simple. To speak about the journey is not easy. To have that journey — to be in the process of that journey, in the company of God — is not given to everybody or to anybody. Not everyone can take it, because you will have to experience physical discomfort, social boycott, and sometimes, even utter neglect from Bhagawan. Yet, you should be able to survive all these challenges.

For those of us, who have spent our lives, which were earlier based on praise, achievements, and all kinds of tributes, to then lead a life as a nameless non-entity is not an easy thing. That itself is the experience. Why? Because this spiritual journey gives us the experience of self-negation, which means that one begins to recognise that: 'I am nobody, Bhagawan. When You are there, I am nobody.'

In the outside world, we go by the psychology that "I am everything", "I am somebody." But, on the spiritual journey, you are not somebody. You are not anybody. You are nobody on the spiritual journey. He intentionally gives you experiences, so that you will remain a non-entity. Self-effacement, withdrawal from all kinds of external show, and such things define the spiritual journey. But, during such experiences, He will hold on to you.

Sai The Dramatist In Action

A few years ago, the *Srinivasa Guesthouse* in Prasanthi Nilayam was inaugurated. For the inaugural function, the Prime Minister, governors, and cabinet ministers were invited to have lunch with Swami.

I was feeling excluded, thinking, 'God, You want the Prime Minister, but You don't want me. You want governors, but You don't want me. You want those people, who come and go on visitors' visas, but You don't want to look at those of us, who have settled here. Swami, what is wrong with me? Or what is wrong with You?'

That's what I was feeling, while I was there in the Eswaramma high school campus, where food and clothes were being distributed.

Suddenly, one gentleman came to me and said, "Anil Kumar, please go to Swami and inform Him that we are running short of clothes. We need four hundred sarees now! People are waiting! Please tell Swami."

So, I took that opportunity and went there. I said, "Swami!"

He said, "Oh, come on, sir."

I repeated, "Swami!"

Swami asked, "What?"

"Swami, they need four hundred more sarees!"

Swami said, "I sent a thousand sarees. There are still two lorries (truckloads) of stock waiting there. This was only an excuse to bring you here. You are feeling badly that I have not called you here. Therefore, I brought you. This is Sai drama," He said.

That was a wonderful experience! A spiritual journey may be a shocking, jolting, or tense affair. But yet, at other times, the experiences can be so blissful. Each such experience creates an eternal memory. Each experience becomes immortal and each experience is unparalleled. That's what He confers in the end.

At Sundaram In Madras

On one occasion, Swami visited Sundaram at Madras (now Chennai). So, I went there to Madras.

Then, Swami asked, "Sir, where are you staying?"

"Swami, I am staying at Madras University Guest House."

Swami said, "No guest house! Come and stay here!"

From then on, I was staying with Swami. At that time, I was serving as the state president of the Sathya Sai Organisation of Andhra Pradesh. I was feeling like I had done something great. That was natural after all, for at that time I used to come and go. I had not lived with Him at the ashram.

Only the wearer knows where the shoe pinches. It is quite easy to talk, standing along the shores. But, come on, get into the sea! Because it is only when we get into the sea and face those challenges that we can say, "We follow You!" Only then can we take our hats off to You!

But, at that time, I did not know all this. So what happened?

Swami called me and asked, "Come on, have you seen Sundaram?"

"No, Swami."

"Come on, I will show you," He said.

He was taking me along the verandas and corridors, when He called out to one *seva dal*: "What is your name?"

The man answered, "Radha K."

"Oh, Radha K," Swami repeated. "How much salary do you make in your job?"

"Swami, one lakh."

Swami imitated him, "Oh, one lakh."

Then, He asked, "What are you?"

"Swami, I am the Director of the Indian Institute of Technology in Madras."

"Manchidi!" (Good!) Swami responded and then, gave me a sarcastic look.

Swami walked a little bit further, saw another man and also asked him for his name.

"Venkataram," the man answered.

"Oh, Venkataraman," Swami repeated. "What are you doing?"

"Swami, I am an electrical engineering professor at Madras Guindy Engineering College."

Swami continued to look at me with some sarcasm. All those fellows at Sundaram were professors or directors and such, doing ordinary *seva dal* services. This experience took me to the next step.

"Do you have such people in Andhra?" Swami asked me. Remember, I was the state president.

'Shall I say I don't have?' I asked myself. 'If I say that, I'll lose my prestige! Shall I say I have? But, I have none! So, what shall I say?'

I said, "Swami, in Andhra, there are devotees that equal Tamil Nadu people with respect to devotion. They may not be equal with respect to position and qualification; but, with respect to devotion, Andhra people are equal."

"What a tactful response, isn't it? You gave a clever answer," He responded.

He then went around to a swing (called a *'jhoola'* in India) there, in Sundaram, and sat in it.

Swami asked, "Anil Kumar, how do you like?"

"It is not nice, Swami."

"Not nice? How dare you say that? It's the best jhoola (swing for the deity)!" He said.

"No, no, I don't think so, Swami."

"Why do you say that?" He asked.

I answered, "If You sit there, it becomes great, but not otherwise!"

"Oh, I see."

"So, how do I look?" He asked (sitting in the jhoola).

"Swami, You look great; but still, something is lacking!"

"What?"

I motioned to Swami that I wanted to rock Him like Bala Gopal.

He said, "Come on, do that!"

So, I did. What an experience! Some of the experiences along the spiritual journey are worth remembering for lifetimes, for many more lives to come! Such an experience will make you forget all troubles and all difficulties you have ever had.

Until such a moment, you may feel all worked up inside; but, once He gives such experiences, all difficulties are gone — simply spontaneously gone! Therefore, it is the spiritual journey that gives such experiences, which ultimately lead to transformation.

Sai Mission And Its Continuity
Part II

(Special Talk by Prof. Anil Kumar
in Kuala Lumpur, Malaysia, October 30th, 2011)

What Is Transformation?

What is transformation? There are many misconceptions about transformation. Is a non-vegetarian, who becomes a vegetarian, experiencing transformation? I don't think so. Can an alcoholic, who becomes a teetotaller, be considered transformed? No, it is not enough.

Some people ask me, "What has been the most noticeable transformation in your life, since you have known Swami?" My answer is, "I never needed any transformation, as I was good enough."

So, what is true transformation? True transformation is egolessness, absence of jealousy, absence of pride, not craving for power, and no arrogance. That is transformation.

There are some people, who say, "Anil Kumar, after coming to Swami, I stopped eating brinjal curry." That is not transformation!

Somebody said, "Anil Kumar, I have undergone transformation, because I stopped eating bitter gourd." I said, "You don't like it anyway, so that is not transformation!"

Some people also say, "Once a month, I don't take food on a Thursday." I tell them, "Not eating once a month is still not enough. It is not transformation."

Others say, "Thursday is Baba's day, so I don't eat. Saturday is Venkateshwara's day (or Tuesday, Hanuman's day), so I don't eat."

I say, "Please stop eating. That will be your day — the final day!"

Such statements are not transformations. Giving up an item at the breakfast table or at the dining table is not transformation.

Baba said in a poem:

Ali Tho Aligi Pastunnantha Maatraanna

Adi Goppa Upavasamaguna

When you have had a fight with your wife, you don't want to eat that night in order to express your anger. But, then you cannot say the next morning, "I have been fasting." Fighting with your wife is not religious transformation!

Preethitho Raathrantha Pekaadinantha
Maatraana Jaagarana Aguna

By playing cards on Sivaratri, all night long, you cannot say that you have been vigilant. Whom are you cheating?

True Transformation

Transformation means feeling that you are nobody. It means seeing your own mistakes and at the same time, noticing the talents in others. To be nobody... that is transformation.

Let's look at external transformation. Some people have three parallel lines (referring to vibhuti marks on their foreheads). Then, what about these other lines? (Professor Anil Kumar points to the lines on the palm of his hands) And a zebra has lines all over its body! So, external marks or markings, even seen in the observance of rituals, are not enough. Perhaps, they can be a beginning, like the first rung on a spiritual ladder.

There was a gentleman, who donated a lot of equipment to the hospital in Puttaparthi. Do you know what that man said? "Swami, this equipment is not mine to give. It's Yours and it is enough, if You accept it. Thank You, Swami." That is transformation!

But, other people will brag that they donated all their savings (or whatever it is) to Swami. Do you know what I say to them? "You will probably need to reincarnate 100 times more, in order to undergo transformation."

Therefore, this spiritual journey is an opportunity, an adventure, and a challenge — a journey from the known to the unknown. It is easy to travel from the known to the known. I know Malaysia and I know India. But, if I were to travel to the moon, it would be an unknown environment. I don't know whether I would return or not.

Transformation Brings Equanimity

So, this spiritual journey is a journey from the known to the unknown. It is quite risky and not that easy. But, experience after experience will make you stronger and stronger and then, you won't be carried away by the currents so easily. You won't sway like leaves in the slightest wind. You will remain like a boulder in the sea. The waves of the ocean crash against the boulders, but the boulders remain steady. This is what experience gives you — a sort of transformation, where you remain steady and blissful.

For example, there was a great scholar, who was in charge of the yagna in Prasanthi Nilayam. Swami materialised a necklace for his wife. Everybody saw the necklace.

I thought to myself, 'If I don't enquire about the necklace, the scholar may feel that I am jealous of his wife. What should I do?' So, I approached the scholar and said, "Sir, I hear that Swami materialised a necklace for your wife."

He replied, "The body is temporary like a water bubble. Do you think that this necklace will last forever? Do you believe that this chain is permanent, when the body itself is impermanent? Mr. Anil Kumar, I didn't expect you to make such a query."

I replied, "I did not want to get myself into trouble, sir. I knew that answer!"

A true transformation doesn't make you feel elated by praise, or depressed by blame, nor affected by profit or loss. Instead, you maintain equanimity.

As long as we crave for power, name, and fame and such, it is not transformation. When my head is full of information, it is not transformation. The spiritual journey confers an experience that leads to a phenomenal inner change without our knowledge. That is true transformation.

Sai Mission And Its Continuity

Now, let me say a few words about the Sai mission and its continuity. Here is what Baba said about it, "You are not the doer." I am sure discovering this has been the experience of every devotee all over the world. It is He, Who prompts, fulfils, and decides, whether you like it or not!

Somebody asked me, "Anil Kumar, do you have sufficient funds to carry on Sai's mission in the future?"

I told that person that the activities of Sai Baba are not based on funds. They are based on a refund, that's all. No funds, only refunds.

We don't have to receive finances from anybody. We decide amongst friends whatever little we can do and then, we do it. That's all. We do not raise funds. The Sai mission and its continuity will succeed, because the strength of the Sai mission is not financial. Please remember, the strength of the Sai mission is faith and definitely not finances.

Need Of The Hour: Strengthen Our Faith

Therefore, the need of the hour is to strengthen our faith. Let our faith grow stronger and stronger, deeper and deeper, so that the Sai procession will move majestically and the Sai mission will continue forever and ever.

Having been Baba's translator, I know many of His statements, such as, "You cannot leave Me. I will not allow you to leave Me. I will chase you and see to it that I accomplish what I want through you. Until then, you cannot be free from Me."

Therefore, there is no doubt about His mission, because He will call and inspire people, talking to them from within, through the inner voice, to get things done.

Do Not Doubt The Continuity
Of Swami's Mission

Here is another example. Madhuri Shah was the Chairman of the University Grants (UGC), the apex body in India that monitors the activities of all universities. She came to see Swami.

Swami said, as if it were a piece of chocolate, "Madhuri, I want a university. Would you give Me one?"

Madhuri Shah said, "That is impossible, Swami."

"Why?" Swami asked.

"It is impossible, because there is already a university in Anantapur; so, another university cannot be built within a 40 mile radius. It is just not possible, Swami."

Here is what Swami said, "Madhuri, it is possible and you will inaugurate it!"

Then, she said, "Swami, I will give You my head if You want, but not the university."

Swami said, "I don't want your head, because it is empty. If your head was full, you would not say that. I will have the university next year and you will inaugurate it."

By the indescribable Divine will of Bhagawan Sri Sathya Sai Baba, it became a reality. The lady said it was impossible, but Swami made it possible and she was the chief guest for the inauguration!

So, why should we doubt the continuity of Swami's mission? Please follow His Avataric mission, His Divine mission.

He Will Accomplish His Mission...
Even Now

A very important person from the United States sent a doctor by the name Robert Bonn Chuck to Prasanthi Nilayam, to attend an International Cardiac Conference.

The doctor said, "I am here as an emissary of so-and-so. I was sent here to study, to see how this hospital is run. I have been here for the last three days, but I am not able to understand how this hospital manages to give free medical aid. Surgery, diagnosis, pathological investigations, and accommodation are all free. Only He could do it!"

Robert Bonn Chuck then made this statement on the dais, in the Mandir, "It is only Sathya Sai Baba, Who could run a hospital like this. No human being on Earth can ever undertake such a job, not a chance of it. Only Baba could do it!"

Swami went to Bangalore to inaugurate the Sri Sathya Sai Super Specialty Hospital there. I accompanied Him in order to translate His talk that afternoon. The chief guest happened to be Atal Bihari Vajpayee, the Prime Minister of India at that time. Another important guest was Rama Devi, Governor of Karnataka. Swami was sitting there like a child — Ananda Sai, Kalyana Sai, Leela Sai, Mahima Sai.

Vajpayee, the Prime Minister said, "It is impossible for the government to construct a hospital of this size even in 9 years, but Baba did it in 9 months!" That is the Divinity of Bhagawan Baba. But, the story doesn't end there.

Rama Devi, the Governor of Karnataka, said: "Swami, the Government of Karnataka undertook a project to construct a hospital seven years ago; not even half of it has been completed yet. But, You managed to build Your hospital. How? Because You are Bhagawan Sri Sathya Sai Baba."

So, there is no need to doubt the continuity of His mission. I am sure that He will inspire people from within. He will not allow you to rest; He will accomplish His mission.

Keep Our Faith

When all is said and done, what is our role here? Our role is to not lose faith. If I lose faith in myself, it's like losing my life. Having faith in yourself is the same as having faith in Baba. That faith is the foundation for this renaissance. That faith is the foundation for our transformation, for the spiritual mission to come in the future. So, our role is to keep our faith.

Ever-existent, Ever-vibrant, And Ever-radiant

More miracles are happening now than ever before. In the South Indian canteen in Prasanthi Nilayam, we have seen the footsteps of Bhagawan on the wall. On the ladies side of the South Indian canteen, nectar is flowing from Baba's photo. At Sundaram in Madras, you find Swami's footprints all along the way.

A Sathya Sai primary school child was ill and could not sleep. Baba appeared in his room, gave him some medicine, and said, "My child, don't worry. I am with you. Don't disturb the warden, the principal, or your lecturers. My child, I am ever with you."

That is Sathya Sai Baba. He is not the physical body, which appears and disappears. **Sathya Sai Baba is the Divine, cosmic energy, ever-existent, ever-vibrant, and ever-radiant! That is Sathya Sai Maha Divya Samadhi.**

Therefore, if anyone asks you, "What do you see there?" just tell them, "Come and experience for yourself!"

Continue To Visit Prasanthi Nilayam

Continue visiting Prasanthi Nilayam. It will recharge you. We all use cell phones; when the charge is running out, what do we do? We charge up our phone! Similarly, when your cells are running out, come to Puttaparthi to recharge there.

Kneel down before the Samadhi, touch your forehead to it, and tell me what happens. He is waiting for you there. Some people feel an electric current, some people experience vibrations, some feel consoled and supported, and some draw strength by doing namaskar to the Maha Samadhi, feeling His Divine presence there.

People go through struggles to reach Lord *Venkateshwara*, the Divinity residing on the seventh hill in *Tirumala*. Pilgrims endure a lot to go to *Sabarimala*; but because of Lord *Ayyapan*, strength is found there. People risk their lives to go to *Kedarnath* and *Badrinath* (in the *Himalayas*) to charge their spiritual batteries. All that is there in Sathya Sai Divya Maha Samadhi!

So, tell everybody: "Why do you say that there is nobody in Prasanthi Nilayam? Bhagawan is there, waiting for you. Please believe this."

When I don't attend bhajans, because I have work to do, I feel guilty. 'Maybe Swami is waiting for me. So, I better go there and carry on this work later,' I tell myself.

Once Swami passed by me in His physical body and said, "Ah, you were not here yesterday and you were not here this morning either!"

The same Swami will miss me this morning and in the evening. Similarly, feel Him and experience Him at the Divya Maha Samadhi. Continue your connection with Him. **Let the Sai mission be our life breath.**

Never Miss A Chance To Serve

I don't know how many of you here are from the Sai Organisation. Many of you may not be, so I want to tell you that we volunteers don't receive funds from anywhere. We are not paid, though we work continuously, and are all over the world.

Sathya Sai volunteers were among the first to visit Bosnia (in their hour of need). *Sathya Sai Sevadals* **were**

among the first batch off to Indonesia and Sri Lanka (after the Tsunami). They were not paid any travel expenses, nothing. They went on their own, spending their own money. That is Sathya Sai Baba. Nowhere else in the world do you find such a voluntary organisation!

In Indonesia, 108 water tanks were built by the Sai youth. In Singapore, the Sai youth is well represented. In Argentina, Sathya Sai Educare has risen to such heights that we cannot tell them anything. They know more than all of us here! Sathya Sai educational activity and Sathya Sai service activities are happening globally. They are no longer mere local activities.

Our role in the Sai mission is to be aware of what is going on in the entire world and to never miss the chance to serve. Some people feel that they are very important and that without them, nothing will be done. Well, my answer to them is that the work will be better without them!

Some people ask me, "Anil Kumar, why have you come to Swami?"

My answer is that the world would have been a better place without me. The Sai movement would have been much better without me. There would have been hundreds of willing translators available to Swami, so I am not indispensable.

I have been given an opportunity to serve. It is not something to feel proud about, but something to feel grateful to Him for. **Therefore, never give up your activity with the Sai mission. If you drop out now, you may have to repent forever and ever. This opportunity has been given to you, because of merits accrued over several lives.**

If there is any movement based on the unity of religions, it is the Sathya Sai movement. Emphasising the unity of religions, having an active and worldwide voluntary organisation, and doing Sai service as sadhana, these are the 'super-specialities' of the Sai movement!

Sai Mission And Its Continuity
Part III

(Special Talk by Prof. Anil Kumar,
Singapore, November 1st, 2011)

Challenging Topic

"Sai's Mission and Its Continuity" is a very challenging topic. And to talk to a Singaporean gathering, known for science and technology, is even more challenging. I have to be logical, technical, and scientific! However, I have had more than forty years' experience with Swami and twenty two of those years were directly working under Him, translating His talks. Therefore, much of His message has gone into the blood, bone, and marrow of this body, so I can't but accept this challenge.

We Should Communicate
Only Sai's Message

It is Sai's message and Sai's interpretation that we should communicate, rather than our own interpretation. Our own interpretation is bound to be wrong. Our own explanation may be imagination on our part, or a psychological projection. Therefore, we should only quote Swami and recount what He did. That is all.

Sai's Mission Is Continuous

The topic is: "Sai's Mission and Its Continuity." So, will it continue? A doubt in our mind led to this question.

There was no such question, while He was physically with us. But, it has arisen now. So, that is one factor. Yet, I can remind you of a second factor, which consists of His Divine promises and declarations. These are the Divine statements, which will support our cause and give us strength and hope to continue with the Sai service organisation. There is no question or question-mark over whether Sai's mission can or cannot continue!

"You Are Here, Because Of My Will"

Baba said, "None of you are here on your own. You are brought here, because of Me, because of My will."

So, we are at the feet of Bhagawan and we are in service to Bhagawan, not because of our own worth, merit, or talent, but because of His compassion and grace. We are selected to be here. What a wonderful statement!

"I Am Always With You"

The second statement is: "I am always with you. Never doubt that; follow Me. Never entertain any idea that I am away from you. I am in you, with you, above you, below you, around you." So, never forget the second Divine promise made by Bhagawan Baba.

"I Will Not Leave You Even If You Leave Me"

The third statement is: "I will not leave you even if you leave Me." So, life with Baba is eternal and continuous. The 'bondage' with Baba is forever and ever. It is not a social or business contract. It is heart-to-heart, love-to-love, an eternal bondage!

"I shall not forsake you even if you forsake Me," says Baba in the third statement. When we are attentive to these words, we can have no doubts about the continuity of the Sai mission.

"I Will Not Leave You, Until I Accomplish What I Want"

The fourth statement (and this encourages us to continue His mission) is: "I will not leave you, until I accomplish what I want through you."

If He wants you to do some work, He will see to it that you do it. You cannot run away from Him. Even if you are halfway home, you return with double-speed to Him, because He will not leave you. He will see to it that His mission is done through you.

"Even if you run away, I will bring you back. I will tie strings to your feet, as they do to parrots when they are bought. My previous *Avatar* Shirdi was the same." So, old habits die hard! Sathya Sai and Shirdi Sai were alike in bringing back those people, who flew off.

"All That You Do Is For Your Own Liberation"

This is the fifth statement: "All that you do is for your own liberation, not for My benefit."

Sai is selfless and total love. He has no expectations in return for what you do. What does it matter to Him, if you do it or not? He can accomplish everything by Himself. But, this opportunity is given to us for our own spiritual growth, upliftment, and liberation.

"Understand That You Are
Only Instruments In The Divine Mission"

The sixth statement is: "Understand that you are only instruments in the Divine mission."

"The Whole Family Is Blessed
If You Participate In My Mission"

The seventh statement is: **"If one of you participates in My mission, you are blessed and all family members are blessed."**

It is a spiritual 'wholesale bargain'! All the children are blessed, the wife at home is blessed, and the in-laws are equally blessed!

"By My Grace, You Will Be Happy
In Spite Of Your Problems"

The eighth statement is: "By My grace, you will be happy in spite of your problems."

You may say, "I am suffering with many worries and anxieties. I have family, business, and physical problems."

But, Baba says, "By My grace, you will be happy in spite of your problems."

We know of many people, who have run away from families and others, living in total frustration and depression. They report, "But, with Baba, I am happy!"

"You Can Never Understand Me - You Can Only Experience Me"

The ninth statement by Baba is: "You can never understand Me. You can only experience Me. Never analyse Me. Realise Me."

Sai is not subject to analysis. We can only realise Him. So, experience Him and do not seek to understand Him.

"You Are Here With Me, Because I Have Known You For Several Lives"

The tenth statement is: "You are here with Me, because I have known you over several lives."

Baba tells us, "You think that this is the first time I have known you. But, I have known you over the last several lives and that is why you are here with Me, now. You have forgotten that in the past life, you wanted to be with Me and to live in My company. You do not know that you prayed for that special grace. You do not know. That forgotten prayer is now fulfilled today."

"I Am With You Wherever You Go"

The eleventh statement tells us, "I am with you wherever you go."

Wherever you go, you will find a devotee saying, "Sai Ram!" Go to Frankfurt for the flight taking you to New York and somebody will say, "Sai Ram Anil, how are you?" I have never even met him before!

Eighteen years ago, at Narita airport, Tokyo, a man said suddenly, "Sai Ram! Good to have you in Japan!"

Wherever you go, you find somebody greeting you in the name of Sai. Or they narrate Sai stories. Some relate how they came to Swami and ask you how you came to know about Him.

Now, Swami says, "This is proof of My special grace. This is enough proof to say I am with you wherever you go. This is evidence to say I have not forgotten you."

The Sai Mission Is A Spiritual Mission

The Sai mission is not a social, political, or religious mission. It is not a status symbol. It is not a symbol of dignity, prestige, or knowledge, no! Our dignity, prestige, scholarship, talent, skill, and all the stuff that we are so proud of has nothing to do with it.

The Sai mission is a spiritual mission. It is an inner awareness, an inner spiritual growth, an inner transformation. It is the experience of oneness or universal consciousness, a transformation from the individual soul to the cosmic soul.

The Sai mission is the identity of a drop with the ocean, or of a spark with the fire. From the small to the mighty, from the microcosmic to macrocosmic — that is the Sai mission! This oneness, this super-consciousness has to be understood and experienced.

That is the purpose of the Sai mission, for which He has built a big organisation with all the convenors, presidents, secretaries, national chair, deputy chair, regional chair, and so on. All these things are established for only one purpose: to realise and experience the super-consciousness, of which we are all a part. We are the sparks of the Divine; we are the embodiments of the Divine. That is the Sai mission. He has gathered all of us for that.

He built a mighty organisation and an infrastructure, a cadre to work together. We are not to fight with each other, but to work together, because the common goal is Baba, not you and not me. The common objective is to see Baba within ourselves. The outside material world is noise, while the inside spiritual world is the inner voice. We are here to experience the inner voice and not to join in and react to outer noise. So, the Sai mission is that.

Swami Expects Transformation And Participation

In Singapore, there are many youth, who have done a lot of work. Very good! Is Swami happy about it? Yes, He is very happy. But, is there transformation in them? That is what Swami asks. **He is not concerned about the magnitude or the intensity, or the quantum of work. He wants the quality of the person. He wants you. He expects transformation, not merely paper reports. That is what Swami says.**

We have committee reports. What are committee reports? They are reports made by committee members that are then discussed over a cup of tea. The Sai mission is not like that. It expects participation. There are some people, who don't participate, but find mistakes in the mission. That is the political approach. There are many, who give suggestions without understanding the mission. That is only a spectator's view.

The one, who is involved, is the one, who understands what it is. As the English proverb goes, "Only the wearer knows where the shoe pinches." Therefore, let us analyse point-by-point and from all points-of-view, the continuity of the Sai mission.

Sai Organisation Posts
Are Appointed By Bhagawan

Here is an incident. It is about a message from Indulal Shah, the World Council Chairman in those days. He is *Bhismaacharya* (a righteous warrior) of the Sathya Sai organisation and he is over ninety years 'young'!

He sent a telegram message: "You are appointed the Zonal Convenor of the Sathya Sai Organisation in charge of Andhra and Rayalaseema." Yes, a good post! I was very happy and excited like any of you would be. I am just an ordinary devotee, not even knowing the *bhajans* completely. I was just sitting close to the footwear and taking care of the kids; in other words, I was always a back-bencher. Suddenly, I was promoted to the ranks of an administrator!

Immediately, I went to Parthi to thank Swami. "Thank you, Bhagawan. Indulal Shah sent me the message that I am appointed Zonal Convenor."

Then, He replied, "Who is Indulal Shah? That fellow has got nothing to do with this. Only I appointed you! He is just a postman, that's all."

In other words, all of us in the youth wing or ladies wing, or at the national or regional level are occupying certain positions, because of Him, not because of the people that nominated us. That is the lesson of this. Nobody nominated you; only He picked you.

No One Can Escape From Sai's Mission

The second incident was when I was about to go to Kurnool in Andhra Pradesh, for a meeting. The chairman of the Sai centre there is Dr. Krishna Rao, a dentist, who has now passed away.

It was raining heavily that day. All buses and trains were cancelled. It was impossible to reach Kurnool. So, I sent a telegram to them to let them know that I would not attend the meeting.

The next morning, there was a feeling within me to go to Kurnool. Yet, the function must have finished by that time and the people must have returned home. 'Why should I go now?' No, go, go! A kind of inner pressure built up and something forced me to go.

I changed buses three times to reach that place, because of the heavy rain. The conference was over and the people were returning home. Suddenly, they saw me coming. All of them started running back to the venue of the meeting — old, young, men, women, girls, boys, all running.

Somebody stared at me. "Is this Anil Kumar or some devil? He sent a telegram yesterday, saying that he is not going to attend. How is it that he is here?"

I attended the meeting and the next morning, I returned to Puttaparthi.

Swami, while giving *darshan*, said to me, "Hmmm! You wanted to avoid the meeting, but I did not allow that, because all those devotees would have been disappointed. I don't want to disappoint them."

And Baba added, "Krishna Rao is the first *sevadal* (volunteer service worker) member in Prasanthi Nilayam, doing work around the whole area. I didn't want him to be disappointed, because you didn't go, so I drew you there. How was the meeting, Anil Kumar?"

"Swami, it went very well."

This proves that even if you want to escape, you cannot. I stand as an example of that.

Nobody Can Harm You
When You Are In Sai's Mission

Once, I went to a region in Andhra Pradesh called Telangana. The towns of Hyderabad, Nizamabad, Adilabad, Khammam, and Nalgonda all belong to Telangana. I went to a place called Nizamabad. The people there invited me, "Anil Kumar, please come to our place also." I have this weakness, where I cannot say 'no' to anybody.

So, when they asked me to go, I said, "Alright, I will go." We were travelling by car towards Ramakrishnapore, one hundred and fifty miles away. The police had information that some anti-social elements, such as terrorists or political activists, were active in that area. Therefore, every car was frequently stopped and the driver questioned each time, at gunpoint. "Where are you going?"

We are teachers and not used to guns. We are not used to facing such serious, severe threats. When the police were pointing their guns at me, asking "Who are you?" they would see Swami's picture close to the steering wheel.

Before I could answer, they would say, "Oh! Sai Baba! You can go!" And like a football kicked from one point to another point, after seeing Baba's picture, the police kicked my car from one point to another!

A couple of days after the meeting, I came to Puttaparthi. Baba said, "You are a fool! Didn't I tell you not to travel after 10 o'clock at night? Why did you go? I had to follow your car all the way, or else you would not have got there!"

This incident shows that when we do God's service in the Sai mission, nothing can happen to us. Nothing! Nobody will ever attack or harm us.

Your Job Is Protected When You Are On Sai's Mission

Swami has also made this promise: "Your job is protected, because of Me."

Some people ask, "How about my job?"

My reply is, "You think you keep the job? It is kept in spite of you!"

Here are two instances that show how Swami protects your job, when you are on His mission.

I once went to Nagpur, Maharashtra, to address the Nagpur University on a bio-science topic and also, to address Sai devotees. On returning, I missed the connecting train and so, was very late getting back to the Christian college, where I worked. They are very strict there. You cannot be absent, without applying for casual leave. So, I felt very apprehensive about being so late.

To my utter dismay, I noticed that the whole campus was empty. Only the watchman was there. I asked him what had happened.

He said, "Sir, today has been declared a holiday, because one lecturer is getting married."

Then, I prayed to my dear Baba to let all the lecturers get married on the days, when I am occupied in the service of Sai!

There was another occasion, when I was again late getting back, because of connecting trains. I thought I would certainly lose my job. But, to my surprise, only the watchman was around. I asked him what was wrong. "Sir, there is a meeting in the auditorium."

I went over there and saw it was a celebration held for the boys of the inter-college cricket match. They were receiving shields and everyone was clapping. I, too, joined the audience and clapped more than those around me! I prayed to Swami to let our boys continue to win in different matches, so that I can keep my job while carrying on His work!

These experiences show that your job will be kept safe while you are on Sai's mission.

The Sai Mission Is Greater
Than Your Comfort And Convenience

I live in staff quarters at Prasanthi Nilayam. They are matchbox-sized, just one room. Somebody said, "Mr. Anil Kumar, how is it that the staff quarters are so silent and spiritual?"

I told him, "My dear young man, you are wrong. There may be silence, but it is because the place is empty during the day. When the husband goes to college, the wife is on duty, or security service in the Mandir (temple). When the wife is at home, the husband is working at the college. Like the moon and the sun, they move in opposite directions. By the time they return home after *bhajans,* they immediately go to bed. So, there is peace abiding and *samadhi* (bliss) granted, because both of them are so tired."

Sai activities are so interesting that you won't care about the facilities, comforts, or your needs. If a guest wants to visit me and stay, then he has to sleep under the sofa. So, no guests come to stay. They just say, "Hello," and then, we arrange to meet later. They know the situation.

But, I do not ever complain. This is the reason: "Baba, there are millionaires and billionaires, with palatial palaces, and they want just a look from You. They want just a blessing from You. They are ready to offer You anything. But, here I am, Swami. You bless me every day with Your *darshan.* You have blessed me with Your Divine touch and You have blessed me with the opportunity to translate Your talks. It is worth several more future lives!" All the luxury and pomp they might have is nothing in comparison to Divine proximity. I tell you this based on my own experience.

Hence, the Sai mission is greater than your comfort and convenience. Your wealth, social status, and contacts are worldly and have nothing to do with the Sai mission, which is spiritual.

The Sai Mission Helps You Do Things That You Yourself Cannot Do

The Sai mission helps you do things that you yourself cannot do. For instance, in our family, I am the only hopeless person in respect to cooking. But, I know one thing — how to make instant coffee. I am an expert at it!

I was brought up by parents, who worked in the education department and who held high educational qualifications. They served as top officers. One was a director and the other was an education officer. So, there was never a need for me to work at home.

Then, later, I enjoyed married life with a wife, who could successfully manage on her own. In addition, my in-laws lived only one and half furlongs from my place. So, if there was a problem in obtaining a meal, for instance, I could go there. So, in short, I was irresponsible, when it came to domestic chores. I am telling you this openly.

The Flood Relief Camp In Diviseema

But, under those circumstances, not knowing anything, such a person like Anil Kumar had to go and participate in a flood relief camp, in the Krishna district of Andhra Pradesh! It was about 1977, when thousands died from the Diviseema flood havoc.

The power of the Sai mission helps you do something that you have not done before. In this case, I was learning to cope with fears and at the same time, handle food distribution. Thousands were homeless with no drinking water or food. There was no power supply. There were dead bodies everywhere. I am scared of a dead cat or dog and suddenly, I had to see dead bodies! I was working there day and night, though I am afraid of the night. And it was dark too, after returning to our place.

Thousands and thousands of homeless people were coming to our camp for food supplies. They sat in lines and we served them food. This went on, until one or two o'clock in the morning!

But, do you know what Baba said on my return? "Anil Kumar, you did nothing! But, what a show you gave, huh? The acting was very good!"

The people were served in batches of two to three thousand. But, there would be many others waiting for their turn. Their places and food had to be made ready before they could start eating their meal.

All Are Happy Because Of Bhajans

So, what could we do to help these people pass the time happily? We noticed that we had musicians, Sai devotees, skilled in *bhajan* singing. The idea of giving *bhajan* sessions came to me! I had these fellows turn the iron baskets, used for carrying cement and sand, upside down. Then, I took two sticks and started drumming and singing, *'Gopala Radhe Krishna!'* That is what I did. Devotees all around joined in and so did the people waiting. By these means, all were engaged happily throughout the night.

I spent one full month there. One full month! Why? It was because of the company of Sai devotees! All were singing Sai *bhajans*, while the work was getting done and all the people were jumping in joy.

Swami said something else after His comment on this 'show'. He said, "Swami is happy, because you engaged those people so nicely. Come on, boy," and He presented me a suit.

The Sai Mission Is To Live, Learn, And Laugh

It is not about the suit or anything Swami may give to you. The point is that He knows I did not do any manual work; instead, I did what I could via dance and music. And yet, He was pleased with that.

This is proof enough to say that the Sai mission does not expect stress or strain from you. We are to take it easy, smile, and relax. Sometimes, people look almost like bulldogs when giving service! You don't have to be like that. We have enough bulldogs in our offices, so why have more in service camps?

Smile, laugh, and sing — that is Baba. Baba is laughter. Baba is music and dance. Baba is ecstasy and bliss. Seriousness is sickness. Live to learn to laugh; do not live to earn, to burn, and to die. Nonsense! In that case, it is not worth living at all. Let us live, learning and laughing. That is life! Enjoy every day with Baba; that is laughter.

Sai Bhajans Are A Boost For All Of Us

You don't need any other boost than Sai *bhajans*. They are more powerful than a multivitamin tablet. Those, who feel weak, should test a 'sample dose' by listening to Sai *bhajans*, because it is pure energy.

However, our habit is that we want medicines and injections, not *bhajans*. Unless you pay, you don't have satisfaction. Money gives it value! When anything is given freely, we don't appreciate its value. Here are two stories that show the value of *bhajans*.

The Effect Of Sai Bhajan
In California, San Jose

In California, San Jose, an elderly lady in a wheelchair was left at home without anybody's help, because both the son and the daughter-in-law were employed at work. One afternoon, she had to go to the restroom. Who will help her? So, she played a recorded Sai *bhajan* and then suddenly, somebody opened her door: "Grandma, I will help you. Grandma, I will come and help you." That is the effect of Sai *bhajan*!

The Effect Of Sai Bhajans
In Jaffna, Sri Lanka

There is a place in Sri Lanka called Jaffna, which I once visited. My children wrote me letters, "Of all places, why do you want to go to Jaffna? The whole area is bombed. We want your safe return, not for you to fly off to the other planet!"

I told them it is more important to go to Jaffna, not to a safe city like San Francisco or London. The Sai mission is a challenge, not a honeymoon trip. It is a spiritual mission.

In Jaffna, driving a car is not straightforward. You will be asked to stop en route and you have to get into a military truck to be taken straight to the airport. On either side, there are military soldiers with their rifles ready. If there is anything wrong with you, it is a non-stop flight straight away! I saw all of that.

When I went to Jaffna, I was told, "Anil Kumar, be careful when you speak. There are some LTTE people (Liberation Tigers of Tamil Eelam) among them. The leaders there will listen to what you say."

I said, "I would be happy to have them sing Sai *bhajans*! They should occupy the front rows. Why not? They are not our enemies."

I started giving the talk, when suddenly an old man sat down by my side. He told me that fifteen days ago, because of heavy bombing in Jaffna, everybody vacated Jaffna, including his children. This old fellow was left all alone at home. Who will cook for him? How does he manage to eat? Nobody bothered. Then, he sat in front of Sai's picture, singing Baba *bhajans*.

Immediately, a little boy came to him, "*Thatha* (Grandfather), what do you want? I will cook for you."

That boy cooked and served him coffee and then, massaged his feet until he went to sleep. He did this for one full month. After that, the situation in Jaffna improved and people started returning. By the time the elderly gentleman's children came back, that boy had vanished!

The children were surprised that the old fellow was still alive. And he told them, "Look here, you left me. But, He has not left me. That is Sathya Sai Baba."

Swami Gives Us Intelligence, Strength, And Initiative To Do His Work

Sometimes, we doubt whether we are able to do our *seva* or not. The Sai mission is stupendous and magnificent. It calls for expertise, total dedication, and no compromise in respect to the standards and outcome. Can we reach those exalted heights? Can we ever attain those expected results?

Sai is perfect. "What can I do, Swami? You are perfect, while I am totally imperfect. Can I ever match You?" That is a doubt we all have.

A long time ago, Swami asked me, "Anil Kumar, come and be the principal of My college at Bangalore." Most people would jump at the opportunity. But, I know that to work with Him is not an ordinary job. It is sacrifice and hard work. It is spiritual exploitation, if you expect to be benefited by His grace and receive His bounteous bliss, and not be prepared to sacrifice and work. And you must be prepared to be part of a community, who knows that well. We have to be prepared to sacrifice. We should be prepared to bear the cross, come what may.

So, after lunch, I was tossing on the bed. "Swami, why do You ask me to come there as the principal? Is it to put me to shame? Is it to demonstrate to everybody that I am incapable? Do you want me to be a laughing-stock, a ridiculous creature now? Swami, please, please withdraw Your offer and I will go home." That was my prayer that afternoon, tossing on the bed.

In the evening, Swami gave a discourse. I was the translator. He said, "Sri Ramachandra (the ideal Man and an *Avatar*) looked at all the *Vanaras* (monkey warriors). He picked Hanuman from amongst them to go to Lanka in search of Mother Sita. Hanuman had never met Sita before and he did not know the way to Lanka. Neither did he know about the danger and threats on the way. But, despite all these difficulties, Hanuman said he would go."

Then, Rama asked him, "Hanuman, how are you going to do it? You have never seen Mother Sita. You have never been to Lanka."

Hanuman replied, "Swami, because You have delegated me to go there, You will give me all the intelligence, strength, and initiative to do Your work and fulfil Your mission."

"Anil Kumar, what do you say about that?" said our Swami.

It was a conversation between both of us! Nobody in the audience understood the underlying message: "You are a fool to worry. When I want you to go there, I will give you the strength and talent to do the job I assigned. Why do you doubt that?"

I replied to Swami's question, "Yes, Swami, yes, Swami."

This is an illustration to let you know that, when Swami gives a job, He will see to it that you are successful and will accomplish it. He will see to it that you get a good name and fame.

Sai's mission is not a bed of thorns; there is a lot of humour, blessings, fun and frolic, and many other things to experience as well.

Sai Makes You Laugh As Well, When You Are Involved In His Mission

In Kodaikanal, during one of the trips, I marked my name as 'KA' on the reverse side of my white shirt. Everyone wears a white shirt and I did not want my shirt to be mixed with the others. The *dhobi* (washerman) put the clean shirt on my bed.

The next morning, our dear Lord saw those clothes in our room. I was not there luckily. He asked, "Why is it marked 'KA'? It should be 'AK' for 'Anil Kumar'."

A lecturer, Gopinath from Bangalore campus, was there. He said, "Swami, he is 'KA'. 'K' for 'Kamaraju' and 'A' for 'Anil Kumar'."

"Oh ho."

After lunch, this lecturer told me what had happened. Then, I knew something was in store for me!

In the evening, He started giving a discourse:

E Desamunandu, E Desamunaku, Bharathiya Sanathana Dharmamunaku

Kavalasinatuvantidhi Tyagaraju Kavali, Yogaraju Kavali
Kani Kamaraju Kadhu.

This country needs Tyagaraju, the king of sacrifice,
And Yogaraju, the king of spiritual discipline.
It does not need Kamaraju, the king of desires!

This is proof to show you how He makes you laugh.
He gives you time to feel free, to have free space and a free
mind, so that you will feel energised to do His work later.

The Sai Mission Gives You
More Than You Deserve

Therefore, the Sai mission is continuous. Swami will
give you the needed strength and talent. He will save you
from all the troubles and obstacles along the way. He will
see to it that you get all your promotions. You will also find
that you get more, much more than what you deserve.

Let any Sai devotee say, "I got what I deserved." No!
You got much more than what you deserved.

One day, Swami was saying, "Anil Kumar, see our
(college) boys. They are very good boys. They study well.
They sing and dance well. They cook well."

At that time, I was at my home town. I felt so bad, when
He was praising the boys like that, since I was a lecturer
teaching boys at my Christian college. We all belong to God.
God cannot say, "My boys," and "Your boys." Hence, I felt
so bad.

Then, He said, "Why do you look like that? Aren't your
boys as good as that? Aren't they so well-disciplined?" He

went on repeating all the great qualities of His boys. It was like listening to a recorded tape with rewind!

Then, I said to Swami, "Oh! Your boys are really great. But, let them come to our place and study. *(Speaking jokingly)* Here, they will become first-class *goondas* (thugs), terrorists, and rowdies! Your boys are talented and excellent, because of You! Let our boys come to You and they will be the best boys ever possible. It is not the greatness of the boy; it is the greatness of Baba!"

Swami answered, *"Manchidi ayya. Poni le, sathyam telusukunnaavu.* (Good, good you have known the truth.)"

Therefore, Sai activity gives us more than what we deserve. And the Sai mission gives us the ability to face things in life, too.

Never Miss The Opportunity Of Being In The Sai Mission

There was a widespread question in India: "After Nehru, what will happen to India?" Well, many leaders came later — they took the opportunity. But, regardless of whether leaders are there or not, India goes on.

Men may come and men may go, but the Sai mission will go on forever and ever. You may choose to lose this opportunity, but He will carry on. In that case, there are better people than you; there are experts far better than you. But, this beautiful opportunity to make life really interesting is given to you.

Service Gives You Greater Joy
Than Any Other Form Of Work

No money, no power, no luxury can give you as much joy as the company of Bhagawan Sri Sathya Sai Baba. No work on Earth could ever give you more happiness than service to Sathya Sai Baba and His devotees.

Service gives you greater joy than any other form of work on this earthly planet. Many people have left their jobs to give service. Why? Because of an inner calling and His grace; not due to any other considerations.

Questions And Answers Session

(Talk by Prof. Anil Kumar, Singapore, November 1st, 2011)

Q: When will Prema Sai be born?

A: No Prema Sai question is relevant, as it has nothing to do with now. Prema Sai is futuristic, while Sathya Sai is presently here, right now. So, enjoy and experience Him! Follow the path that He has shown. That is enough. Forget about Prema Sai. Why?

Lord Krishna came and said to Hanuman, "Hanuman, I am Krishna."

Hanuman said, "So what?"

Then, Krishna said, "I am the same Rama, do you know?"

"Nonsense! My Rama had only one wife, whereas You are a romantic guy. My Rama was a plain man, whereas You are a diplomat. So, I don't accept You!" Hanuman replied. So, Krishna had to go back, change his make-up, and then, appear in front of him as Rama!

That should be our devotion! **Anytime, anywhere Sathya Sai!**

Q: What is happening in Parthi? Is it business as usual?

A: What is happening in Puttaparthi? Puttaparthi is undergoing a transition from physical proximity to spiritual experience (from person to presence). Puttaparthi is shifting from a state of many residents to a more floating population.

Earlier, Puttaparthi was a place where Bhagawan gave us *padanamaskar* flowers. Today, Puttaparthi is a centre for His Maha Samadhi, which is as vibrant, resplendent, radiant and powerful as an international, thermal power station! More powerful than electro-magnetic waves!

If you go to Shirdi's Samadhi or *dargah* or Jerusalem, you will have the same experience. So, we are travelling from form to formlessness. Puttaparthi is going through this type of spiritual evolution and revolution!

Q: Next set of questions are quite an ego boost for you. We thought people would only ask about Swami. No! They want to know about you, too! So, the first one is a very pointed question: Are you also missing Swami? If yes, then how much?

A: Yes, I miss Swami just like any of you. Perhaps, I miss Swami an extra amount, because of the extra love He showered upon me, because of the extra lovely Divine romance, closeness, and intimacy that I experienced with Him. I can say, in front of the Lotus Feet and subject to verification, that no other person ever enjoyed so many funny moments with Bhagawan as Anil Kumar did. Nobody!

You can ask thousands of students of our institution and thousands of members of the Sai Organisation about this. Swami and I always joked. He never treated me as a grown-up man. He treated me as a child, joking about clothes and food among other things.

Q: So, you actually led us up to the next question: Are you going to actually write a book about all these stories that you mentioned? Did Swami give you any personal message? Did He convey something to you, before He actually left the physical world?

A: Yes, I started writing "Memories and Memoirs with Swami." I don't know how this thought came to me. They will be appearing monthly in Telugu *Sanathana Sarathi*, from this October. I gave enough material for 4 issues, including my experiences, the organisational growth, along with the undercurrent of Sai's message. These articles have already been contributed to the Telugu *Sanathana Sarathi*. Also, arrangements are being made for an English translation by Prof. Ramesh Datta, from the United States of America. So finally, they will come in a book form.

Regarding any final message, God gave us a message — in fact, He gave us hundreds of volumes of messages! So, there is no 'extra' message. We have to understand all His messages and put them into practice every day.

Q: There are some questions about things, like how do we do sadhana and how do we become the person that Swami wanted us to be. How do we do chitta shuddhi (mental purification)? Then, there are people, who are also asking if they need to have other goals in life, or is loving Swami enough?

A: The greatest *sadhana* is to give up envy, pride, and jealousy. Do not compare yourself with others, do not compete with others, and do not feel jealous of others. Feel satisfied in one's own Self with a spirit of acceptance, whether circumstances are positive or negative. That is the *sadhana* we should undertake.

Q: Next one: In this world today, everything is two-minute Maggi style. So, what is the two-minute solution to Sai realisation?

A: Why two minutes? I will give you a half-minute solution: *prema* (love). Two seconds, that's all! Love is enough, and everything else will be added unto you.

Q: *Sometimes, it is painful to think that Swami is not in His physical form. Please give us some realistic advice on how to get over this. You mentioned stories, which have happened in the past. Do you know of any experiences, which devotees have had in the recent past, after Swami physically left us?*

A: Don't feel sorry about His physical withdrawal from the body. Instead, feel the presence of Sai. Whenever you sing His glory, whenever you read His literature, whenever you participate in service activity, whenever you love, whenever you are giving and forgiving — there is Sai! You are Sai! Sai and you are one, forever and ever.

Today, more miracles are happening than ever before. Earlier, very few miracles happened in Puttaparthi. We fellows there learned about your experiences and spoke everywhere about them. But today, more miracles are happening in Prasanthi Nilayam. Perhaps, He thought we needed some more 'medical treatment' or even 'surgery', I do not know. That's how I take it.

Never before have so many miracles happened there, as are happening today. In the South Indian canteen, on the wall, there are Swami's footprints. In the South Indian canteen on the ladies side, close to the storeroom, there has been a continuous flow of *amrith* on Swami's picture, for the last one month.

Vibhuti is pouring out from one of the photos in the North Block or Round Block. In the village of Puttaparthi, *amrith* is flowing from the feet of a statue made by a Muslim and *vibhuti* is pouring from its head as well.

Sathya Sai Baba is eternal, immortal, blemishless God, Divinity, incarnated forever and ever more!

Q: There are two questions seeking personal advice: a person says he recently got transformed by Swami. But, he is undergoing the consequences of his past. Swami says we are free to shape our own future and therefore, sufferings are not His Will. So, how should this person proceed?

A: This person should feel that he could bear this suffering for so long, while still staying alive, because of His grace. Or else, he would have been in search of some poison to end his life! So, He is still carrying on, only because of His grace.

Q: This question is from a very young friend, a 13-year-old boy. He says that since Baba is no longer physically with us, he finds it hard to feel Baba's presence, especially during bhajans or silent time, no matter how hard he tries. How can he invoke the feeling of His presence?

A: Don't listen to *bhajans*; *bhajans* aren't for listening. Participate in *bhajans*! Sing in chorus! It is not a concert of M.S.Subbalakshmi or M.L.Vasantha Kumari. No! You should join in as a lead singer. *Bhajan* means participation and involvement; it will connect you to God.

A simple example: If I have pain here *(showing his feet)*, I could murmur *(in a whisper)*, "I have pain, I have pain, I have pain, pain, pain," or I could shout, "PAIN!" What is the difference?

Similarly, if you whisper, you won't be heard. SAI *(shouted loudly)*, say loudly! *(To the audience)* That's not loud enough! Say again, "SAI!" *(A loud 'Sai' is heard from the audience)* Louder, SAI! *(An even louder 'Sai' is heard from the audience)* He is listening now! So, that's what *bhajan* is!

Q: All the questions from the audience are over, but I have one question. It is of a personal nature: Did you ever imagine, in your wildest dreams, that the part you would play in the Sai mission would be much greater today, when He is not among us physically, than when you were the translator or when you were closest to Him? Personally, did you ever imagine and feel that today, our role is actually much more important as His emissaries, rather than when He is physically present here?

A: I feel the need to meet the devotees all over the world. I feel the need to go around the villages, towns, and cities in India and tell devotees that Swami has not left us. He is with us. Don't cry and don't change your political parties. Religion is not politics, so don't be carried away by rumours and don't listen to TV channels and newspapers. That is nothing but cooked-up information.

Establish yourself in your faith. Sai is with you. These are the things I want to tell everyone. So, given the chance, I don't want to rest for even a day. I want to travel forever and ever, to give more courage and faith to the devotees of Bhagawan Sri Sathya Sai Baba.

One Guru, One Focus, One Goal
Part I

(Special Talk by Prof. Anil Kumar,
Singapore, November 2nd, 2011)

We have so many *gurus*, so why do we say that we should have only one *guru*? And how do we judge a true *guru*? How can we determine who is a *guru* and who is not? Who is genuine and who is a fake? Who is worldly and who is spiritual? Who is wise and who is otherwise?

We have got to know the *guru*'s concepts. It is most unfortunate that in this land of *gurus*, the concept of *guru* is most misunderstood! We call everyone a *guru*. At the student level, some of the students even call their friends '*guru*'. That is the situation today.

Peace Of Mind In The Presence
Of The True Guru

Next to Adi Shankara, Ramana Maharshi was the greatest teacher of non-duality. Adi Sankara was top-most in the theory of non-dualism. Next comes Ramana Maharshi of Tiruvannamalai. What does he say about a *guru*?

He says, "He is the *guru*, in whose presence you feel peace of mind." Let us question ourselves in this way: Do we have peace of mind in the presence of all of our so-called *gurus*? That is up to the individual, who will decide based on his experience and, above all, on his expectations.

First of all, we should feel peace abiding within us. What is peace? We might say, "He is peaceful." How do you know when he is peaceful? The face is the index of the mind. When we see the faces of people, we can note how peaceful they are. There are those, who preside at peace conferences, yet they are totally restless and agitated! Their faces are full of fury and jealousy, which makes them look horrible. It is common to find many people like this presiding at peace conferences.

So, peace is evident as an expression on the face itself. For example, look at the pictures of Buddha and Adi Shankara: there you will find peace, supreme peace. Lord Buddha was the very embodiment of peace and Jesus Christ, the king of peace.

So, a *guru* is the one, in whose presence you will find that level of peace. We may ask ourselves, 'Why is it that a *guru* is so peaceful, while we are not?' Take, for example, Bhagawan Sri Sathya Sai Baba, Who is peace itself. He is peace-embodied, peace-personified, the very metaphor of peace, and the very symbol of peace.

At any moment, the President of India may be on an official visit to Prasanthi Nilayam. But, our most peaceful Baba does not change His dress. There is no *hungama* (commotion), no advance *darshan,* no delay of *darshan,* no special *darshan,* no special welcoming board, nor any special decorations put up. The President of India silently comes and goes, while Swami talks to primary school children, college students, and jokes with staff members.

Finally, Swami talks to the President of India at the end of *darshan.* So, the 'first citizen' is the last to be spoken to, because Swami has no preferences whatsoever. He does not see people in terms of citizen number one, citizen number two, or first-class or second-class, so He is at peace. Baba is peaceful, because He has no cadre. He does not take someone's political qualifications or status into consideration; therefore, He is at peace.

We can also be at peace, if we are like Him. That is to say, we can treat everybody with love, talking to everyone with love and treating everybody equally and unselfishly. Only then can we remain in peace. And so, a true *guru* is the one, in whose presence you experience peace.

In The Presence Of The Guru, One Is Thoughtless

Secondly, a true *guru* is the one, in whose presence you are without thought — completely thoughtless.

Someone may suggest, "Sir, I am thoughtless." But, there is something wrong with their understanding, because the mind will never be quiet on its own. It is a bundle of thoughts. It goes on entertaining thoughts and counter-thoughts, *sankalpa* and *vikalpa*. *Mananath ithi manaha:* It is the mind that recalls, memorises, recollects, lives in the past, and worries about the future. The mind is always shopping in the marketplace.

However, in the presence of the *guru*, one is thoughtless. What does this mean? It means that the mind is withdrawn. The mind is silenced, becoming passive, inert, and functionless in the presence of a true *guru*.

When you go to Swami with a letter, Swami will stand in front of you, but you forget to give Him the letter!

Then, some of us have problems, like knee problems and joint problems. Those, who were romantic at one time, turn rheumatic later! Naturally, we go from romanticism to rheumatism; it is a natural shift in life. So, people want to tell Swami that they have some problem with their eyes or bones, with their family, or some other kind of problem. Then, Swami will call them for an interview.

He asks, "How are you? How are your children? How are they doing?"

Then suddenly, He starts speaking about philosophy: "See, here is a kerchief. The kerchief is white and bright. The mind is like that, too. But, if you go on making use of a kerchief, it becomes dirty. Similarly, the mind with worldly thoughts becomes dirty. A quiet mind as such is pure, but a mind with thoughts of the world becomes dirty." He goes on like that, explaining spiritual philosophy.

Then, you come out of the interview room with *vibhuti* packets, having totally forgotten to ask Him about the relief of your joint pains! As you forgot to ask, your joint pain remains. Why did you forget?

Sometimes, when Swami stands in front of you, you ask about something other than what you wanted to ask about. Why does this happen? You ask about your grandfather, who is no more, but you wanted to ask about a great-grandson, who is yet to be born. Or you ask about everyone else, but you forget to ask about yourself. What makes this happen?

Or while sitting in front of Swami at the dining table, you go on mixing *sambar* with *rasam*, *rasam* with *sambar* and curd, and so on like that. (Normally, these two dishes are never mixed together in India.) Why do you go on looking at Him and forget what you are eating? Outside you may feel, "Hey, wow! What wonderful items were offered there, but I lost focus on them. I should have concentrated on the food. I don't know what happened!"

In front of Swami, you forget all your choices, all your preferences, all your goals, and all your desires, petitions, and requests. Why? The steering of the mind is in His hands. He will apply a brake and the mind stops. The mind stops functioning in the presence of Swami. Therefore, we tend to forget to submit our requests and special prayers to Him, because our mind stops. That is the effect of the presence of a true *guru*, the presence of a Divine Master.

Waiting For Swami Compared To Waiting For A Flight Or Train

In Prasanthi Nilayam, people would wait and wait. We never knew when Swami would come out to give *darshan*. We did not know. We would be waiting from 6:30 am. He might come at 7:30, 8:30, or 9:30 am, or He might not come at any of those times and only come in the afternoon.

No one would ever get vexed, or disgusted, or bored, while waiting for Swami. Am I right? One hour might pass, but you are not bothered, because you know Swami will come. Even after two hours, it does not matter. After three hours, Swami comes and you forget all about the stress and strain of waiting. It happens like that.

Outside the *ashram*, when flights are delayed by half-an-hour, you go on cursing, "Flights! Malaysian airlines, Indian airlines, British Airways! These fellows do not know how to run flights." You go on getting upset for just a half-an-hour delay!

If you have to wait at the bus or railway station, or for an interview with a big man, it is boring, vexing, and troublesome. You don't want to wait patiently. But, when you're waiting for Swami, you don't feel this impatience. Why? It is because your mind is focused on Swami.

At the bus station, airport, or railway station, the mind is focused on the place of our destination, the person with whom we work, or the number of files kept pending for disposal. Our minds are filled with thoughts — first about our enemies, then about our friends, or we think about our boss and then, our colleagues. All of the vexing, boring thoughts that fill the mind arise from the mind itself.

We Forget About Time And Body

We are dealing with two things here: time and mind. Mind is time and time is the mind; mind is thought and thought is the mind. You are thoughtless by nature, when you have withdrawn your mind. You are timeless as well; you are beyond time. So, while waiting for Swami, we don't bother about time; we forget about it. This does not happen in the outside world.

Not only do you forget about time, you also forget about your joint pains. In the *ashram,* it is necessary to sit on the floor, sometimes sitting with legs tightly crossed for three hours minimum. This is no joke and definitely not an easy thing to do. Just try this at home; you can't do it! You can't do it at home, yet you will do it every day in Puttaparthi.

Pain at home is a gain (not felt) at Prasanthi Nilayam. Why? There, in His presence, you are beyond the body. You don't feel the temperature, you don't feel the inconvenience, and you don't feel the discomfort. You are beyond the mind, being timeless. You are beyond the mind, being free of thought. You are beyond the body, unmindful of its discomfort or inconvenience. That is the effect of being in the presence of a true *guru*.

Even if the most charismatic film actor appeared before you on stage, you could not sit cross-legged for hours on end. You would eventually say, "Mister! Observe the time, okay! Otherwise, come and sit down here with me, so you will understand my plight."

A Divine Master is One, in Whose presence you go beyond the body, mind, and time. This is a Divine Master! When you go to Prasanthi Nilayam, you forget the date and even what day of the week it is. This is the experience of everyone.

The Guru Is Omniscient And Omnipresent

K. Munshi was the Chairman of Bharatiya Vidya Bhavan in Bombay. He served as the Governor, also and was a great exponent of Indian culture and spirituality. K. Munshi wanted to get an interview, because he wanted to ask Swami some questions. So, he did his homework, wrote down all of his questions, and kept that letter in his pocket.

Swami granted him an interview. During the course of regular conversation, Swami began answering one question after another, without the letter even being taken out and without the questions being posed. He went on in this way, answering all of his questions. At the end of the interview, Swami said, "Munshi, I have answered all of the nine questions, but you have forgotten to write the tenth question."

He said, "No, no, Swami! I have written it."

"No, you have forgotten the tenth question. What is it? Your hands are shaking; your fingers are shaking. You are not able to keep them steady. You forgot to write that, right?"

"Oh, Swami! I know that."

Then, Swami picked up K. Munshi's hand and began to massage it. Since then, the hand, the head — everything has been steady. Munshi wrote an article in Bhavan's journal in his own hand. This is the kind of transformation that has taken place in the Divine presence of Bhagawan Baba.

So, you may write nine questions and you may have another question — a tenth question, which you may forget to ask. It means that He is absolutely all-knowing, all-pervasive, all-powerful, omniscient, and omnipresent. He knows them all, without any of them being specifically mentioned. He is a True Master. He is a True *Guru*.

The Guru Loves Unconditionally

A true *guru* is one, who loves you unconditionally. But, we only love people under certain conditions, taking into consideration their bank account, official status, and age before loving them. So, every relationship on Earth is conditional. Swami Himself gives us an example. A newly married couple comes to Singapore on their honeymoon. They go around sightseeing, looking at all the greenery here.

These newlyweds are strolling through the lovely lawns and gardens, when the young husband suddenly spots a thorn ahead on his wife's path. He shouts, "Oh, dear! Honey, be careful! There is a thorn on the path. It might prick your lovely, rosy feet and I can't bear that. So, be watchful."

The girl is extremely happy, thinking, 'This husband of mine is heaven-sent, so worried about a little thorn hurting me. My foolish father paid only ten *lakhs* dowry, not knowing the great concern he has for me. He should have paid him twenty *lakhs*!' This makes her very happy.

Now, six months have passed and they are visiting the public gardens in Hyderabad. (Singapore was only for their honeymoon) Now, six months later, she goes to the public gardens in Hyderabad. This time, when the husband spots a thorn, he shouts, "Look here! Be careful as you walk! Do you understand?" The girl is shocked! The same fellow, who six months ago expressed his loving concern, now shouts at her. "Now be watchful!" he says, indicating that fifty percent of his love has gone.

After one year, with a child in her arms, they are in Singapore again — this time for shopping. There is greenery everywhere here, so just in the normal course of walking, her husband spots a thorn. "Don't you know how to walk?" he reprimands. "Where are your eyes? Where are you looking? Be careful! Otherwise, most of our money will be spent on medical bills, understand?!"

She understands. Now, within one year of their marriage, the percentage of love is zero. Later, it deteriorates into minus marks! This is common all over the world. There are no exceptions. So, love in human relationships is conditional.

Here is another example. In India, in the olden days, windows of houses were very small and the doors were small and narrow as well. Why? This was to prevent any theft or robbery. So, most of the houses were like that and even today, in the villages, we see small windows and narrow doors on houses.

One day, it so happened that a householder, who had a sufficiently aged and hefty body, died. His body was very wide on account of his being so generous and kind-hearted, and accommodating whatever food came his way! Everyone wondered how to take the body out, as the doors were very narrow.

Somebody suggested, "Let us break the door and take the body out."

His wife — his legal wife — told everybody, "Don't break the door. Why do that? It will take time to build the doors again and that is expensive. It's better to chop off the hands and legs with a woodcutter, so you can take it out easily. It's not necessary to spend money." That's love! We may call that genuine love, but it is really conditional love.

Bhagawan gives us another example: In those days, even youngsters attended spiritual classes in the evening. Today, we don't need spiritual classes, because we are very busy watching TV shows. Why are we so interested in TV shows?

An actress is paid according to the amount of tears she can produce. Once, an actress went to a director and said,

"Sir, I want to act." The director said, "Bring two buckets. Now, come on and cry. If you can fill these buckets, I will make you the heroine of the movie." That is why TV shows are so popular, because actors and actresses are paid to cry. We pay people to cry! We also end up crying as well, while later watching their show!

Therefore, since we are busy, we don't need any classes. In the olden days, even married people, householders, usually attended some spiritual classes, some *Puranas*, *Hari Kathas*, discourses, or some type of *satsang*. That is the tradition of this land.

A married fellow attended one of these talks. The *guru*, who spoke, was enthusiastic and articulated on truth (*sathya*) with expertise for two hours. This fellow went on listening for a while, but finally said, "Master, shall we continue tomorrow?"

He replied, "Why? I have not yet finished speaking about truth. There is more to talk about."

"My wife is waiting at home. I must go there."

"*Arre*! (Hey!) Useless fellow, don't worry about it!"

Then, this boy said, "*Guru*, you are not married, so you don't know the love of a wife."

"Now, follow this." So, the *guru* went on speaking about truth for fifteen minutes more.

Then, this young man said, "Sir, enough. My mother is waiting at home."

"*Arre!* What mother! Don't worry!"

"Oh, Master! You left your home long ago. You don't know the love of a mother or a wife, so you speak like that."

Then, the *guru* had a master plan: "Boy, come along with me. Let us both go to your house. I will give you a glass of water to drink. You will drink it and then, immediately fall down unconscious as if you have died, but you won't die. Don't worry! I will give you *guru* 'insurance coverage', so you don't have to worry. You will just lie there and listen to all that is happening, but you won't die. Okay?"

"Oh good. I won't die, but I will be able to hear everything. What does it matter? It's only water."

So, they arrived at his home and the *guruji* gave him water. As he drank it, he fell down unconscious.

His wife ran from the kitchen straightaway, fell on the body, and began carrying on and on, crying: "How can I live without you? The sky without stars is useless. The ocean without waves — of what use is it? And a flower without fragrance is no more than a plastic flower. What is the use of all this? How can I live without you?"

Then, the *guru* said, "Don't worry! Bring a glass of water and I will give a *mantra*. You will drink the water and die, but then this man will get up and live! Are you ready?"

She said, "*Guru*, please wait!" And immediately, she said, "Why should I die along with him? It is not necessary! After all, we got married only last year. I have so many years ahead of me. Why should I die with him? No, Swami. I am sorry."

This fellow had heard all of her romantic poems and songs earlier, so he began to reminisce. But suddenly, they all became meaningless now.

Then, the mother came in and lamented, "*Arre,* my boy. How can I live without you? You are my only son. I thought that you would take me to heaven, crossing the *Vaitharani* (a symbolic river of life, which is full of difficulties; 'river of blood' in Hindu mythology) *Punnaama Naraka.* You are my son. Now, who will take me to heaven? You are gone, so how can I live? At this age, how can I carry on for the rest of my life?"

Then, the *guru* tells her, "Amma, don't worry! Drink this water. You will die, but your son will come back to life. You have lived for eighty years — long enough to have children and see your grandchildren. But, this fellow is young. Drink this, so your son will live, though you will die."

"I am sorry, sir. I want to see the marriage of my grandson. It is too soon for me to die now." (The grandson is just a few months' old baby, yet she wants to see his marriage!) This fellow heard all of this.

Then, *Guru*ji said, "What can I do now?"

Both the mother and wife then came to the *guruji,* "You have no mother, you have no wife, and you have no family. Drink this water so that this fellow will live. You made all of this up, so you drink the water. Nobody is there to miss you."

Then, this fellow understood what life is all about. He got up immediately and said,

Maatha Nasthi, Pitha Nasthi, Nasthi Bandhu Sahodara
Artham Nasthi, Gruham Nasthi, Tasmaat Jagrata Jagrata.
Sampraapthe Sannihithe Kaale Nahi Nahi
Rakshathi Dukrinkarane
Govindam Bhaja Moodhamathe

The meaning here is that no one will come to your rescue. No one will ever solve your problems. When the end approaches, no one is dear and no one is near. Think of and sing to Govinda: *Govindam Bhaja Moodamathe*.

Therefore, only Divine love is unconditional. Divine love is not limited. The true *guru* has that unconditional love. Having the quality of unconditional love and the ability to make you love unconditionally, immersed in Self-contained peace and having the ability to grant you that same peace — having all these qualities, that is a true *guru*. We are not capable of those same feelings on our own.

The Importance Of
Focused Attention Or Concentration

One-pointed focus is absolutely necessary in life. If you work in a bank and you don't have focused attention, there will be wrong entries in the bank's ledger. You will find yourself dismissed immediately and out of work!

As a doctor, if your attention is not focused, you may leave the Turkish towel in the abdomen. Then, we will read in the newspapers about a surgeon forgetting a Turkish towel in the patient's abdomen. The operation was successful, but a Turkish towel was left inside! These incidents are written up in the newspapers. Scissors are left in the abdomen, which becomes something like a zip-lock bag. They drop it in and collect it later — safe, customs-free. Anything can be stored in there! Why did this happen? There was no focus of attention by the doctor.

Even as a lecturer, you may have problems, if you are not focused. I met a lecturer at the college, where I serve. That gentleman taught for the whole semester. At the end of the term, he told me, "Everything I taught for this semester is part of the syllabus for next semester." So now, he has to prepare fresh for the next semester! Some of the boys know who he is, so they are smiling. Students had already completed the whole syllabus that belongs to the next semester, because he had no focused attention.

As you drive home, if you are not focused, you won't reach home. You will reach the orthopedic ward, due to an accident! So, focused attention is required in mundane living also. In worldly life, in every human effort, in every human endeavour — even in little subtle things, focused attention is required.

While giving a talk to the boys in Brindavan, Swami looked around and said, "*Arre*, boy. You are not following Me properly; instead, you are thinking. Something is wrong with you." He will immediately identify and diagnose the monkey mind of anybody, no matter who he is, his age or his position. The mind should be concentrated and focused.

All these examples are from Swami's literature.

In those days, Rani Rasamani built a temple in Calcutta for Sri Ramakrishna Paramahamsa. She also attended the *satsang* of Paramahamsa. One time, Paramahamsa suddenly got up and slapped her. Everybody was wondering what was wrong with this mad cap! She was a great philanthropist and a very rich lady as well. She had built a temple for him, yet he dared to slap her. What was wrong?

Then, Paramahamsa said loudly, "Better you stay back at home, rather than be here with a deviated, diverted, disturbed, and perverted, non-focused attention." If you can't pay attention to the topic being dealt with, to the subject being spoken about, it is better to stay at home.

Why is it necessary to concentrate? Even in the classroom, if a student has no focused attention, his life and studies become difficult, because he cannot concentrate. One-pointed attention is necessary and even more so in spiritual life. Focused attention is called concentration and concentration is single-pointed.

There is attention and there is concentration. Concentration is focused attention. Concentration is absolutely essential in spiritual life. But, what is happening today? We have Sathyanarayana *puja* at home. The priest tells us to put a flower or a leaf here and there, on this or that. Well, we have no focused attention, so we put the flower on the head of the priest, instead of on Sathyanarayana Swami! That actually happens! And some people go on inquiring, "Is the *prasadam* ready? Sir, carry on, carry on."

See how ridiculous it is. All that we have been doing in the name of religion and in the name of ritual. I don't know if it is just vanity or what. No, it is neither vanity, nor charity, nor clarity, nor dignity, nor simplicity — just foolishness. This is all because we don't allow the priest to read the five chapters of Sathyanarayana Swami *katha*.

Even during a wedding, somebody may announce that the *muhurtam* (auspicious hour) will be at 12:15; but then, they decide to wait for the photographer and begin instead at 12:30. They think they can easily move the time to 12:30. They want the photos, but not the auspicious *muhurtam*. Therefore, we have no focused attention in spiritual life either.

Meditation

Our meditation has become ridiculous, particularly when we sit for meditation. It is then, that the minds of ninety nine to one hundred percent of the people become full of unwanted thoughts! Try it for yourself tonight.

You will start recalling your enemies, right from your childhood. You will start recollecting the fights between you and your mother-in-law, right from the first day of your marriage. You will also start remembering the teachers, who didn't give you the marks you wanted. You will think about the boss, who is torturing you — all this in the name of meditation. That's what happens.

Some of you might say, "I pray to the Lord. I have done meditation for the last several decades. I meditate every day for one hour." No, no, no! Why do you speak like that? Some of you may really talk like this.

If you have that truly meditative, sensitive, and receptive mind, as you come out of meditation, you should be calm and peaceful. How many of you are calm and peaceful after meditation? Most are much worse off than those people, who do not meditate. You come out of the meditation room and expect a hot cup of coffee from your wife, immediately. If it is delayed, you get angry. That is the result of your meditation!

"Where is the servant maid? What in God's name are you doing? Don't you have extra milk packets?" You go on shouting like this as a result of meditation.

It is better, if we don't meditate. Why? Meditation should make you more loving and forgiving. Meditation should make you friendlier and make you begin the day with love. But, we don't do that.

Some say, "My meditation time is from 5 to 6." How do you know when it is 6 o'clock? Do you set an alarm? Do you tie a string to your foot, so that your son will pull the string and get you up? How do you know?

Therefore, know that meditation is timeless. Meditation is the absence of thought. Meditation is beyond space. It is the withdrawal of 'I'. With 'I'-ness gone, ego is submerged. Mind is passive. You do not know where you are. That is true meditation, not meditating from 4 to 5, or from 5 to 6. That is only plastic meditation. We have synthetic foods, food in ten minutes, coffee in five minutes, meditation in ten minutes, and madness in one minute, because we don't have properly focused attention.

True Spirtuality

We call ourselves highly religious. No. We are ritualistic, but not religious. Being ritualistic is different from being religious. Ritualism is pomp, show, advertisement, and publicity, whereas true spirituality is inward and personal. A truly spiritual man does not make his spirituality known to anybody.

Here is another simple example from Baba: A queen went on complaining about her husband. She said, "You see, I think of God morning, afternoon, and evening, but my husband doesn't think of God at all. This is nonsense! What's wrong with him?"

She went on like this, feeling badly about her husband. One day, she overheard her husband saying, "Ram, Ram, Ram."

"Ah, my husband is saying Ram!" Before he even got up, she called everybody, "Today is a day to celebrate! Let there be a festival. Let the cookies be made. Let there be beating of drums everywhere, because my husband said 'Ram'."

When the king got up, he noticed all sorts of paraphernalia — all the *hungama* (commotion) going on, so he called the queen to ask what was happening. "Oh, I heard you say 'Ram', so I am celebrating."

Then, the king humbly said, "I am sorry, dear. I am very sorry. I should not have said it out loud. The relationship between God and me is totally personal and intimate. It is not to be publicised, nor expressed openly. I am sorry, when you say that you have heard me. I am unhappy about that."

Baba says that many people may not look spiritual, but are actually more spiritual than those, who sound spiritual. He adds that this is because the spirituality of those, who sound spiritual, is ritualism and not true spirituality.

True spirituality is inner transformation, lack of ego, absence of pride, and absence of pomp; it is humility. A fellow can say, "I am a spiritual man," but he, who says so, is not even a human being, let alone spiritual. When there is no humility in you, when you are all ego and arrogance, it is a disgrace to spirituality.

Therefore, not ritualism, but focused attention is true spirituality. Focused attention is religiousness, not religion. So, to be known as a religious man, one must practise focused attention. This is a well-known fact. Therefore, we say, "One *guru,* one focus."

One Guru, One Focus, One Goal
Part II

(Talk by Prof. Anil Kumar,
Singapore, November 2nd, 2011)

Omkara

There are four components in *Omkara*: 'a', 'u', 'm', 'mm'. The *Chandogya Upanishad* explains clearly the four components of *Omkara*: 'a' stands for creation, 'u' stands for sustenance, 'm' stands for annihilation, and the fourth sound is beyond the three.

'A' also stands for the waking state, called *jagrata*. 'U' stands for dreaming state or *swapna*. 'M' stands for deep sleep, *sushupti*. The final sound stands for *turiya*, or eternity.

Jaya Guru Omkara means He is present in the waking state, in the dreaming state, in the deep sleep state, and He is eternal, *turiya*, the ultimate.

Satguru Omkara: here, *sat* means 'existence'. You cannot say, "I met my *guru* yesterday," or "I plan to meet my *guru* next year." Are you sure you will be alive till then? You cannot say, "I am going to meet my *guru* after one year," or "I was with my *guru* last year." That is philosophically a blunder! Why? Because the *guru* is present in your waking state, your dreaming state, and in your deep sleep state: *jagratha*, *swapna*, *sushupti*. He is eternity, *turiya*, the ultimate, Who is present in all the three states of awareness or consciousness.

The Guru Is Present
In All States Of Consciousness

Baba gives a beautiful example. There is an actor in Andhra Pradesh, named Mr. N.T. Rama Rao. He has played Krishna, Karna, and Duryodhana - all three roles. But, he is not Krishna; he is N.T. Rama Rao after all! And he is not Duryodhana. He is a good man, better than Duryodhana! He is not Karna; he is not as charitable as that! He is N.T. Rama Rao; but, when he plays the role of Krishna, yes, he is Krishna. Similarly, the *turiya*, the ultimate, or the *Vaiswanara*, is present in all the three levels of awareness or consciousness: *jagrata*, *swapna*, and *sushupti*.

So, *Jaya Guru Omkara* means He is *turiya*, the ultimate, the *Vaiswanara*, Who is present in all the three states of awareness or consciousness.

Satguru Omkara: *Sat* is the ever-existent. You cannot say He was. You cannot say He will be. He is! That existence, that moment, that existential, experimental, and experiential reality is *Satguru Omkara*!

It is this *Satguru*, about Whom we will talk for some time and understand how He takes us to the goal.

He is the Divine Master, Whose Presence we feel in every breath, every pulsation, every vibration, and every thought. We cannot forget Him. We cannot be away from Him, having been with Him. If one does forget Him, there cannot be a more unfortunate person on Earth! We can afford to lose anything, but not Baba and our devotion to Him! We cannot ignore Him. Wherever we go, we feel His touch.

Swami's Presence In Argentina

A couple of years ago, I went to Buenos Aires, Argentina. They took me to see the Iguazu Falls. To reach the waterfall, we had to walk through the forest. There were iron bars on either side for safety, because there were wild animals around. There was water everywhere. The moonlight on the water reminded one of Kailasapati Bhagawan Shankara - Sainatha Bhagawan! How beautiful it was!

We travelled by train. A boy named Martin escorted me. Do you know what he said? He said, "Mr. Anil, Kadugodi Railway Station is near Brindavan, right?" In Argentina, he was thinking of the Kadugodi Railway Station, Brindavan, and Bangalore! That is Baba!

All over Argentina, cows are very beloved. Just as we decorate Ganesha, Argentineans decorate cows in different fashions! They had some cows dressed in military clothes and some with post (mail) bags! A lady named Moina Perodan was my translator. She said, "Anil, is this cow carrying letters to Swami?" A cow carrying letters to Swami. See that! Where is Argentina and where is Bangalore? What is this identification to Kadugodi? What is the similarity between that cow and letters to Swami? Another lady named Wesley, also a translator, said, "Mr. Anil, this is the *Gokulam* of Sai Baba."

Swami Has No Limits

Baba is not limited to a geographical space. He is not limited to a nation and He is not limited to a province. He is not limited to a couple of individuals, who think they are important, certainly not! God is neither in form, nor out of form, He is uniform! You have to understand that.

For functional purposes He may call you, that is all. But later, you are a nobody; that we have to understand! Bhagawan Baba is not limited to anyone. He is not limited to any nation or any language. Please believe me! Baba belongs to all languages, all countries, all castes, all creeds, and all nationalities. That is Sathya Sai Baba. You cannot limit Him.

He Is Truth, Goodness, Beauty

Bhagawan Baba is not limited to time and He is not to be identified with the space, where He spent the maximum amount of time. Then, Who is He?

Where there is truth, there is Sai Baba. Where there is goodness, there is Sai Baba. Where there is beauty, there is Sai Baba. Truth, goodness, and beauty - *Sathyam, Sivam, Sundaram* - that is Sathya Sai Baba!

The beauty of Singapore will remind one of Sathya Sai Baba, why not? It has the clean air Swami loves! Think about it. He named the Brindavan campus *Brindavana*, meaning a garden. The campus in Ooty is called *Nandanavana*. He loves gardens, He loves greenery. So, wherever there is greenery, there is Sai Baba.

Once, in Kodaikanal, we had the opportunity to have individual photographs with Swami. There were some lovely potted plants with flowers there. Swami stood on one side and some lucky individual stood on the other side.

When my chance came, being crazy, I moved very close to Him.

You know what He said? "That flower is praying to be photographed. That flower is also waiting for My visit. The flower looks more beautiful than you. So, better give it some space and let that flower also be in the photograph."

Truth, goodness, and beauty are our *Guru*, our Divine Master, Sathya Sai Baba. This is one dimension of one *guru*, one focus, and one goal.

You Are Divine

There is another dimension: the *guru* and the goal are not separate. The *guru* is the goal and the goal is the *guru*. What is your goal? *Guru*! Who is your *guru*? My goal! So, the goal and the *guru* are not separate. But, this perceived separation is due to the absence of focussed attention or concentration. You consider the *guru* and the goal as separate, because there is no focus. Once you are focused, you will know that the goal is the *guru* and the *guru* is the goal.

Someone said to Ramana Maharshi, "Swami, I am going back to my native place. Please help me." Ramana Maharshi replied, "You are going away from me? Impossible! I am there also. You may travel from India to Canada, but I am in Canada also!"

What is a goal? A goal involves distance and it demands time. You might ask, "How much time do I need? How many kilometres should I travel? Which airline will help me?"

You are That! You are Divine. *Tat Tvam Asi,* meaning 'That thou art!" That Divinity is the Self! Not only that, *Aham Brahmasmi* means "I am That, I am God." Then, there is no question of a goal. You are That.

Suppose I say, "Where is Anil Kumar? Who is Anil Kumar?" Then, you will immediately reply: "Let me call the organisers and find out why they invited this fellow! He does not know who he is! He wants to know where he is! He must be crazy!" It is an act of ignorance to search for myself! To search for a goal in spirituality is equally foolish, because you *are* the destination. You are the goal. You are the beginning and you are the end.

What is the goal? *Sathyam,* or truth is the goal. What is truth? You are the truth. God is truth. Who is God? God is truth. What is truth? "Truth is God. Live in truth," says Baba.

Science Is True, But Not Truth

I will tell you a small anecdote. Swami visited Hyderabad to inaugurate the *Sivam* building. We had lunch and then, Swami started talking to me:

"Hmm… what subject do you teach?"

"Swami, science," I said.

"Ha, science! Okay, I have a simple question, sir."

"Yes, Swami?"

"What is truth?" He asked.

I answered, "Swami, science is based on truth. There is no science without truth. Truth is scientific. Science is truthful. Truthfulness is science and technology. It cannot be false." I used all my vocabulary in an utter state of ignorance! Some people speak in front of Swami to exhibit how foolish they are and I am no exception.

Swami said, "No, sir, science is not truth."

"So, science is false? Swami, science is...."

Swami said, "Just wait. Today, you are wearing a black suit. Yesterday, you wore a blue suit. Two days ago, you were in a pyjama-*kurta*, is it not true?"

I answered, "Yes, Swami."

"It is true, but not Truth," Swami said.

Why? It is only a fact. A *kurta*-pyjama is a fact. The black suit is a fact and so is the blue suit. They are true, but not the Truth. Why? The clothes change, the colour changes, and uniforms change. That which changes may be true, but it is only a fact. So, science speaks of facts, but not of truth. Then, for the first time, I understood what truth is!

Next, Baba said, "You may be changing the clothing, but you are the same. The one in that suit the other day and the one in these clothes today is the same person. That is Truth. That, which is *nithya* or eternal, is *Sathya*. That is Truth. All that changes is fact." That is Sathya Sai Baba! Nobody else can speak like that!

The Real Meaning Of Technology

Once, some students and professors were given an interview. Swami asked one student,

"What are you doing?"

The student replied, "M. Tech., Swami."

Swami said, "M. Tech., hmmm. What is 'tech'?"

"Tech means technology, Swami," the student answered.

Swami said, "Ah...technology."

Then, He asked another student, "What is technology?"

"Swami, applied science," the student answered.

Swami said, "O, ho! If applied science is technology, you can call it applied science. Why call it technology?"

Swami asked again, "What is technology?"

"Swami, science is theory and technology is application," the student ventured.

Swami replied, "*Arre, emi gas ra*? Is it all gas(a lie)?"

Then, He asked the professor, "Professor, tell Me, what is technology?"

The professor thought Swami had no knowledge! "Swami, technology and the different fields in technology...," he started explaining.

Swami allowed him to talk, until the gas cylinder was empty! Then, suddenly He said, "*Arre*, how wrong, *ra*! That is not technology! What you speak of as technology is really tricknology, only tricks. But, the real technology is 'take knowledge' - take My knowledge! Take My knowledge for your progress, for your welfare. Take My knowledge for a matter of service. That 'take knowledge' is 'technology', otherwise it is tricknology." That is Sathya Sai Baba! Who can speak like that?

Therefore, Sathya Sai Baba is the eternal, the immortal, the blemish-less, unpolluted, crystal clear, non-dual, spiritual truth or *Sathya*, on which He reclines and which He represents! Sathya Sai Baba is that eternal truth, that immortal truth, that nectarine truth. That is the truth of eternity! The one of continuity or eternity is Sathya Sai Baba.

Swami Is The Best Chef

On one occasion, my wife prepared a sweet dish called *badshah*, I believe, and we sent it to Bhagawan. He said, "This is not nice, *ra!*"

"Why, Swami?" I asked.

Swami said, "You should mix some curd (yogurt) in it. It will be crisp and very nice."

"Swami, you speak of cookies and home science techniques!" I said.

Then, He said, "This chutney is very nice, but there should be less salt."

He tells you about all delicious items and gives you recipes far, far better than all the ladies here.

Swami, The Fashion Guru

Now, let me tell you about His selection of *saris*. He selects *saris* of beautiful colours! You may not know what colour suits you best, but Swami knows! During Dasara and

Birthday celebrations, He distributes *saris* to the ladies. Ladies are ladies all over the world! They don't want to wait! They will wear the *sari* that same evening! Can't they wait and wear it the next day?

Then, our good Lord, the Divine Master, starts walking during *darshan,* looking at how well the *sari* suits each recipient. If you look at Him when He looks at you, He will look elsewhere! He wants to look at you without your noticing it!

Usually, Swami distributes white *saris* to very elderly widows, who love their husbands and spend their time in the Mandir. One day, He gave a very colourful *sari* to an elderly widow, "Wear this *sari* now and your husband will come immediately from heaven! Come on, he is waiting!"

Sai is romantic. He is very conscious of the clothes we wear. He will notice what you are wearing and say, "You are wearing a new suit. Let me see...you walk this way...now walk that way...hmm, okay."

Do Not Imitate Fashions Indiscriminately

I have a fancy for new clothes. While I was in Brindavan, a Punjabi student named Ajay Rana was wearing a *kurta* pyjama that went down to his knees. The boys were doing a Punjabi dance with a fast beat. I like to dance, though I do not dance often. I saw the boy doing the dance well.

I said, "Is that a Punjabi outfit?"

"Yes, sir," he replied.

"Very nice!" I said.

"Do you like it?"

"Yes!" I replied.

Please believe me, within twenty-four hours I received a Punjabi outfit from his parents!

Whenever I have new clothes, I first show them to Swami. Swami went to Madras on a visit. I wanted to wear the Punjabi outfit; but, if there is a public meeting and I wear a Punjabi dress, it may be risky! If Swami doesn't like it, I would have to zip my bag and leave the place! I know it is risky. So, I took a formal suit.

In the early morning, there was *nagarsankirtan* at *Sundaram* in Madras. How many of you have seen *Sundaram* in Madras? It is the most beautiful piece of architecture in Madras. Swami gives *darshan* at the end of *nagarsankirtan*, early in the morning. A few thousand devotees are seated, all lights are switched off, and floodlights are focussed on Swami. He stands in the centre, while the whole area is dark in the early hours of the morning. Such a magnificent sight! A most wonderful sight: God descending on Earth, Love on two feet, the orange robed Bhagawan like a rainbow in the firmament of the sky, adding beauty to the dark blue backdrop of the sky!

At the end of *darshan*, He walks through a corridor to go into His room. So, I went and stood near the corridor in my new Punjabi outfit, so that He could see it.

Swami came towards me and stopped. "Hmm... *Kottha* dress *darincheve*," meaning, "You have put on a new outfit."

"Yes, Swami. How do I look?" I asked.

Swami asked, "Has your wife seen you?"

"Not yet, Swami! I wanted to show You first!" I replied.

"Shall I tell you how you look?" Swami asked.

"Yes, Swami, that is why I came here," I said.

Swami said, "You look exactly like a Punjabi truck driver!"

Swami Is Beauty And Energy Personified

The beauty of Swami is not based on cosmetics, face powder, or make up, no! His beauty is natural. For example: He starts at five in the morning from Bangalore and reaches Kodaikanal at six in the evening, with no washing or change of clothes. He eats nothing, yet He is as fresh and active in the evening as He was in the morning!

Whereas we fellows, who join His entourage, have tea and lunch, then snacks, plus boxes of sweets and fruits in the bus, but we feel weak. Swami, on the other hand, is *Mita Smita Sundara Mukharavinda*, meaning the beauty of a fresh, blossoming flower. That is what we see on His face! All our energy is based on food, but Swami's energy is never based on food.

One day, I said to Swami, "Swami, we are eating and You are not eating. We feel embarrassed, when You are not eating. Please Swami, eat something."

Immediately, Baba said, "You need food, because you need a lot of energy. I don't need food, because I am energy." "I am energy" - that is Sathya Sai Baba! His energy is not based on the food He consumes; He is energy!

Smita: smita refers to Swami's lovely smile. When Swami smiles, we like it. Some people's smiles are sarcastic, others' smiles seem villainous. But, when Swami smiles, we feel relieved of our problems. His smile is a solution to our questions, His smile clarifies our doubts and kindles and awakens our intuition! That is the beauty of the Divine smile!

A baby's smile represents innocence, whereas we represent ignorance. Innocence is Divine, it is spiritual. *Nandalala* refers to the eternal Child, Who smiles. So, Baba is that eternal *Sundaram*, He is *Sathyam Sivam Sundaram*.

Know that you, too, are *Sathyam Sivam Sundaram*! The feeling of permanence, the feeling of eternity within you is *Sathya*. We know that we are sure to die, but we still have that feeling of permanence or eternity, which is *Sathya*. You are *Sathya*. You know what happened yesterday and what happened today; you know what is good for you and what is not. That awareness is *Sivam*. Everyone wants to be handsome, everyone wants to look beautiful. So, you are *Sundaram*.

Loyalty To The *Guru* Is Essential

Stay with one *guru*. Do not change your *guru*. There are some people, who say, "Sir, I have started visiting this *guru*, I have started visiting that *guru*..."

This is not a shopping mall of *gurus*! There is only one *guru*. Once, someone went to Shirdi Bhagawan and said, "I want to change my *guru*." Shirdi Bhagawan was violent, as you all know. He gave him two doses immediately! "Idiot! Do you change your father? Do you change your mother? Dirty fellow, get out of Dwarakamayi!"

The one *guru* you believe in has all the potential to turn the potential into the actual! Therefore, don't change your *guru*. If we keep changing *guru*s, what happens? A rolling stone gathers no moss: you don't get anything!

Ramakrishna Paramahamsa gave this example. One fellow wanted to dig a well. He dug a hole six feet deep, but there was no water. So, he dug another hole ten feet deep, still no water. Then, he dug yet another hole twenty-five feet deep - again, no water. Finally, when he had dug a hole forty feet deep, he found water. Ramakrishna Paramahamsa said, "Had you gone forty feet deep with the first hole you dug, you would have reached the same water. But, now you made the whole land full of pits!"

If you dive deep, explore, excavate, and experience your *guru,* you get infinite, fathomless depths of bliss, brought out like a fountain by His grace. Never change your *guru*, because religion is not like politics - jumping from one party to another party! Religion is not a job you change just for a small raise! No, my friends, any *guru* likes loyalty. Your family expects loyalty, your employer expects loyalty, but the *guru* expects total loyalty! "Come what may, You are my Lord, You are my Lord."

Never Give Up Your *Guru*

Hiranyakasipu, father of Prahlada, was ready to excuse him only if he said, "*Om Namo Hiranyakasipaya*," instead of "*Om Namo Narayanaya*." But, Prahlada refused to give up Narayana! He knew only one *guru*, that is all! His father threatened to take his life, but Prahlada remained focused on only one *guru*.

Swami mentions the example of Mansoor. Mansoor was a great devotee. He always said, *"An Al Haq."* An Al Haq means "God is, God is."

The King felt insulted. "What! God is and I am not, is that so? Put him in prison."

But, Mansoor went on repeating, *"An Al Haq, An Al Haq."*

The King was very disturbed. He brought Mansoor in front of him and asked his fellows, "Come chop off his legs and hands." But, Mansoor continued chanting, *"An Al Haq, An Al Haq."*

"Throw him into the fire," the King said.

Baba says that even in the flame, in the rising ashes, Mansoor listened to the sound *'An Al Haq, An Al Haq... Allah Malik Hai, Allah Malik Hai.'* That is devotion! That is devotion to one *guru*!

We cannot be like Judas, who betrayed Jesus Christ! Some fellows come to Swami and say, "Oh Lord, You are everything!" But, then they cheat Swami and cheat devotees also! We have some people like that! "Swami, this life is for You, this body is for You," they say, but they are the first ones to leave Swami!

This is not new — there were many people like that around Jesus also!

"O Lord, You are my life," one said.

"Oh stop it! You will deny Me tomorrow before the cock crows thrice," said Jesus Christ. The next morning, Jesus was betrayed by Judas and Jesus was crucified! Should you and I be like Judas? **It is better not to live than to lead a life forgetting your *guru*, or being disloyal or ungrateful to the *guru*!**

Worldly Positions Are Temporary

Ramakrishna Paramahamsa said, "At the time of sunset, glow worms shine. They think they are bright, but after some time, stars appear. So, glow worms are nothing. Stars think they are superstars, but when the moon appears, the stars appear like dust after all! Then, the moon thinks it is great, until the next morning when the sun comes up!"

There is always someone, who can exceed you. We don't need to crave for this position or that position! Baba gives an example of two fellows passing each other. One fellow was on the horse, the other was carrying a pillow. Many thought the fellow carrying the pillow was a menial fellow, a servant, and that the man on the back of the horse was the master.

Then, it rained. The fellow on horseback got down, tied up the horse to a post outside a temple. Then, he slept under the horse, because he was afraid someone may take it away. The fellow with the pillow went into the temple, put the pillow under him, and sat cross legged. Then, people thought he was the master and the fellow sleeping under the horse was the servant! Tell me, who is the master and who is the servant?

A Real Beggar Has No Satisfaction

It is only a question of time, a question of position or fortune, as well as His grace. God is always with us. His grace we need and His benediction we want. Without Him, all these tinsels fall into nothing.

Once, on a rainy day, Alexander the Great was riding on his horse. He stopped his horse when he saw a fellow, naked and shivering, under the tree. Alexander offered him a blanket, "Oh beggar, take this," he said.

The naked fellow declined the gift, saying, "My Lord, give it to a beggar, not to me."

"You are a beggar! You are shivering and you have no clothes to wear. You seem beggarly enough. Why do you say that I should give this to some other beggar?" asked Alexander.

Then, the fellow asked, "Oh King, where are you going?"

Alexander replied, "I am going to the neighbouring kingdom to conquer, because I am Alexander the Great."

Then, the fellow said, "Oh King, with all the kingdoms you have, you are not satisfied. You want to conquer the neighbouring kingdom! You are the biggest beggar! You can keep the blanket for yourself."

So, it is that want, desire, and possessive instinct that is beggarly! To be beggarly is a lot worse than being a beggar.

Therefore, when we think, "I am rich enough. I have God's grace with me, I have satisfaction, I am content, and I can face the challenges of life," that is His spiritual gift to mankind! Not the sound of coins, or lifeless currency notes! That is Bhagawan Sri Sathya Sai Baba.

"I Wait For Your Love"

Once, there was an important union minister, who came for Swami's *darshan,* but Swami had left the *darshan* hall already. I wanted to see what would happen. I hid behind a bush near Swami's residence in Brindavan. There were a number of cars carrying ambassadors, district and national level officers, but Swami did not come out of His residence.

In the afternoon, He called me: "What were you doing this morning?"

I said, "Swami, I was behind the bush watching."

"Don't you have college?" Swami asked.

"Yes, Swami," I replied.

"Then, why were you there?" Swami asked.

I replied, "Swami, I wanted to see what You would do, because I noticed an important central government minister waiting for You!"

Please note what Baba said: "Everyone will have to wait for me. I don't wait for anyone. I don't bend down before anyone. But, I wait for your love; I wait for your devotion. I wait for my devotees, not for men of stature or wealth." That is Sathya Sai Baba.

He Looks At Your Heart, Not Your Clothes

Another example: a gang of nomads, whom we call *lambadis,* were once given an interview. They are nomads, so they don't have a permanent place to live. Instead, they move from place to place. Swami gave them an interview. I noticed that they were stinking; I don't think they had a bath once in their lifetime!

Swami called them into the interview room, "Come on, come on."

I was wearing good clothes and I had even applied perfume. Why did He not call me? He gave the *lambadis* an interview. At the end of the interview, they came out with beaming faces and bags full of clothes, watches, chains, and cash!

Swami came close to me and said, "Why are you looking like that?"

"Swami, why did you give an interview to those people?" I asked.

"When I am giving, why are you crying?" Swami said.

"Swami, You can give, but those people are stinking, Swami. The interview room must have been spoiled by now!" I said.

Baba said, "I don't see their clothes, I see their heart."

That is Sathya Sai Baba. He sees your heart. He doesn't look at your dress; He doesn't look at your jewellery. He does not look at your attainments, achievements, scholarships, bio-data, or CV! He looks at your heart!

Therefore, remember one *guru*, Bhagawan Sri Sathya Sai Baba. Focus your attention on Him. Our goal is Sathya Sai Baba. Once again, the only requirement is focus.

Questions And Answers Session

(Special Talk by Prof. Anil Kumar
in Singapore, November 2nd, 2011)

Q: What was Baba's last message to His devotees?

A: Baba's first message was also His final message:

Manasa Bhajare Guru Charanam,

Dustara Bhava Sagara Taranam.

**O Mind, without worshiping
the Lotus Feet of Guru Sai Natha,
It is not possible to cross the ocean of life and death.**

That is Baba's first and last message to us, and it is also His future message. It is His message even now: *Manasa Bhajare Guru Charanam!*

Q: We are keen to do seva projects, but in our organisation, there are many protocols that must be followed. These protocols often delay us in achieving our mission. So, what shall we do?

A: Protocol is different from reverence and protocol is different from respect. Protocol relates to the official, while respect and reverence relate to the spiritual. So, in the Sai organisation, let us place the emphasis on reverence and respect rather than on so much protocol. This is fundamental as ours is a spiritual organisation, not a bureaucratic officialdom. Our emphasis should be on total respect, not bureaucracy.

Q: *So, how do you advise our organisational leaders to overcome the restrictions of their positions and titles, in order to be spiritual in their action?*

A: Oh, it is a psychological problem. It is like this: While occupying a certain position, I have developed an image. With this position, I have developed my personality, received some respect, and gained some sort of status. However, when that position is gone, I am suddenly nobody! So therefore, I am not prepared to quit the position!

Let us take Baba Himself as an example. What position does He have? He is not *samithi* convenor, nor is He a state president. He is also not a national coordinator. He is not even a rich man, as He has no bank account also! He has no high Ph.D or D.Sc degrees. In fact, He dropped out of school in the seventh class! Even His body is not completely fit — only one ear can hear and only one eye can see; but still, He is totally Divine! That is Sathya Sai Baba.

So, if you rise above your position, then you are like Baba — Divine! You are egoless. It is only a question of transition, of evolution, under His guidance and grace. **Those, who have Divine grace, will rise above their position. Those, who enjoy His blessings, are not conscious of their position, because ultimately a position is an imposition!** So you are free.

Q: *Swami's love for His devotees is unique and it always leaves me in awe and wonder. Can you please share some personal examples of how His love is so unique?*

A: Yes, Swami's love is unique! He speaks to a primary school child with the same affection as He does to a college student. He speaks to a professor with the same concern He has for a student. He talks to *ashram* authorities with the same love He has for the professors. When He talks to the President of India, the Prime Minister, the King of Nepal, or the King of Greece, He speaks to each of them in the same tone and with the same love.

That is the uniqueness of Sathya Sai Baba's love! He shares the same love with all, whereas you and I do not. When we speak to our boss, we treat him very differently from a subordinate. If there is a question of cash involved, we will treat someone differently. But, Swami showers the same love upon everyone. He shares the same love with all, whether a servant, a maid, a student, or anyone else!

So, what should you do if someone says to you, "Swami loves me more!"? Pity him please! He doesn't know what he's talking about. That fellow is still under the spell of delusion. Baba loves everybody equally and entirely. So, if any fellow says to you, "The sun shines mostly on me," then just let him enjoy his madness! Baba loves everyone equally. That is the uniqueness of Sai's love.

You may be a sinner or a saint, virtuous or debauched, a scholar or an illiterate fool; you may be doing *sadhana* or not. Our Sai is high, infinite, and above all these things. No matter what you are, He loves you just the same. He loves us in spite of all our mistakes and in spite of all our pitfalls! Nobody else will love us like that. That kind of supreme love is above duality. It is continuous giving and forgiving. That's what He is — the Divine embodiment of Divine Love!

Q: Lately, I have been attending a 'Hare Krishna Satsang' led by a guru. I am a Swami devotee. Is it wrong to attend the satsang of another guru?

A: There are some *gurus*, who show you the true way. Suppose you take me to Singapore on a tour and you arrange for a guide to show us around. (We went on such a duck tour here, where another 'duck' was explaining what was happening!) We might learn a lot from this guide about Singapore. So, it's the same with a *guru*. It doesn't mean that this *guru* is the ultimate, but he has shown me what is true. So, true *gurus* show the way.

However, Baba is the way and the goal. So, there is a double benefit! In the *Holy Bible*, it is written, "I am life, I am the goal, I am the way!" That 'I am' is Sai Baba! That 'I am' is Sathya Sai! So, He is the goal and the way.

Q: Could you please advise us what an individual should do to be a better teacher (for example, a guru at a Sathya Sai Education in Human Values centre)?

A: It's probably better that we don't call the teacher '*guru*', because it is a name that carries a lot of responsibility. '*Gu*' stands for '*gunatita*', which means 'attributeless, without attributes', and '*ru*' stands for '*rupa varjitah*', or 'formless'! *Guru* illuminates; it is He, Who dispels darkness. We teachers don't do that. We are only teachers.

So then, what should we do to be good teachers? Do you want me to tell you my secrets? Okay then! First secret: A teacher is not merely a DVD or CD, there to repeat information over and over again. No! When you teach, you must be lively. Children don't want monotony and repetition. You must infuse your teachings with life! When I teach *Balvikas*, I infuse them with life.

Second secret: A teacher must make himself presentable. You cannot come to class in some horrible, ugly dress, with your hair uncombed and your face unwashed. We are teachers, not vagabonds! A teacher has got to be presentable. So, first dress and then, address! I repeat, a teacher has got to be presentable.

Third secret: A teacher has got to be resourceful. He's got to know a lot of information. He's got to know more than what's in the syllabus and he's got to know more than the students do!

Fourth secret: A teacher should be impartial. He should treat everyone in the same manner. "He is Indian," "He is South Indian," "He is my neighbour" . . . A teacher, who separates people like that, is not a teacher at all! He is not worthy of the name of a teacher. He should be equal to everybody! He cannot be a linguistic chauvinist or a regional 'leper'. He should treat everybody the same, impartially.

Secret number five: A teacher should have wit and humour. "Take down the notes... Newton's Law of Science..." *Abba!* Then, add a little humour! He must bring a sense of humour into his classroom — some of wit and a sportsmanship spirit.

Six: A teacher does not complain. I must not say to my new class, "Last year's batch was better than your group!" If you feel a need to say this, then resign. Just go! Who asked you to stay? Resign! A teacher should not complain.

And finally, secret number seven: Inspire! Be inspiring. Make your students say, "I want to be like him!"

When I was a student, some of my teachers were heroes to me. Take my English professor, for example. He used to wear the loveliest suits. I used to take so many notes about the colour of his suit and his ties! They were so nice. I always wanted to be like him, because he dressed and addressed us with such style! He was so engaging that, when the bell rang to signal the end of class, we'd want to shoot the peon, who'd rung the bell! So, the teacher should be a role model.

God blessed me to work under him and with him for a decade and half! Whenever I wore a new suit, he would say, "Good, Mr. Anil!" He used to call me to his office to serve me a cup of coffee, a fresh cup, when I wore a new dress.

Then, whenever there was a mistake, he used to immediately, quietly correct me then and there. For example, once I was in a bit of a hurry, so I sent a notice: "Few of students will be going on biological tour. They may be permitted to leave." I sent that notice. What's wrong there?

My professor saw that and right away, I was called to the office! "Anil Kumar, come to my office!" So, I went there.

The teacher asked the peons to close the door. "I don't expect you to write like that! I don't expect such grammatical mistakes to be committed by you. You write 'few students', which means 'nil students'. You should write '<u>a</u> few students'... '<u>a</u> few students'. Do you understand that?"

"I am sorry, sir!"

"No, nothing doing! I don't expect it from you!"

Immediately, he would say, "Peon, open the door! Give him a cup of coffee. Nice boy!"

That was the style of this teacher. So, a teacher should inspire his students by virtue of his personality, his resourcefulness, his ready wit, his example, and his perfection!

There are even some girls, who imitate their teachers. If the teacher wears a rose flower here, they will also wear it there. So, teacher has all sorts of influence. In fact, students believe such a teacher more than their own parents. For example, if I were to say 2 X 2 = 6, even if their mother says, "No, it equals 4!" their response would be, "Shut up! My teacher told me so!"

Q: How do I know and realise that Swami is with me always?

A: How do you know that Swami is with you? Since you are here, you know that Swami is with you. Many people are not here, because they are not aware of Swami, without or within. Swami is with them, in them, above them, below them, and around them, but they are not aware of it. They are not aware of Him. Since you are aware of Him, of His presence, you have chosen to be here. That proves that Swami is with you. He blesses you, forever and ever! Have no doubt about it!

Q: My question has two parts. Given the requirements of daily work and other stresses in life, how can one keep one's focus on the goal? And secondly, in this fast-paced, stressful world, how can one maintain calm, meeting everyone and every situation with love and peace?

A: Though those may indeed be two questions, the answer is only one. A simple advice: When you are stressed, don't talk to anybody. Particularly not to the wife. That's because, if you talk to her when you are tense, she will give it back to you for a week! So, be careful!

Also, don't talk to your children when you are stressed. They will remember your transgression for a lifetime! So, when you are tense, when you are stressed, don't speak! Be silent. Have a glass of cold water. Stand in front of the mirror and see how you look when you are stressed and tense. A donkey looks better than you! Take a walk. Feel the cool breeze. If you do, then slowly you will calm down.

Now, what can you do to reduce tension during your busy work day? What can you do to relieve stress at the office?

Well, you have an iPod, so listen to Sai *bhajans*! As you listen to Sai *bhajans*, Sai will console you. When there is a problem at the office, sing *'Daya Sagara Karunakara, Daya Sagara Karunakara'*. When you sing that song, I swear in the name of Baba that you will receive Divine help. You will receive immediate help! So, sing *bhajans*. Sai *bhajans* create solutions for your problems.

I know of a case, where a child was suffering from dysentery. This child was having fifty or sixty motions per day! If this continued, he was sure to die soon. And finally, this boy turned blue! His whole body turned blue. And so, the mother took this child and sat with him before Baba's picture and started singing, *'Sarva Jeeva Vasa Narayana, Sarva Jeeva Vasa Narayana'*.

Now, of course, Swami saw all of this. So, as the mother sang, the child started to move. He started moving his limbs and the blue in his skin faded and his normal colour returned. All this was achieved by singing only one song! All of this happened, because the mother simply started singing *'Sarva Jeeva Vasa Narayana'*.

So, just remember that Sai *bhajans* relieve your problems, your stress, and your strain. You don't need to pay someone to teach you to meditate, to relieve your stress.

Who is the fellow, who takes your money to teach you to be peaceful? He is a businessman, not a spiritual man! Why? No saint ever took money to teach meditation! The one, who expects money from you, is no *guru* at all. If he teaches you meditation and takes money for it, he is not a *guru*. The wind is free, the earth is free, and water is free! But, your meditation classes are so costly!

So, just sing Sai *bhajans* and you won't have to pay anything to get immediate relief. Immediate relief! These *bhajans* are more powerful than penicillin or Zandu Balm! So, Sai *bhajans* are the way to relieve stress and strain. That's why I have invited our brothers here to sing today — so you won't have stress and I won't have strain!

Q: Since Swami is everywhere, is there a need to go to Puttaparthi?

A: If God is everywhere, then why do you go to the temple? You can sleep in any room, so why do you need a bedroom? You can cook in the veranda or on the street, so why do you need a kitchen?

Baba is everywhere. He is like a current, which exists everywhere all at once. His energy and power are omnipresent. But, Puttaparthi is like a thermal power station. It is like a power station, from which the energy is sent forth out into the world. And so, you come here. You come to be near that source of Divine energy.

Q: Swami's ending is hard to accept, because of the way He left. We did not expect Him to go that way! What are your comments please?

A: We did not expect Him to leave like that. But neither did we expect Him to arrive in the way He did!

He was born in the early hours. Why not in the daytime? Why not in the afternoon? When He was born, musical instruments began to play. Why? When He was born, a cobra was found near His body. Why? In spirituality, to ask "Why?" isn't helpful, because the explanations are beyond earthly reasoning, beyond the rational, beyond the scope of our logic. So, God is beyond mind and reason.

Then, about Baba's withdrawal, He gave us 27 days' time to adjust, while He remained in the hospital. Actually, I don't believe that Baba was in the hospital for 27 days. I don't believe that! His body was there in the hospital, but He was 'touring' elsewhere — maybe Singapore, China, Taiwan, or America — wherever His devotees are!

"Why do you say that? Are we fools to believe you?" Some double fools may think like that.

This is my reply: Our students and staff, who saw Swami at close quarters, reported that His body was softer than rose petals, softer than butter! How could such a soft form withstand so many needles poking into His body? His Feet were so tender that when those, who were present, pressed them, the press marks remained on His Feet! Then, how do you expect Him to cope with the ventilator and all the other kind of treatment?

So, my answer is always this: Baba was showing, "Come on! Do whatever you can with this body, but I know when to go! You cannot fix My timetable! All 'arrivals' and 'departures' are in My hands! So, even My departure is in My Hands! So, you can use any instrument, or give any number of injections for any number of days — I won't be bothered." Then, He simply left the body there in the hospital like that, while He went on visiting everybody!

Perhaps, it was to give time for us to withstand the shock of His departure from the body. Had He left immediately in one day, perhaps thousands would have also left this planet. Thousands could have died in shock! So, as Baba's devotees are spread all over the world, time was needed to prepare the devotees to receive this huge shock.

Then, *lakhs* of people came there to see His body. There was no accommodation, no food, no shelter (as so many were here). Simply they were all lined up watching. So, if Swami left the body immediately when He fell sick, all these people would have left for heaven, not remaining further here on Earth!

So, two points are clear: First, He has withdrawn as per His decision, in spite of all medical treatment. And second, He was not there in the body in the hospital. He gave His body to the doctors for treatment, while He went around visiting everybody.

That visitor, that global visitor, that cosmic visitor, that real Sai, Which is super-consciousness, is ever-present as *Sat-chit-ananda*. That's the true Sathya Sai Baba!

Q: *Who is a living guru, now that Swami has left His form? Do we need a living guru?*

A: *Guru* has no birth and no death! Teachers are born and teachers die; but, *guru* has neither birth, nor death. Shirdi Bhagawan is *Jagadguru*. Shirdi Bhagawan is *Sadguru*. What did He say? He said that His bones will speak, that His tomb will speak! The moment you enter Shirdi, all of your problems are solved.

And what did Baba say? "Puttaparthi is verily heaven on Earth!" That's what Baba said! He said, "The moment you come here, I shall wipe all your tears of grief, so that you will shed only tears of joy and jubilation thereafter! Leave all your burden at My Feet! Go back filled with *ananda*!" That's what Baba said.

So, Baba has not 'left', because He never 'came'. He has always been ever-present!

Chaavu Puttuka Lenatti Saswathundu
Adi Madyanta Rahithudu Anaadi Vaadu
Taanu Puttaka Chaavaka Champabadaka
Anthata Alarunatti Sarva Sakshi

Means -

He has no beginning,
He has no end.
He is not born to die,
Nor can He be put to death.
He is eternal!
Sadguru is the Reality, Sadguru is Existence.
Sadguru is not mortal, but immortal.

That's what we have to understand!

Q: Yesterday, you asked us to forget Prema Sai and just concentrate on Sathya Sai, but there are many, who have been contemporaries of both Shirdi and Sathya Sai. Some of us have also dreamt of living to experience both Sathya Sai and Prema Sai. Is there any chance that this dream might come true?

A: Don't dream and don't listen to dreamers! Don't believe dreamers. Dreamers spread rumours. They create gossip and vain talk. Never believe that! It is utter nonsense. Dreams are individual, just for the dreamer, and should never be generalised.

Prema Sai is the future and that future is not yet here. You are here now, in the present, while Prema Sai comes in future. Future is uncertain, so live in the present. Why do you think of Prema Sai? Live in the moment, never live in the future. And never live in the past. Past is dead. Past is history, while future is mystery. So, present is life. Live in the present. In the present, here and now, is Sathya Sai Baba!

Ethics And Moral Values
In Daily Life
Part I

(Special Talk by Prof. Anil Kumar,
In Brunei, Southeast Asia, November 3rd, 2011)

I first heard the name of this country, Brunei, when I was doing social studies in 11th class. Then, I didn't hear anything more about it, until Brunei was mentioned recently.

I was also told that there is a very small family of Sai devotees here. Even though you are fewer in number, it does not mean that I would treat you in any way less for that reason. I sincerely believe that numbers are not important in the spiritual field. In our history and spiritual literature, you will not find any *guru* mentioning the number of people around him, whether in the thousands or not.

Bhajans In Brunei Are Superb

I do not usually praise people, unless I feel they really deserve it. So, please believe me when I say that the *bhajans* (your devotional songs) in Brunei are superb! They are so melodious and they take one to the fathomless depths of devotion!

It really is Swami's benign grace. From the discipline you have as you sing, it is obvious that you are not missing Swami's physical form, because you feel Swami within you. Otherwise, it would not be possible to sing this way.

Only In Silence Is The Voice Of God Heard

The quietness you have here is not due to a small population. Indeed, two people alone can make a lot of noise! Small families with only two or three people may argue and afterwards, the whole street gets involved in their fight! So, silence cannot be credited to a small population.

Silence seems to be the discipline of this place and that is most convenient for a spiritual life, because it is only in silence that the depth of God is felt and the voice of God is heard. Therefore, when I learnt that Baba has been here for the last nineteen years, it came as no surprise. He will continue to be here for the next ninety years to come at least!

When Morals Are Taken Care Of, Ethics Are Ensured

Today's topic is: "Ethical and Moral Values in Daily Life." Are ethics and morals the same? If they have the same meaning, then why have both words, 'ethics' and 'morals', in the topic title?

Each word has its own importance, something special to convey. As I look at it, ethics are applied to a community, a society, and a generation of people, while morals relate to the individual's attitude and code of conduct.

When morals are taken care of, ethics are ensured. You cannot have ethics without morals; you cannot have the second floor without the first floor. So, first, we have morals, and then ethics.

Baba Is The Ultimate Communicator

Baba has defined all morals and ethics with these three words: "Love for God." Sri Sathya Sai Baba, the latest God Incarnate, is the *Avatar* of the computer and electronic age, Who epitomises all values and ethics.

An iPod, iPad, a phone, or any other media could never convey messages the way Bhagawan does. He belongs to this atomic age and so, He appeals to the modern generation. That's why Bhagawan Sri Sathya Sai Baba is so popular all over the world. If He were to draw illustrations from the Stone Age and the cow-dung era, nobody would listen to Him.

But, He speaks about electronics, laser sciences, cardiology, neurology, and engineering. Moreover, He also speaks about the quality and colour of *sarees* that women wear! So, Baba is down-to earth and close to everybody.

His discourses apply to every person, not to just a select few. There are *gurus* (spiritual teachers), whose talks are meant for enlightened and intellectual people (though they themselves may not be). Those, who call themselves 'intellectuals', are not at all intellectual. (No intellectual would ever call himself an intellectual, unless he is stupid!) So, Baba's talks appeal to everybody, from a tiny tot to a youngster, from the illiterate to the literate, from a boy to a grandfather, from a rural resident to a city professional.

Please consider this total appeal that is a special Sai feature. It is unique! If my talk is appealing to graduates, children will get bored. If my talk is appealing to children, others will check their watch to see how much longer before

I finish! But, here is Baba, whose talks are as interesting for children as they are to a grandmother. In the same congregation, all people listen as if with one ear. There is only one Divine Personality, Who is able to impress everybody on the same topic and that is Bhagawan Sri Sathya Sai Baba!

The scholars say, "We have not heard that interpretation, until now." The children say, "The stories are very interesting." The musicians say, "*Arre,* what melody there is in His voice!" Women discover, "Baba knows more about cooking than I know."

So, Baba is the ultimate in every aspect of human life, mundane or spiritual, momentary or eternal, phenomenal or ephemeral. It is, therefore, no surprise that He defines ethics and morals by these three words: "Love for God." That is the greatness of Baba.

Love Of God And Fear Of Sin

Daiva Preethi means 'love for God'. You should love Him intensely. If you love God, what will happen? You will have *Paapa Bheethi,* 'fear of sin'. What does fear of sin lead to? *Sanga Neethi,* or 'morality in society'. So, we have *Sanga Neethi,* ethics based on morality, and *Paapa Bheethi,* fear of sin, and these are based on *Daiva Preethi,* love for God.

People may ask you to do a lot of things that nobody else wants to do. But, when you love God, you will do it. Before coming here, I was watching the rain from the hotel window. I thought that perhaps you would not get here. But, you came in spite of the rain, out of love for God. This love will never allow you to commit a sin. When we have fear of sin, we ask ourselves, "How would Baba feel about it? How will He take it? What will He say?" It is these two — the love of God and the fear of sin — that are necessary for the upkeep of *Sanga Neethi*, or morality in society.

The Five Human Values Constitute Ethics

The ethics of the community are based on the five human values of *Sathya, Dharma, Shanthi, Prema, Ahimsa*, which mean Truth, Righteousness, Peace, Love, and Non-violence. These five basic values constitute the ethics of society. This is because, they are eternal. *Sathya*, truth in India is not different from *Sathya*, truth in Brunei. *Sathya* in Indonesia is the same as *Sathya* in Malaysia. What *Sathya* was ten years ago is the same today, still the same truth. So, the basic, primordial principles of life that constitute ethics are *Sathya, Dharma, Shanthi, Prema,* and *Ahimsa*. This is the lighthouse that sets the standard of the culture of the nation.

Morals May Change According To Society

Morality may change according to the society; however, ethics are changeless as they are consistently based on the everlasting five human values.

Some examples of how morality changes over time: Once upon a time, it was a sin in India to go abroad; but today, it's more like a sin if you do not go! In days gone by, it was the custom for a girl to marry at the age of eight. Today, if anyone performs a wedding at that age, they will be put behind bars!

Morals are the 'norms' of the society. They are the behaviour of the community. Morals constitute civilisation, whereas ethics constitute culture. Culture and civilisation are different. The culture of the nation, family, and community are eternal and everlasting, whereas morals differ from place to place.

What is right in India is not right here. If you are a woman wearing trousers to the rural villages, all people will stare at you; and if you wear *sarees* to work around here, you will be dismissed! So, it is not possible to standardise as far as morals are concerned, because they vary so much.

Ethics, however, are eternal. They remain the eternal values in a changing society. Morality, as you have learnt, demands some kind of discipline according to the individual circumstances. For example, in some places, to arrive late is not tolerated; while in other places, if you are punctual, you are the odd-one-out, because everybody else is late!

The point is that morality constitutes the very personality of an individual. Having good manners, dressing appropriately, and speaking politely are the traits of a gentleman and this is to have good morals.

The Manners Of Each Generation Change

On a larger scale, like the customs of a country or the manners of each generation, the morals of civilisation are subject to change.

An example is in India. Students stand up, when the teacher arrives. But, in certain countries, students remain seated. *Aaah*! It was a shock to me. I will not mention the country, because it is their way of life. Who am I to comment?

So, morals that direct our daily conduct and attitudes are changeable. For instance, look at our families: the people of my generation never said, "No," to our parents. We would not dare! On the other hand, nowadays the young do not heed their elders.

The lady sitting there is my wife, Vijaylakshmi. She came from the same area as myself; but, please believe me, I only first saw her on our wedding day.

A lot of discussion went on amongst the two families. "What is their family like?" "When and where should we celebrate?"

Nobody bothered to ask me what I would like. So, I went to my younger brother. "*Arre*, tell mother that I want to see the girl first, before I marry her."

And my younger brother hesitantly said to my mother, "He wants to see the girl before he marries her."

My mother replied, "Shut up! What does he know! I have seen her! Can he see better than I?"

It was the same for all of us from that generation. It was, "You do that!" Then, in the next generation, monologue turned to dialogue, "Daddy, shall I do this . . . ?" And the answer was generally accepted.

These modern days, we see a confrontational dialogue! "Why? Why? So what!"

In this generation, a parent might say, "I would prefer this colour for your suit." And the answer from the youth is, "No, daddy! I prefer a different colour!"

The Generation Gap

I don't blame them, the winds of change are blowing; it is so all over the world. A child of today plays on the computer, while I can't. The child is only six years old… *pat pat pat,* he taps on the keyboard.

I asked my grandson to teach me PowerPoint. He was brought up in America and is very fast. It was hard to keep up. "*Arre,* you are a useless fellow!" I told him, "You must slow down and let me take some notes. Then, I can do it."

My grandson said, "It is boring teaching you. How many slides do you want? I will do the PowerPoint for you."

"*Arre,* useless fellow! I have been a teacher for forty-four years. If I were as impatient as you, how could I have been a successful teacher?" So, today's children are very intelligent, critical, and have sharp minds.

So, today, we parents are helpless; we cannot tell children anything. They will only say, "What do you know?"

Long ago, I asked my son to study mechanical engineering.

He said, "What do you know about mechanical engineering?"

Then, I said, "In my day, there were four branches of engineering — electrical, mechanical, civil, and chemical."

He replied, "There are forty branches now! You were born at a time, when there were only four branches. Why do you want me to study mechanical engineering?"

For the first time, I understood what 'generation gap' meant. I realised that children know more about the present than all of us, so I don't blame them. We cannot command and dictate what they should do. Yet, at the same time, morals are at stake and so, ethics have been shaken to the ground.

Fortunately, at this time Sathya Sai Baba, the Divine parent, appeared in our midst as an *Avatar*. **Had this *Avatar* not been here, the young generation would have been completely spoilt!**

Baba's Greatest Gift Has Been To Grace Countries Outside Of India

God has blessed me to visit about twenty-five countries. I have found the youth that have been through Bal Vikas training (a spiritual education programme for children), or that are serving as *seva dals* (service volunteers) are a million times better than those, who have not had this training. You can see this in certain places, like the United States, the United Kingdom, and Canada. There is a noticeable difference between the children of the Sri Sathya Sai background and other children.

The greatest gift of Sri Sathya Sai Baba has been to grace the countries outside of India. How else would the Japanese recite the *Vedas*? Could you have ever imagined the Chinese, the Iranians, and Iraqis reciting the *Vedas*? How is it possible? It is only possible due to Sri Sathya Sai Baba.

Sathya Sai Baba Is Truth

Sathya, truth, is at the physical and spiritual level. At the worldly level, a promise made should never be broken. Once you give your word, you should adhere to it, come what may.

Bhagawan Sri Sathya Sai shows us the working principle of truth. Forty years ago, He announced publicly that there would be a college in Anantapur. Later, He walked into the dining room, where members of the Trust (Sri Sathya Sai Central Trust, which runs the Sai institutions and *ashrams*) were sitting.

One of them asked, "Swami, how can You start a college next year?"

Baba immediately said, "It is My problem, not yours."

Then, the man said, "Excuse me, I ask, only because there is no money in the Trust. Building a college requires at least fifty *lakhs* (1 *lakh* = 100,000 *rupees*). How will You do that, Swami, when there is no money?"

"Don't let your blood pressure shoot up! Please calm down. Swami will take care of it."

Believe me, I am speaking in the Divine presence of Bhagawan. The very next day, one *crore rupees* (100 *lakhs*) was deposited into the account of the Sri Sathya Sai Central Trust!

Then, Swami called that member of the Trust and said to him, "When Swami says it will happen, it will. It cannot be reversed."

That's what truth is. Truth is unshakable and has no fear. Truth has no hesitation or ambiguity, and cannot be doubted. That's what Sathya Sai Baba is and after all, His name is Sathya.

Baba Himself declared, *"Aham Sathya Bodhakaha"*. ("I am the propagator of the principle of Truth.")

The Dharma For Each Phase Of Life

Dharma is a word that has several meanings. Some people rightly believe that *dharma* means donating to charity or feeding people. But, *dharma* also has another meaning. This is observing the phase of life that we are currently in.

A celibate, college student, or an unmarried man needs a certain type of discipline in his lifestyle and this is called *brahmacharya* or celibacy.

Next, as a married man, you have certain responsibilities and have to follow certain principles. This stage is called *grihasta,* householder. As a parent, you have to raise your children, look after them, guide and help them.

Slowly, you reach the age of retirement. That is called *vanaprasta,* recluse.

Then, the final stage arrives, when you are not bothered about worldly matters. Your son comes up to you and says, "Daddy, what should I do about the business?"

"Do what you want to do," is the reply.

"Daddy, shall I stay here in Brunei, or go to the United States?"

"Stay or go, wherever you will be happy."

This is the *sanyasa* stage of renunciation and detachment.

All these phases are *dharma*, doing one's duty according to the age and stage in life.

A bachelor or celibate cannot have a married life. And a *grihasta* cannot be a celibate, unless there is a medical reason. Furthermore, none can remain at the same stage for the rest of their life.

In certain families, the father is still dictating to his grown-up son of forty years, who has children of his own: "Do this, don't do that." What is this? It is so ridiculous.

So, we earn well and look after our children, preparing them for life. And after that, all we can do is to give advice.

When becoming a *sanyasi*, you live for yourself, disengaging from material and emotional ties and seeking a spiritual understanding of your life: "What am I, who am I, and why was I born? I have to leave my family one day or another. Where am I going and from where have I come? What happens in between one life and another?"

These are the concerns of a *sanyasi*, a renunciate. But, a householder has different concerns. His are family duties. If a son-in-law does not behave properly, the father-in-law must take charge, because he was responsible for marrying his daughter to such a useless creature.

This is how *dharma* works at the various stages in life.

Dharma Is One's Own Duty

Bhagawan teaches us where our responsibilities lie. Some ladies came to the *ashram* saying, "Swami, we want to stay here."

Swami's reply is, "Go home and serve your husband and take care of your children."

And there are some people, who say, "Swami, I want to do service."

Swami says, "You have enough service to do at home. Look after your children and husband."

Taking a broomstick and cleaning the streets is public service. Those, who do public service, do disservice privately. They have four sweepers working in their home, while they sweep the street! This is not correct.

Dharma is one's own duty. For example, I am a professor, so I am supposed to teach. To sing and dance in the classroom is not my *dharma*. Doing the appropriate duty is *dharma* and this is called *vyakthi dharma,* or individual duty. (*Samishti dharma* is the duty of a community.)

Finally, here is an example of *dharma* from our Swami: Many people came to thank Baba, "Baba, thank You! You have spent seven hundred *crores* to provide us with drinking water."

Do you know what Baba said? "It is My duty, sir, you don't have to thank Me. Do you thank your father and say that he is great for having given you some new pants?"

Peace Is An Experience

A *Bal Vikas* teacher, a knowledgeable and senior lady, once gave a speech on the five human values. At the time she was speaking, I was the state president. She kept on saying forcefully, "Do you know what *Santhi*, peace, is? What is peace? Peace means..."

At the end of the talk, I said, "Madam, you yourself have no peace, yet you are speaking about peace! The subject is good, but there was not even a piece of peace in what you said!"

Peace cannot be expressed; peace is an inner experience. You cannot say, "I am very peaceful." Politicians are good at appearing peaceful, but they have high blood pressure. So, this is synthetic peace, not natural peace. So, peace is an experience.

Bhagawan gives an example. Bhagawan Buddha was once passing through a village and some young people gathered around and started to mock him.

They said, "A prince, with a shaven head, wearing ochre robes, walking barefoot along the street with a begging bowl, and a married prince too!"

To the young fellows, Buddha looked like a fool. They were calling him names and making fun of him, but Buddha was simply smiling.

After some time, Buddha said, "Have you had enough now? Have you run out of gas? Right, be happy. I am going on to the next village, where the local villagers are happy to receive me. But, if they hear of your mockery, they will beat you up and I will feel hurt."

"Now, I am happy, because you are happy. Criticising me makes you happy and the other villagers are happy to praise me. I am equally happy and positive towards both — whether it is praise or blame."

That is peace! Peace is that, which cannot be disturbed. We lose our peace, when the first cup of coffee is delayed. Or we lose our peace, when the annual increment payment is delayed for a couple of days, or when we don't get a promotion or VIP treatment. That is not peace; that is ego.

"Oh, I am peaceful." Well, why not... when you are receiving VIP treatment and in a top position? No, no! This is ego satisfaction. When people praise or blame you, and you don't lose your calm and composure, that is true peace!

Bhagawan Sri Sathya Sai Baba is the embodiment of peace.

Ethics And Moral Values
In Daily Life
Part II

(Special Talk by Prof. Anil Kumar,
in Brunei, Southeast Asia, November 3rd, 2011)

The Peace Of Swami

Someone said, "Swami, people are writing nasty things about You in the newspapers. People are speaking ill of You. Swami, we feel so badly. We know You, but those fellows, who are doing that, don't know You. Shall I reply to them? Shall I write an article, countering these attacks?"

This was Baba's answer, "Look here, all those, who praise Me, are the size of a mountain. All those, who criticise Me, are also the size of a mountain. I am in between, blessing both of them. Why? Your happiness is My happiness."

That is called peace. Whether you praise Him or condemn Him, He will never lose His calm and composure. That is peace. He wants us to be peaceful like that too.

On several occasions at Prasanthi Nilayam, during Birthday celebrations, Dasara celebrations, and Sivaratri celebrations, hundreds of thousands of people gathered here. Five hundred thousand people, or even more, were present when it was fully occupied. Our Lord walked in with a smile and talked to people nicely, whereas when you and I invite four people for lunch, we have a curfew in our family from the early hours of the morning! We make everyone stand on their heels! Why? Four guests are coming!

But, here is Baba with four *lakhs* (four hundred thousand) people and He is peaceful; everything is all right. That is true peace. In spite of provocation, in spite of agitation, in spite of disturbance, turbulence, opposition, criticism, mud-slinging, and character assassination, if one remains unruffled and undisturbed, that is called *prasanthi* or supreme peace.

Prema - Love

Darussalam, which is the full name of Brunei, also means 'the Abode of Supreme Peace', just like Prasanthi Nilayam. Prasanthi Nilayam is Darussalam. So here, with this name, you won't be allowed to forget Prasanthi, supreme peace, or *sathya, dharma*, and *santhi*. Next, we think of *prema*, the ethics of love! *Prema*, what is this *prema*?

Love is not seasonal! At the time of examinations, science students love their teachers, because practical examinations are approaching and the teachers have to award marks. And Ph.D boys love their guides, as their dissertation is getting ready. That is only 'seasonal love'.

Some people love their boss, but that is conditional love. Why? If the boss asks you to leave, then you will not love him! So, it is conditional love. But, Baba's love is not conditional love or seasonal love. It is unconditional love. Unconditional!

Love demands that whether He talks to you or not, whether you get an interview or not, receive gifts or not,

have your desires fulfilled or not, you still continue to love
Him. That is *prema,* or love. That love is unconditional.

Love Is Unconditional

Love is unconditional. I often tell everyone that it may
look like Swami has extra love towards a particular devotee.
It may appear like that. While I was the State President of
Andhra Pradesh, Swami was talking to me every day. Every
day! All the devotees present there considered me a world-
class devotee, with a Ph.D in devotion!

But, what was He talking to me about? First day: "You
are a useless fellow." Second day: "You are an irresponsible
fellow." Third day: "You are unfit to be the State President."
Fourth day: "You will be awarding a prize to a district from
another state, where you have never been." The following
day: "How do you give a prize to that district, when you do
not know what is happening in other districts?" The next
day: "Why don't you raise your voice at the World Council,
protesting that prizes should not be given in the Sathya Sai
Organisation?"

Swami Loves Everyone

Everybody thinks, "Swami is talking to you, sir, how
great!"

How can I tell them? "Yes, yes, yes," I said, while I
was crying inside. I know the music going on inside!

Therefore, Swami appears to be close to some people,
but He is close to everybody. Never think that you alone
are close. You are close to Him in order to get a responsibility
from Him, to be assigned a duty; it's not that you are close.

A simple example: We have a servant maid. I go on talking to her every day. "Get me a cup of coffee, get hot water ready, wash the clothes." I don't have time to talk to my son, but that doesn't mean I love the servant maid more than my son!

Swami talks to some people for assigning responsibilities, or to delegate some power. For that reason, He may talk to them, but He loves everybody.

Swami Tells Important Things To Important People

It was the time of the inauguration of Sathya Sai University, thirty years ago. Swami was moving in that silver chariot along with the Chief Justice of the Supreme Court, Justice Chandra Chood.

You know what Swami was talking about to the Chief Justice of the Supreme Court? "Look here, Chandra Chood, these are not my true devotees. My true devotees are those, who are in the sheds, those, who are staying under the trees. My true devotees are those, who are exposed to sunlight and rain, not those people, who stay here." So, we see Swami talking to Chandra Chood, but He is speaking about you and me.

Swami calls the President of India. What does He say to him? He does not speak about politics. No! He does not say this man will get another term. He is not interested in that. He will tell them that they should work for the people. He will tell them that the welfare of the community is important, that nationality is important, that education is very important, and that water and food are very important.

He will tell such things to important persons. But, we may think that this person got some personal interview. Yes, he did. But, what is it about? He is simply reminded of his duty. Baba speaks to those people for our benefit. He talks to those people in order to help all of us. That is the reality. Whatever He may talk about to them, it is for our benefit.

Swami's Loving Words

He may talk to Sinclair from Connecticut, United States of America; He may talk to Tigrett, or He may talk to Dr. Narendra Reddy from Los Angeles, United States of America. What does He talk to them about? He will say things like, "Take care of the patients; build a nice hospital; the equipment should be modern; we should not charge anyone; be kind to the patients; when you give an injection, be kind to them, talk to them, engage them. Don't arrive with a stern face to do the injection!"

These are Swami's words. You can watch videos. Swami stays on the dais to talk to doctors about these things. I translated His talks, so I am the witness. He advises that when a doctor gives an injection, he should smile and talk, enquiring about the family. The doctor should smile, giving a hope to the patient. That is what He talks about to such people.

Therefore, that is love: to explain the duties and responsibilities of the doctor to their patients and to speak about their obligations to their profession for the benefit of others. That is His love. His love is not calling you inside just to give you a silver cup or a bag of currency! What would you do with that? So, that is Swami's love.

The Definition Of Himsa (Violence)

Himsa means violence. What is *himsa* — killing an animal? Yes, it is *himsa* or violent. But, Baba's interpretation of *himsa* (violence) is different. Some people's looks are very violent. 'Why is that fellow looking at me like that? What is wrong with me? What is wrong with him?' So, looks can be violent. Some people can hurt you by their stares, looking at you as if you are a criminal or a terrorist. Thus, you can hurt people with your eyes.

You can hurt people by your words. Some people speak certain words to us, which are so hurtful that we will not forget them for a lifetime. Our thoughts are also so hurtful.

Therefore, violence means hurting people through your thought, word, deed, or simply by your looks. Swami gives the following example: Suppose you can eat three or four *vadas*, *bisibela* (type of *sambar* rice), or *maddur vada*.

The point is that in this process, I can eat four *vadas*, for example. But, if I eat six *vadas*, I am sick to my stomach. I can look at an ordinary light, but if I look at a thousand candle bulb, it violently hurts my eye. I can listen to sounds of some intensity, but if I start listening to a very high-pitched sound, it is violent to my ears. So, you can be violent with all five senses.

Swami's Style Of Ahimsa

Baba says, "*Emappa, baguntiva!* Oh boy, how are you? *Emma Bangaru, Eppudu vachchevu*? When did you come?"

"Amma, where is *manmadha*? Where is your husband?"
When He looks at the wife and asks, "Where is *manmadha*?"
He is talking about her husband. *Manmadha* means 'a most
handsome fellow'. When Swami says, "Where is *manmadha*?"
the wife is very happy. In fact, he is not *manmadha* at all!

Baba knows how to make people happy. Then, He
comes to the husband and asks, "How is your wife?" The
husband thinks, 'Aaah! When am I going to ask Him about
my life? Why, when I am here, is Swami asking about my
wife?' Why? Swami is concerned about His family. Swami
cares about His family, His children. He loves us all. These
words of enquiry prove that He takes care of all of us. That
is the boost.

Suppose something is wrong with the husband, or
something is wrong with the wife. He will call both of them
for an interview and then, tell the husband that the wife is a
very good lady. He will say that the husband would not
come to this position but for her, and that she is managing
and taking care of the whole family.

The lady will be ecstatic! He will give them *vibhuti*.
Then, both of them try to leave the interview room. But, if
Baba leaves them at that stage, the husband won't
understand. He was praising the wife, so what to do? The
husband cannot say, "Swami, please stop, I have a problem.
Please praise me also for some time." He cannot say that.

So, when they are about to leave the interview room,
Swami will look at the wife and say, "See, your husband is
a very noble man, a very kind-hearted man. Because of
troubles in the office, he is sometimes angry. He is very busy
with the files and he is going on tours, but he thinks of you

with all his heart." Finished! That is how peace is established: that fellow got corrected naturally, with Swami's style of *ahimsa* or non-violence.

Swami Corrects A Student

Suddenly, Swami will call a student along with his parents and tell his parents that their boy is the best student in our university, and is very, very well behaved. He will go on about how he is a singer, an actor, and does a lot of work in the hostel. "We are very lucky to have him, a very nice boy!"

After the parents leave, Swami will close the doors. "Boy, come here! You are misbehaving, I know! I know what you are doing in the hostel. You are not attending prayers. You failed in two subjects. You are a rowdy, an idiot, a donkey, stupid, and a pig." He will talk like that.

Finally, Swami will tell the boy, "I praised you in front of your parents, so that you will know how to be and how not to be. The words spoken to your parents are how you should behave. Listen properly. I did not tell your parents that I love you more than them. Behave yourself." Then, He gives the boy a chain.

The fellow, who was talkative, is changed in that moment, like an iron that melts in the steel plant is now polished, refined, and more cultured after coming through Swami's furnace. The moment he comes out with a slightly serious face, you think, 'Aaah! What happened to this fellow?'

Swami also tells the student, "Don't tell anyone that I scolded you!" This fellow nods his head, saying, "Yes."

"Hey! Swami gave you interview?" The student simply nods his head, indicating yes.

"What did Swami say?" Again, he nods his head.

"He praised you?" Again, the nodding of his head! The student will not open his mouth, because of this steel plant processing.

This is non-violence — not insulting grown-up children in front of everyone. Getting things done without condemnation, that is Sai's technique.

Swami Will Not Hurt Anyone

Once, a student came and said, "Anil Kumar, sir, Swami is calling you for an interview. Go!"

"Oh, I didn't hear my name!" I said.

"No, sir, we heard your name. You go." The boys love me and I love the boys. Be they of any class, I love to spend time with them and tease them. Unless I tease them and joke, my digestion will be affected for the day. That is why I call them and joke like that.

The boys said, "Sir, Swami is calling you!" They love me. They must have heard my name, so I went there.

Swami said, "Come here!" I sat there, but He didn't call me. The boys misunderstood my name, misheard it. Now, see the Divine Master's style!

"Hmmm, good. All are here. Oh! Principal, you are also here, good! Anil Kumar, find out where Radhakrishnan is." Radhakrishnan lived with Swami for twenty years, a very good boy who was like Swami's shadow. "Anil Kumar, call Radhakrishnan," said Swami.

I came out of the interview room and went looking for Radhakrishnan. I went to the car shed, where there was a driver by the name of Unni. He said, "Sir, Radhakrishnan? Please come." He made me sit on a chair and offered me a glass of water, and then he said, "Sir, Radhakrishnan is only there with Swami. He is with Swami only. In order to send you out, He told you to find Radhakrishnan, where he is not."

Swami has not offended me and He got His work done. That is Divine technology. We've heard of B.Tech and M.Tech, but Sathya Sai Baba is D.Tech, meaning Divine Technology. *Ahimsa*! He will not hurt anyone, by any gesture or action.

Another example: I started speaking three to four times a year in the Divine presence of Baba, starting from 1978. When you go to Him, He gives *padanamaskar* and then, you give a speech. Please watch the DVD's and you will see. He will keep His hands under the table. Why? When you are getting up after doing *namaskar*, your head may hit the table. So, to protect you, He puts His hands there. This is Sri Sathya Sai Baba. That is why we love Him. So, these are His ethics.

Swami Has Supreme Tolerance

Now, about morals, just a few points: He has supreme tolerance. Tolerance is a moral value. How can you say Baba is tolerant? He is tolerating all of us. In fact, most of us are useless being here. Most of us are unfit to be here. We never follow what He tells us and yet, He never tells us to get out, no!

Is there any bulletin board, saying that certain people are allowed and the following people are not allowed? It's not like that. We are all allowed a multiple-entry visa to Prasanthi Nilayam. Anyone can come, anyone. This is tolerance.

One fellow fell on Swami's feet and said, "Sorry, Swami, I made so many mistakes. Swami, please excuse me."

"Forget about it! Forget the past. The past is past. Be happy! Why do you say that? You are my child, don't cry." That is tolerance. Tolerance is forgiveness. Any number of examples can be given.

Attempts To Harm Swami

In His childhood, Swami was served *vadai*. A householder, who invited Swami to dine, mixed poison into the *vada*. People started scolding her, "Why did you invite Swami? Why have you mixed poison in the *vada*?"

Swami said, "Don't scold her, don't scold her."

After some time, that lady invited Swami again.

Then, Baba said, "A normal *vada* is enough. I don't need any special *vada*." That is tolerance from Baba.

Once, when Baba was sleeping in a hut, people wanted to set that hut on fire. Some enemies brought a match box. Swami, Who was speaking to everyone, suddenly got up and went outside. All were worried and wondered what had happened. He went outside and saw those fellows trying to light the match. Swami said, "Ah, the match box is wet! Next time, bring a dry box." That is tolerance. That is Sathya Sai Baba.

He is always practising these moral values of tolerance, forbearance, purity, and cleanliness. Swami, how clean He is! His nails are cut very close, so you can see the flesh also, totally clipped. Sometimes, He looked at my nails. If He calls me, He'll ask, "Are you a ghost or a human being?" So, He's very neat!

How about His clothing? *Pakka*, neat, everything folded neatly. He does not like exposing flesh by wearing shorts, no, no, no! He wants you to be modest and He wants you to be fashionable, that's very important. That's also a moral value.

Patient Listening Is A Moral Value

A doctor is talking to Swami and Swami asks him, "How do people get a heart attack? Oh, I see. Cholesterol? Oh, I see. Blood pressure? Ah, I see!" as if He has never heard of it! This is patient listening.

Finally, He says, "Look here, doctor, very nice. You are a very good doctor; but, I think only three things are responsible for heart attacks: hurry - worry - curry. That's all." This is after the doctor has just given a one hour lecture on heart disease! So, patient listening is also a moral value.

Then, He will be talking to the Ph.D boys: "What happened to your research?"

One of their subjects is leadership. The Ph.D management boys had written that paper and one fellow wrote his thesis on leadership: "Who are the leaders and how they function."

"Aah... aah... good, but you missed one thing!"

"What, Swami?"

"Baba is the leader, but you have not mentioned that! Swami is the leader and these others are followers. You have no brain!"

Swami attained only a seventh grade education, yet He speaks on all these subjects, patiently listening to others, giving value to what others say and giving respect to elders.

Respecting Elders Is A Moral Value

Now, consider elderly people, who were once the organisation's state presidents, but are not officers now. Swami respects elderly people. When Swami visits their houses, do you know what He does? He immediately goes to the elders. "How are you, Amma? *Bavunnava!* Oh, joint pains, okay, I will take care of them." "How are you, sir? Blood pressure? Be happy, no BP."

Then, He will go to the *pooja* room. "Aah, it is nice!" He materialises some Siva *lingam* for them. He knows their house in more detail than they know it. He immediately goes to the dining room. "The dining room is not proper. You Brahmins are like that. What to do? Brahmins don't maintain their kitchen properly. Notice Swami's kitchen is dry, with no water dripping, whereas yours is a swimming pool." And finally, He says, "Amma, *Gruhalakshmi neevu.* You are the wealth of this family, very nice. Good!"

So, He compliments others, recognises their talents, and encourages them with their talents. It is really marvellous to see and hear this.

Questions And Answers

Q: What must a person do in order to take away jealousy and anger from another person?

A: What you can do is first, be free from anger and jealousy yourself. Then, naturally the other person will also become free from anger and jealousy. One has to work at it; we cannot do it for others. One has to know that anger is dangerous.

I read somewhere that when you are angry and shout, your energy gets so used up that you have exhausted the equivalent supply of electricity for twenty-four hours. Know that anger is dangerous. Therefore, when you are angry, just drink a glass of water, or stand in front of the mirror, or take a walk on the veranda in the cool breeze. You will cool down.

Jealousy: the secret to overcoming jealousy is the following. Let's say you think, 'That man is very tall, but I am short, so I am jealous of him." Immediately, then add, "But, I am fairer than him." Or another example, 'That man is very rich, but I am healthier than him." Or, "He can sing, but I can dance."

We are all Baba's children. He gives one gift or another to everyone. If you discover your own talent, if you discover your own Self, there is no one to compete with you there, so there is no one, of which to feel jealous. Yes, why not?

He plays *tabla* and I play *harmonium*. But, if I also want to play *tabla*, there starts the problem. Why? It is not necessary! I've got my own thing. Please discover yourself. This is what is called the art of self-discovery. The art of self-discovery is the way to win over jealousy.

Q: How do we find a way to obtain Baba's guidance all our lives?

A: The only way is *bhajans*. Sing *bhajans*, read His literature, participate in His service activities, and do what He likes.

Suppose you want to please your father, what do you do? First, give him a cup of hot coffee without him asking. Now, he is twenty-five percent favourable towards you. Then, keep his shaving set ready. *Aha*, fifty percent favourable! Serve him breakfast, and get his shoes and socks ready. You're finished! You can ask him for anything and he will give it to you!

How do you please your mother? Help her with the cooking, help her by carrying all the bowls and plates, and tell her that her cooking is very nice. Don't eat like a buffalo and then, leave. "This curry is nice and the *chutney* is nice, too." Say it!

I really don't like fellows, who simply eat and leave. There is no difference between zoo animals and such fellows. Can't you say that the food is very nice? "*Amma,* the food is very nice." *Amma's* food is mother's food, why not? Done! When you do what your parents like, they will guide you.

Similarly, when you do what Baba likes, He will protect His children. What does He like? Service! What does He like? Singing His glory with *bhajans*, that's all. It's very easy to please Baba, very easy.

Q: What was your best experience with Swami?

A: There is no question of a good experience, a better experience, and the best experience. They are not relative. Every experience is the best unto itself, nothing is separate. Everything is the best experience.

This visit to Brunei is the best experience. I am letting you know that I was supposed to leave on a particular morning and on the immediately previous evening, at 7pm, I got my passport and visa. Impossible! I told that gentleman that had I been there, in that position, I would have said, "*Anatha Natha, Deena Natha, Sai Natha, Hari Om!*" So, don't worry! Everything is the best experience.

Q: I notice some people having a dream and then, trying to push their idea in the Samithi. Can you tell us a little about these dreams?

A: Dreams are individual. Suppose I dream that I am the President of the United States of America. If I then tell everybody that I am the President of America, they will say that not only am I *not* the President of America, but I am the President of the Madcap Association!

Or if Swami blesses you in an interview, then you repeatedly say that Swami blessed you in an interview. He blessed you, but why do you keep telling me?

So, dreams are meant to be personal, not for general sharing. They are not for publicity, advertisement, or propaganda, and definitely not to be imposed on others.

There is one lecturer in our college, of whom people are afraid. He starts with his dreams, even in the class; so, when he walks this way, people will go that way. Unfortunately, I had to face him once. I already had two years of listening to his dreams. That time, he was about to tell me again. I quickly spoke first, "*Array,* Babu, Swami appeared in my dream last night and told me not to believe your dreams, not to trust you. Even better, He said in my dream that I should avoid you." After that, this fellow stopped speaking about his dreams.

So, don't believe these dreamers and don't believe their dreams. They may be true at the individual level, but not at the general level.

Visit To Brunei

(Special Talk by Mrs. Vijaya Lakshmi Kamaraju,
November 3rd, 2011)

"Don't Scold Anybody If You Are Angry, Scold Yourself!"

If you respect Swami as your mother, He will come to you as your mother and protect you. If you think of Swami as your grandson, He comes to you in that form. He satisfies our desires and He responds to our prayers. I have a few experiences I would like to share with you.

While I was attending daily *bhajans* in the Mandir, it was almost like attending school, where you learn so many things. There are double *bhajans* (morning *bhajans* and evening *bhajans*). At that time, there was also morning *darshan* and evening *darshan*. We learned so many things there, if we would only sit and silently observe Swami's gestures and the people, who waited there for Swami. There are so many experiences we can observe there, from which we can learn.

So, one day, I was sitting in the *darshan* line, but Swami didn't come. Everyone was waiting for Swami. Finally, Swami came towards the line. When Swami comes for *darshan*, we must concentrate on Swami. Only then can we get some vibrations and messages from Swami. So, that day, when I was sitting in the Mandir, I heard Swami say, "*Neeku buddhi ledhu.*" It means, "You don't have any common sense." That's what He said. I couldn't understand why Swami said that.

Whenever Swami says anything, I go to Ganesha and inquire as to what mistake I have committed that morning or throughout the day. So, I wondered within myself what it was that I had done that morning. I had come straightaway for *darshan* in the morning. It seemed like there was no time to commit any mistake!

So, I started inquiring into myself and then, I found out that there was a message coming on the TV, where Swami was giving His discourse, saying, "If you are angry, scold yourself, not others." That is what I heard Swami say in His discourse. But, I had not paid any attention to that. I straightaway came for *darshan*. However, earlier that day, I was so restless, because the servant maid had not come. I was so agitated that I ended up scolding her, as she was not coming to work for many days in a month. So, that was the message for me. That's why, when I came for *darshan*, Swami gave me this message: "Don't scold anybody. If you are angry, scold yourself!" So, that was the message I got that day.

Swami Always Conveys Messages Through Different Forms

Whenever Swami wants to convey something to us, He does it through messages — sometimes through books, sometimes through people, who come to us at our house, and sometimes even through cats and rats.

One cat used to come to our house daily. My husband is allergic to cats. So, whenever he was not home, the cat would come to my house. I used to feed that cat. I got so many messages through that cat! My husband used to criticise me and make fun of me, because so many cats would come, but I would entertain them.

One of my friends told me not to feed the cat and not to allow it to come to the house. But, I did not find any issue in that. The cat used to come and I fed it milk. At that time, I was reading a book. In that book, I read, a Chinese lady used to keep some milk near the altar. After some time, she realised that the level of the milk was going down. She was shocked, but then, she understood that Swami used to take that milk, which was kept next to the altar. I couldn't believe it at that time.

After sometime, I read in Kasturiji's book that even his wife would keep a tumbler of milk for Swami near the altar. One day, Swami told Kasturiji, "Today, the milk was very hot, so I couldn't drink it."

Kasturiji did not understand anything, because He did not know his wife was keeping milk near the altar. So, he came home and asked his wife and she said, "Daily, I am keeping a little milk for Swami." Only then he could understand that whatever is kept next to the altar also goes to Swami. That means that the level of the milk was going down there, also.

So, from that time onwards, having observed the experiences of Kasturiji's wife and this Chinese lady, I started keeping some milk near the altar. So, that's how it went on for sometime. In the beginning, I couldn't understand that Swami was coming and taking the milk in the form of a cat. For some days, it went on like that.

There was a lady, who was the principal of some college, I think. She used to stay in Prasanthi Nilayam. She asked me to write one article. So, I said that if Swami tells me to write something, then I can write; otherwise, I cannot write anything on my own. She gave me one week's time. Six days passed. And on the last day, while I was cooking and cutting the vegetables, this cat came. I gave it some milk and it drank. Suddenly, I got a flash of continuous thoughts to write the article then and there. Thus, Swami used to inspire me through so many objects like that.

Swami Inspired Me To Write Poems

On another day, I had a jasmine flower. I usually decorate all the photographs with jasmine flowers. On that day also, I decorated the photos with a garland. So, my friend, who likes to decorate all idols, made a thick garland that day. *Bhajan* was going on and she invited me; so, I went and attended the *bhajan*. The garland began dancing, though there was no fan blowing near it. I could not understand why the garland was dancing like that; that too, according to the rhythm of the *bhajan*. I was shocked! After *aarti*, when I came home, I could suddenly write a poem about this garland. That chrysanthemum garland was there and so, I could write the poem. Just like that, Swami used to inspire me to write poems.

One day, it was Ladies' Day festival on the 19th in Prasanthi Nilayam. All the women celebrate Ladies' Day on the 19th. On that day, so many ladies were there. Swami was distributing *sarees*, while so many VIP's from Madras, playback singers (recording artists), and many other people were present.

Everybody was sitting there and I was sitting in my usual place. Swami was on the veranda, calling people one-by-one according to a list. Mrs. Shouri (in charge of the ladies' side) was holding the list. She was announcing the names and giving the *sarees* to Swami. One by one, these people were going. Looking at the scene, I thought I could write a beautiful poem about the *sarees* and these receiving ladies. With this poem also, I was inspired by Swami.

Karunantha Rangude Kadhali Vacchi
Komalanganala Rammani Piluva
Sahaja Soundarya Sarasijaakshulu
Paruvuna Swami Dhari Chera
Idigo Suseela Soundaryalanchu
Varada Hastaala Vastraalanicche
Mugdala Momuna Moda Muppongaga

That is the poem. Here is the meaning of the poem:

See this compassionate and loving Lord,
When He is calling these ladies.
These beautiful tender ladies are running towards Swami,
So that they won't miss namaskar and the sarees.

According to their complexion, Swami was distributing the *sarees*. He was selecting and then, giving the *saree*. You see, usually when Swami gives a *saree*, it will suit every lady, all people. No matter what their complexion is, it will suit them perfectly. It won't make a difference, because whoever wears a *saree* given by Swami will look wonderful and beautiful.

So, that day, this beautiful scene was going on with all these people. Their husbands were also watching this scene. Swami was distributing the *sarees* and I was sitting in the line. I thought I would get a *saree,* so I was waiting for my name to be called. But, they didn't call my name. Swami came close and looked at me as though He wondered whether I was jealous of these people, who got the *sarees*. He was teasing me, but I could balance myself. I never showed any expression. So, silently I went away.

After sometime, in the evening I think, my husband was there. Swami asked him, "Did your wife get a *saree*?"

"No, no! Her name is not on the list. So, she didn't get a *saree*," my husband explained to Swami.

Then, Swami said, "But, I already sent the *saree*. Didn't you get it?"

That day, while I was sitting in the line, this is what happened. Swami came over there and gave a *saree* to the lady next to me. He looked at me, purposefully avoided me, and then, He went away. I thought to myself, 'Why is Swami doing this?' I couldn't understand the meaning.

A Witness To Our Innermost Thoughts And Future Plans

You see, there are so many times, when we cannot understand the meaning of Swami's words and Swami's gestures. He says something, but we cannot understand it right away. We have to think and re-think about it. That is my personal experience.

One day, He said something while I was in the line. He came to the line and said, "*Nee mogudu to ooregu.*" It means, "You go along with your husband." Why was Swami saying that? I could not understand the meaning at that time.

Only after ten years, I could understand the meaning of Swami's words: after ten years, I started accompanying my husband wherever he went, determining what kind of service I could do. I also started participating in that program. Of course, Swami could see what would happen ten years ahead. But, at that moment, we could not understand Swami's words.

So, that day, he purposefully avoided me and didn't give me the *saree*. After that, he sent it through my husband. Usually, Swami used to send the *saree* through my husband only. Only once or twice, I got a *saree* in the line.

He observes us and how our feelings will be. If someone gets a *saree,* another person will be jealous of her. How we feel — every movement with every gesture — and even our inner feelings are observed by Swami. That is my personal experience.

Some Swami Lessons

At one time, I wrote a book in Telugu and kept it near the altar. Usually, whenever we celebrate Ganesh Chaturthi, all the books of our children and even office papers are kept on the altar. Just like that, I kept the book there. So, for the whole day, the book was there next to Swami's altar. The next day, I went for *darshan*. I took the book also to get it blessed by Swami.

Then, Swami came to me and said, "You gave the book already! Why did you bring it again?"

I couldn't understand His meaning. 'Why is Swami saying this? This is the first time I am bringing the book to the Mandir!' Only after some thought, I could understand that even if we keep anything near the altar, it will be blessed by Swami.

At another time, for a few days, I had the opportunity to cook for Swami. That day, I thought of cooking some particular item; but, when I went there, the total programme was changed. I thought of making *upma*, but I made *kheer* instead. I didn't know how Swami's idea came into me. So, I sent the item. After some time, I learned that it was somebody's birthday on that particular day. So, He changed my idea of *upma* into *kheer* for that purpose.

One day, I was sitting in the line, holding a letter. Then, Swami came along the line, so I gave Him the letter. As He took it, I was about to take *padnamaskar*.

Swami said, "Why are you taking *padnamaskar* now? Why do you want *namaskar* every day?"

I couldn't understand His meaning. But, I thought that there must be some inner meaning there. Then, I remembered that daily, before coming for *darshan*, I touch the feet of Swami's on a photograph before I come for *darshan*. So, Swami must have been referring to that.

Swami Always Guides And Teaches Us

He used to teach me everything and guide me all the time. We cannot learn these things outside; nobody will tell us. So, that's how Swami guides us and teaches us how to conduct ourselves in the family, how to treat guests, and how to treat anyone, who comes to our house.

One day, a lady came to my house. (All these are personal experiences, but they all have inner meaning.) She was very worried about her son, because they spent *lakhs* of *rupees* sending him to the U.S. He was in the computer field. Halfway through, he came back. He discontinued his studies and came back to India. She was very worried, because so much money was already spent. So, she came to my husband and asked for advice as to how to get him to go back to the U.S.

Continuously for three days, she came to my house. I was so restless to see this lady coming to my house and crying daily. I don't like anyone coming to my house and feeling like that. That was what was going on. I never talked to her. That was the mistake I made.

That day, when I went for *darshan*, Swami didn't look at me. He turned to the other side and went away. Swami usually smiled at me daily, but on that day, He didn't look at me! So, I started inquiring within myself and I realised the mistake I made: I didn't respect that lady and I didn't even offer her a tumbler of water or coffee. So, Swami must have been disturbed, I thought.

The next day, when she came, I gave her coffee and talked to her. I could understand her problem and she was so happy. That day also, Swami smiled at me nicely. There was an immediate response from Swami. Whenever we do good, we get a good response. If our actions are hurting anybody, that's all! Immediately, He will give you that same dose also.

Swami Clears Doubts Immediately

On Thursdays, I will make *dahi wada* sweets. So, I used to send that through my husband. He used to dine with Swami every day, for 3 or 4 years, in the Mandir. I had a doubt in the beginning: 'Is Swami eating all this or not? Or am I just simply preparing the food?' That was the doubt.

Swami clarified my doubt. Just see how! One day, I saw Ganesha, Who appeared in my vision, and His mouth was completely smeared with curd. Then, I could understand that Swami was enjoying whatever I cooked.

Another day, Swami appeared in my dream in the flames. I couldn't understand the meaning. I asked one of my friends, who was there. Then, she told me, "You are doing *yajna*. *Yajna* Purusha appeared in that vision. The meaning of *Yajna* Purusha is that whatever you are offering, He is accepting. So, Swami is taking what you offer, don't worry." That's how the other doubt was clarified. Just like that, Swami used to give me so many messages.

Ladies Must Be Patient
And Have A Forgiving Nature

One time, my sister, who lives in the U.S., was fixing up her third daughter's marriage. Suddenly, it got arranged and she wrote a letter, asking me to buy all the *sarees* and arrange everything.

That time, it took me one month to buy all the *sarees* and matching blouses. I got pure silk *sarees* and cotton *sarees* — a good variety for the wedding. But, in my heart of hearts,

I was worried that I was wasting my time. Usually, in my leisure time, I used to read or write. But, during that month, I was only doing that shopping. In between this, Swami gave me a poem:

Kottha Koka Etanchu Kulikedu Nokakodalamma
Kalikithuraayi Sahanamu Nee Sommu
Katina Sila Karinginchu Karuna Needhani Nammu
O Kanaka Mahalakshmi Idhi Nee Atta Swanubhavamu.

The meaning of the poem is this:

One daughter-in-law came to her mother-in-law's house.
She wore a new saree and was dancing in ecstasy
Because she was so happy wearing the new saree.

See, these sarees and ornaments don't add anything to the personality of ladies.
Patience and a forgiving nature will add to your beauty.
This is your mother-in-law's experience.

That is what Swami told me. Here, 'mother-in-law' refers to experienced ladies, who will be giving advice (whether we follow it or not). That indicates that ladies must have patience and a forgiving nature, compassion and kindness.

Unity, Purity, Divinity

In one of my dreams, long back, around ten years ago, Swami appeared in my vision and told me that ladies must have all these qualities: knowledge, beauty, compassion, and intelligence. He was going on telling me like that with affection.

Then, I asked Swami why He was telling me all this. "Why are You telling me all this? I am not giving speeches! Go and tell my husband. He is the one, who is going to speak." That's what I said. I could not understand at that time.

However, after ten years, I started speaking in Telugu for the first time. I only started speaking in English in the U.S., when my daughter was delivering. I used to stay there for five to six months at that time. As there are so many centres in the U.S., they used to ask me to speak about Swami.

That time, I didn't know anything about Swami. But, if they would ask me, I would have to speak of something. In the beginning, when I went there, I was avoiding speaking, postponing it. But, one day, the centre people asked me to speak in one centre. Then, I said that I wasn't in any position to speak, not being part of the organisation. I said that I was not a Mahila wing coordinator, not part of a study circle or a *balvikas* teacher. I could not speak from any of these positions. But, they said it wasn't a problem, I could speak anyway.

I thought that I must get some clue from Swami — only then I could speak. Then, that day, when I came home, I was reading a book. In the first book itself, I got my message. It was a Joy Thomas book. She was doing a lot and giving a lot of lectures on Swami.

After sometime, she came to Swami and Swami gave her an interview. When she entered the interview room, Swami stared at her and looked into her eyes. She was afraid and was wondering why Swami was doing that. 'Perhaps,

Swami didn't like me giving speeches like this,' she wondered.

The next moment, Swami changed His expression and said, "Oh, you are giving nicely! Go on giving lectures everywhere. You are doing it nicely." That's what Swami said. Then, she thought that was her answer from Swami. After that, she became a writer as well as a speaker. So, I took this message in a positive way and gave the speech at the centre that day.

Next, I thought, 'Swami has let me know it is good to speak, but on which subject should I speak? That also You must tell me.' I didn't know anything about speech topics. Then, Swami gave me a clue: "Unity, Purity, and Divinity." These three words He told me within. Then, I wondered how I would compose the speech on Unity, Purity, and Divinity. Without some inspiring ideas, my thoughts on this subject would be over in one minute! At once, Swami suggested three stories about this topic. That was my first experience in the U.S.

Swami Helps And Trains Before The Time

After that, Swami guided me and helped me to give so many talks there. Even before going to the U.S., Swami prepared me for that. One year before that, Swami gave me training. How?

Many people used to assemble in the Samadhi of Swami's parents. This Samadhi is there, just opposite our house. So many ladies from villages would come there and read some books on Swami daily. Then, I thought, 'These old ladies are reading Swami's literature. But, if there was somebody to explain all that, it would be very nice.' I used to go to the Samadhi every day, to do *namaskar* (pay my respects) to Eswaramma.

That day — I don't know how it happened, perhaps just a coincidence — those people came to me and asked me to explain something about Swami. Then, I said that I was very busy and that I could not say anything. But, they encouraged me to speak to them about Swami for at least half an hour.

So, that's how I used to go there, for half-an-hour in between *darshan* time and *bhajan* time. Every day, I used to go there and tell them something. That's how it went on for one year. So, like that, before going to the U.S., Swami gave me that training also.

In that way, whatever Swami does is for a 10-year plan at least. But, at the moment, we cannot understand anything about it.

Swami Gives A Warning To The Disease

One day, I was sitting in the line. I was suffering from back pain. I thought that I didn't want to tell anything to Swami about my pain or other personal things, because there are so many people, who worry Swami about their personal problems already. I did not want to worry Swami unnecessarily, unless it was an emergency. I thought it was not important.

Patiently, I was suffering, bearing the pain, taking painkillers and all that. This went on for three months. In between, my husband's sister came for Swami's *darshan*. We both were sitting in the line, when Swami came there. I was holding a letter. In the letter, I wrote, "Swami, my sister-in-law has come. Please bless her."

That's what I wrote in the letter. So, I was holding the letter and Swami came there. Then, I gave the letter. But, instead of writing, "My sister-in-law has come," I suddenly wrote, "I am suffering from back pain."

For three months, I could resist writing that. But, when I saw Swami, I told Swami. Then, Swami joked with me and said, "Give a stick to your husband." All the people were smiling at me. I felt so embarrassed. But, there is meaning even in that. After Swami said that, I never had that pain again. It means that He is giving a warning to the disease.

One day, a lady came to Swami and told Him that she was going for an operation. Then, Swami said, "Go and die!"

Then, she wondered why Swami said that. She thought that when she comes to Him in a state like this, Swami should bless her before she goes in for the operation. But, instead of blessing her, Swami said, "Go and die!"

After one month, she went to Swami and He said, "Still, you haven't died!?"

Again, she felt so embarrassed. But, after sometime, without any operation, she was cured of the disease!

Swami's Words Are
Powerful, Unique, And Special

Even the words of Swami are so powerful. They are unique and special. They help a lot. These words of Swami will give you messages, will cure our health, and will confer wealth and health on us. They are so powerful that we cannot understand them. They are Divine gems.

One day, a group of business people came to Swami. They wanted their business to grow. They requested Swami to give them something, so that their business might grow. So, Swami created one coconut and gave it to these people. Swami moved the coconut like this and there was a sound of coins in it. Swami advised them not to break the coconut, until they reach their native place and then, to keep it near the altar. He asked them not to touch it, so that way their business would grow.

But, these people could not resist. On their way, they broke the coconut and Lakshmi came out. They felt so sorry and came back to Swami again. They asked Swami to excuse them and they asked for another coconut.

"No! I told you not to break it, so I am not going to give you another."

So, we have to follow the teachings and the words of Swami. Only then can we enjoy whatever is in reserve for us.

Swami's Blessings Are Limitless

A tobacco merchant of our native place earned *crores* and *crores* of *rupees* from business. But, after sometime, he lost everything and came to Swami.

My husband accompanied him and brought him to Swami. He was lucky that Swami gave him an interview. Swami created a Lakshmi idol and gave it to his wife. When

Swami created it, He told her not to remove the Lakshmi pendant from the chain.

So, again he went home. He earned and got everything he wanted. He cleared off all his debts. He was so happy.

When Swami creates anything purposefully, it will become '*akshaya.*' If He gives gold, it will be limitless. If He gives you *sarees*, continuously we will be getting *sarees*. If He blesses our books, speeches, or songs — or if you are interested in *bhajan* — everything will be limitless, if Swami blesses you.

Questions and Answers Session

(Prof.Anil Kumar talks to Overseas Devotees,
November 12th, 2011)

The Explanation Of
Sai Baba's Mahasamadhi

Q: Would you please explain to us about Sai Baba's Mahasamadhi (His sacred tomb shrine)?

A: In general, a Mahasamadhi is the place where the body of a saintly person is laid to rest. However, Baba's Mahasamadhi is not an ordinary one. It cannot be compared to others. There are Samadhis (tomb shrines) that are located in other places. In Shirdi, we have a Samadhi for Shirdi Sai. Gurudwara is another Samadhi, a Sikh shrine. There is Buddhagaya, the tree under which Buddha became enlightened. Sanchi-Sarnath has a Buddhist Tooth Relic temple and in Kandy, Sri Lanka, there is another. Saints from the Islamic faith have Dargahs (Samadhis). The Temple Mount in Jerusalem attracts Jewish and Christian worshippers from all over the world. Bethlehem is another city with religious meaning for Jews, Muslims, and especially Christians from every denomination. And the building of Kaaba (the House of Allah) in Mecca, Saudi Arabia, is a vital pilgrimage centre for Muslims everywhere.

These are all holy places, where the body of noble souls have been laid to rest, or where they lived and moved among people, working for everyone's spiritual emancipation.

Places Of Worship Are Important

While going to the temple, we are sincerely reminded of God or at least we have some spiritual feelings. So, to caution and remind us, to put us back on track, we go to temples or places of worship every week. It may also be a mosque, church, synagogue, or monastery. Therefore, these places of worship are always important.

In this manner, the Sathya Sai Divya (Divine) Mahasamadhi is one such sacred place, informing us time and time again that the *Poorna Avatar* (full incarnation of God) took birth here, in this place. It identifies this as the place, where He moved about, doing His Divine mission. Therefore, devotees from all over the world are drawn to this spot.

Swami did not go to any other country (except once long ago to Africa for just a couple of days). So, one hundred per cent of His mission and the spreading of His message started here, expanded from here, and concluded here.

Mahasamadhi Is A Special Spiritual Centre With Focussed Energy

The importance of this place is similar to that of a beacon. Here you feel spiritual vibrations and the awakening of intuition, just as you do when you prostrate before the Christian cross, or kneel down in a church, or see a statue in a temple. You experience a state of equanimity, mental peace, steadfastness — a balanced state of mind. You are encouraged to take up the spiritual path, depending upon your own capacity, willingness, and yearning for God. You also experience desires being fulfilled here.

Therefore, the Mahasamadhi is most important, being a special spiritual centre with concentrated energy. You can say this is a powerful, spiritual thermal station. Electricity is everywhere, but a thermal station is different. It is from the thermal station that we receive our electricity supply.

So, never in your wildest dreams take the Mahasamadhi lightly. If I put my fingers into an electric plug and don't get an electric shock, it means something is wrong with me or the plug, or there is a power-cut. Similarly, if someone does not experience the energy of the Samadhi, it means that he is not mature or ready enough, that he has not done enough homework, or that he has no deep yearning. He may have a mundane attitude and thus, doesn't expect any kind of transforming thought or vibration flowing into him.

That is my answer when comparing Sai Baba's Mahasamadhi with other relics, pilgrim centres, and sacred places of worship elsewhere.

Baba Is Always Transcendental

Q: Now that Sai Baba is in the state of Mahasamadhi, what do you think is the impact for the Sai bhaktha and the organisation, as Baba is a very strong figure for His bhakthas?

A: The framing of this question is itself wrong. Here, it is said, "Baba is in the state of *samadhi*." Wrong! *Samadhi* is a transcendental state. It is the state that you reach at the higher levels of meditation, as you progress along the spiritual path, and it is within everyone's experience.

But, to say Baba is in 'a state of *samadhi*' is wrong, because He is always in that state. He is always in steadiness, balanced, transcendental, and beyond the senses. Therefore, He is not in 'a state of *samadhi*'.

A Sincere Devotee Feels Swami In Every Thought, Word, And Act

Then, the second part of this question is about the impact on the Sai *bhaktha* (devotee) and the organisation. The impact on the Sai *bhakthas* is not going to be something new that would affect their devotion. Many people all over the world are experiencing Swami's miracles today, more than ever before. I have authentic proofs and addresses to supply to any number of doubting Thomases. We are all brothers, so I don't blame anybody for doubting. Nevertheless, I have been successful in challenging doubting Thomases for quite a long time. So, for the sincere *bhakthas*, this present situation has no effect at all.

But, for those, who are in between — not yet sure about Sai, His life, and His message — they will be affected. It is good, if they are affected. At least their fate will be decided now: either they will decide to follow Him, or they will stay on the other side of the fence. This type of person is present in every field, particularly in politics. So, those, who are undecided, are politically motivated in the field of religion. Those, who are political in this way — with self-interest, self-glorification, and self-praise as their motivating force in religion — will experience an impact. They will be naturally influenced by the situation of Baba leaving the physical body. But, I know this is not the quality of a sincere devotee.

A sincere devotee feels Him more and more in every thought, word, and act, as he does not rely solely on His physical frame. If the absence of Baba's physical frame deludes, deviates, diverts, or takes you away from the path of religion and faith, then life is gone. In that case, you may be unfit to be in this spiritual life.

This should be our attitude: We have a commitment and hold fast to that. Come what may, we can't lose anything, because we don't aspire for anything. We don't use our religion and faith for personal prospects, or to advance our name or fame. So, in fact we are not at all affected.

The Hindu Influence In Bali

Q: What is your impression about the bhakthas and the organisation on your second visit to Bali? Where do you think things need to be improved?

A: Bali (an island in Indonesia) is a place, where ninety per cent of the people are Hindus. It is interesting to note that the people are highly committed and totally devoted. You will see them carrying all the materials needed for daily worship on their heads. You will also find a little altar or place of worship in front of every residence or shop.

Bali is also interesting in the sense that you have statues of figures from the ancient Hindu epic, the *Mahabharatha*. There is a forty feet high statue of Ghatothgaja (a fighter renowned for magical powers and loyalty). There is also a big statue of Lord Krishna and Prince Arjuna, whose famous spiritual dialogue is recorded in the *Bhagavad Gita,* a well-known Hindu scripture. Though Bali is in a Muslim-dominated country, in a Muslim-ruled country, yet we see many people (including Sai devotees), who keep to the path of Hindu thought and action.

Sai Gatherings In Bali

Every meeting here was challenging as regards to whether people would turn up or not. Often, there will be tremendous downpour of rain, thunder, and lightning. One option was to cancel — why inconvenience the people? But, from experience over a long period of time, we have discovered that Sai gatherings cannot be cancelled and will not be cancelled. And to my surprise, I would find thousands of people attending (with their kids too) despite the rain! And the *bhajan* standard (devotional singing) was so high! It was on a par with that in Prasanthi Nilayam. So, it is narrow-minded to think that Prasanthi Nilayam is the only place for good *bhajans*. Wherever there is genuine love and devotion to Swami, you will find its expression in the melodious singing of *bhajans*.

The Bhakthas And Sai Organisation In Bali

I was asked, "What do you think now of the *bhakthas* and the Bali organisation?" Well, nobody needs 'to think of' the *bhakthas*. One has to be a *bhaktha,* or to think about becoming a *bhaktha*. But, do not think about other *bhakthas*. Who are we to judge? A true *bhaktha* will never judge. The Sai organisation in Bali is clever and modest enough not to embarrass me by insisting on a generalisation about its *bhakthas*.

Regarding the organisation in Bali, it is very ideal, because they all stand united. Many, many more are attending Sai centres, because of their unshakable faith and steady devotion. This sets an example for everybody. The people are middle-class or lower middle-class. So, those, who wish to lead a righteous life by coming to Swami, should come to Bali and see the true benefits of joining a Sai organisation.

All the worldly accumulations and the possessions that one holds are nothing in front of the devotion of Bali *bhakthas*. So, I can give the answer that there have been no negative changes. In fact, it is expanding more and more in devotion day-by-day.

Sai Teachings Have To Be Applied In Daily Life

Q: What do you think about the application of Sai's teachings in Bali?

A: This could be a question that relates generally to all Sai devotees. The answer is that Sai's teachings have to be applied in daily life, not merely quoted. Quoting teachings and speaking about His teachings (as I am doing now) is nothing in comparison to the person, who practises His teachings. The practitioner of Sai's teachings is a billion times closer to the spiritual ideal than a speaker on His teachings.

This is because, listening to a speaker or a person quoting these teachings is no different from hearing His teachings on a DVD or a CD. But, Sai's teachings have to be practised! It is not enough to speak about them or just listen to them. To know is to do! It is not to know only in order to acquire knowledge. Then, it becomes dead knowledge or second-hand information, pomp and show, arrogance and ego. In that case, it is just the experience of somebody else, a repetition in which we have no personal experience.

But, knowing in order to do, in order to act, is different. That way, we experience the taste of the pudding by eating it. **Therefore, Sai's teachings are not merely to be known, recapitulated, and memorised. They are what we are to apply and do in our daily lives, even more so now.**

Our Lives Should Be His Message

Up until now, people were most interested in Baba and less mindful of us (devotees). We were overlooked and even they ignored some of our mistakes. Now, our individual lives will be scrutinised. Are we following His teachings for personal favours or self-glorification? Is there a selfish reason? Are we genuine? What sacrifices are we making? Sacrifice is the proof of love. When there is no sacrifice, it is not love but selfishness. People will look at us now to see.

"My life is My message," Baba would say. Today, *our* lives should be His message, because people will look at us, the world of Sai devotees.

The Ideal Vision For The Sai Organisation

Q: What is your ideal vision about the Sai organisation in Bali for the present and future?

A: This is also a question that applies to all Sai organisations, not just Bali. The ideal vision is this: we should understand the basic principles of the Sai movement. We should be in touch with the fundamentals of Sai's teachings, living according to them and participating closely with others in service activities. So, when we work with people in the company of fellow Sai devotees, all will know the manner of our work.

By understanding that work is 'Love in Action', we will certainly develop a true vision. A true vision includes unity of religions, simplicity, humility, frankness, selflessness, and sacrifice. It is not self-glorification or self-effacement. In fact, until this 'I'-ness is gone, we have not been successful on the spiritual path. This 'I'-ness is an indication of the existence of ego. Until that goes, however great or accomplished one is (in the spiritual parlance), we have yet a long way to go.

Self-effacement And Egolessness

On receiving the Nobel Prize, Mother Teresa said the award is not an achievement at all. For her, it was not an honour or a pomp-and-show exhibit to add to her bio-data. No! She said the award shows that the world acknowledges the need for service to the poor and needy, the sick and orphaned. **Service to such people is better than the recognition of the service.** That is what the award meant to her and that is spirituality.

Swami Ranganathananda (from the Ramakrishna Mission, someone who did much social service) declined the Padma Vibhushan award for distinguished service to the nation. He said a national honour like that cannot be conferred on him as an individual, instead of being awarded to the Mission he represented: "I am not an individual here; we work collectively." That is spirituality!

Self-effacement and egolessness are evident in Swami. Every act, every gesture, every word speaks of utter simplicity, total humility, and absence of ego. These are all to be learnt from Swami.

So, the vision for Sai organisations (as I see it) is more brotherliness, more lovingness, and more friendliness. It is not to focus on identity; instead, it is to mingle with everybody and not feel special or greater than anybody, at any point of time. When Baba Himself feels that He is very ordinary, how can you and I feel extraordinary?

The Bali Music Video: "Your Life Is My Message"

Q: To celebrate Sai Baba's Birthday anniversary this year, we are producing a music video with the theme, 'Your Life Is My Message'. This video clip will be aired at a local TV station in Bali for approximately one month. Will you please kindly us give a short speech to be used as the opening or introduction for the music clip?

A: I have already done the speech as was requested. It is very good that Bali is producing the music clip. But, why just for the Birthday anniversary? Have it on air every day if possible.

All over the Spanish belt — Argentina, Mexico, Peru, and Venezuela — the people have a daily telecast of Sai messages on several TV channels. Right from childhood, my mother used to say to me, "The nearer to the temple, the further away from God." I did not realise its truth then, but I do now.

People living far away from Prasanthi Nilayam have not lost their faith and are not confused after Sai has left the physical body. They are experiencing Him more than before. The doubt has arisen in the minds of those, who are neither near nor far, a psychological hybrid of a spiritual variety! So, the Sai TV telecasts all over the Spanish-speaking regions, which is really quite amazing.

The Visit To Langkawi

The first place we visited was Langkawi Island in Malaysia. Langkawi is such a beautiful place. There are caves to see, nice places to walk, and a boat available for hire. It has wonderful gardens with greenery everywhere. It's quiet and tranquil and less populated — so, there is more oxygen to breathe!

There were two meetings organised there. One was for a wholly Chinese group with a translator. I am quite happy to say that the translator of the talk into Chinese language did a better job than the main speaker!

I am telling you this, because people who speak different languages and live in far-off places know Sai Baba's message a million times better than all of us put together! To think that only I or we know is just self-deception. This Chinese translator was freely translating with no inhibitions or fumbling for words, quite fully equipped with the Sai message.

There was a sizable number there and in the evening, we had a mixed audience. Langkawi has a huge theatre, so it was very good. That was the first visit.

The Visit To Penang

The next visit was to Penang, another island in Malaysia, and a very nice place with water everywhere. You have to go there by ferry or boat. On the mountain top is the handsome building of Penang University, where the meeting was organised. It was no use saying, "Rain, rain go away, come again another day." It was rain, rain every day! There is no question of 'another day', because every day was a rainy day there!

But, see Baba's miracle! All the devotees and the professors from Penang University (along with their families) attended and there were a number of questions they wanted to ask. The Penang meeting was very successful by Bhagawan's grace.

The Visit To Kuala Lumpur

Then again in Malaysia, in the capital of Kuala Lumpur, a meeting was held by the Telugu association. The Kuala Lumpur Telugu association is very capable and some years ago, they hosted the International Telugu Conference. I was able to meet and talk with them. Later on, we had a meeting for devotees in the biggest auditorium in Malaysia. It could accommodate no less than twenty-five thousand devotees!

This is a good time to let you know that Malaysia is a region, where the Sai Organisation is very strong. It has a maximum number of youth and a maximum number of books on Sai literature, published by the Malaysian Sathya Sai Organisation.

Malaysia is ruled by a Muslim government. Yet, the Prime Minister and Cabinet Ministers participate in the Sri Sathya Sai activities. They attend every meeting, because the Sai message of service has gone deeply into their hearts. All that is amazing! So, you don't need to first spell out Who Sai is and you are not there to spread His name or message, because they are all very well informed.

The Visit To Johor Bahru

Then, there is another city, Johor Bahru, in southern Malaysia. It is an important commercial centre, with health care services and many hospitals. There was a big auditorium for the sizeable number of devotees, who attended there as well.

The Visit To Singapore

The Republic of Singapore has one main island and many smaller ones off the southern tip of Malay. The city is also called Singapore and it was my third visit there. We had two meetings on successive dates. The questions were quite interesting with lots of participation. (Singapore devotees come over here in large numbers, as you might know.) The Sai service activities are very well known in Far East countries and Singapore has a very strong, powerful Sathya Sai organisation.

The Visit To Brunei

And then, I went to Brunei. It is a sovereign state on the island of Borneo. The rest of the island belongs to Malaysia and Indonesia. Brunei is a place that is less visited by people, because of visa restrictions. They don't give visas easily. It is again a Muslim country with a population in number similar to Puttaparthi, so it's a very small place. They don't allow anybody in — nor do they let them out! It is like that. But, see how Baba gets in! There could be an iron wall or an impenetrable building, but He can go through any obstacle. He has gone into Brunei!

There is a small centre in Brunei, managed by a doctor and his wife. They were hesitant to ask, wondering whether I would go there or not. They said, "It is a small family, Anil Kumar, a very small centre. Would you be willing to come?"

I said, "I am not for numbers. Our meetings are not political gatherings for thousands. They are not meetings for crowds, like those for Anna Hazare (a political activist), Sonia Gandhi, or Advani (politicians). I am a simple humble servant of Baba — a servant of servants. I don't need thousands there at all."

If we look at history, no spiritual leader addressed large gatherings. Jesus and Ramakrishna Paramahamsa (a Bengali Hindu saint) had only eleven disciples each. Ramana Maharishi (the 'Great Sage') had one or two (or none), because he liked silence. Shirdi Baba (the first Sai *Avatar*) attracted few people, because He would severely chastise those, who did not listen properly! So, no spiritual leader ever wanted to attract thousands of people.

Therefore, if you want people to come in large numbers, it shows you are political, misdirected, or vain. That is what I told that family, "I am not here for that; I will certainly come."

There were very few people at the residential centre. And yet, everyone, including the children, was singing *bhajans* in proper Prasanthi style and they all had their eyes closed. It was amazing! So often, what happens is that our concentration is on wanting to know who is singing, who is absent, who is important, and how to contact that person. This reveals how silly we are. I am not blaming anybody. So, it was a small *satsang* (spiritual gathering) with good *bhajans* at Brunei.

The Visit To Jakarta And Medan

From Brunei, I went on to Indonesia. Indonesia, Malaysia, and Brunei are all Muslim countries — only Singapore is not. Indonesia is special in the sense that the Sai youth there constructed three hundred and twenty water tanks for the poor people, on their own.

It is natural to think of Sai youth as talented young people with the ability to speak and sing, fond of being in the public eye, and always career-oriented! Here in Indonesia, three hundred and twenty water tanks were constructed solely by the youth! As a result, the system here, where previously water could only be purchased or collected by going a long distance to fetch it, now there is a pure drinking water supply! The whole country is very grateful to the Sai youth in Indonesia. So, it is a pleasure to know these details.

Jakarta, the capital of Indonesia, has a centre, where every meeting is attended by at least five thousand people, due to the large number of devotees.

Medan, the capital of the North Sumatra province in Indonesia, was another place I visited. It was again a rainy day, but yet the conference hall was full. Medan has a large number of devotees, the majority being educated youth. The food was made by the Sai *sevadal* (volunteers), most of whom are indigenous to that area.

Visit To Langkawi, Malaysia

(Special Talk by Prof. Anil Kumar, November 28th, 2011)

Expectations Of Sai

Today's topic is: 'Expectations of Sai, the Avatar'. So, what is meant by 'expectations'? Parents, for example, have expectations regarding their children. Parents spend a lot of money on their offspring and sacrifice both time and energy, expecting something in return later. The boss at work is often very demanding and always expects results. A wife expects her husband to behave properly, fulfilling all his duties to the family; and in turn, the husband expects his wife to be both obedient and also a good cook!

So, professional and familial relationships are built on expectations. Even your nation expects loyalty from you and in return, you expect services and income tax exemptions from the state! So, the whole world revolves around expectations.

But, there is one relationship in your life that is not based on such expectations. There is one, who just keeps giving and giving, without expecting anything from you in return. There is one relationship in your life, in which nothing is expected from you, in which nothing is sought. That is your relationship with the Source, your relationship with the Divine. That is your relationship with Bhagawan Sri Sathya Sai Baba! He doesn't expect appreciation or recognition from you. He doesn't expect these from anyone. He does not seek popularity or publicity. No! **The 'expectation' of the Avatar is 'not to expect'!**

One day, a student said to Baba, "Swami, I promise to give up all my bad habits and hold on to You only!"

Baba said in reply? "You promise, but you break sometimes, so I don't believe you." The only One, Who will never break a promise is Bhagawan Sri Sathya Sai Baba!

Baba always smiles. He is always happy. Why? He has zero expectations!

So, if you want to be happy, never expect anything from anybody! Don't expect anything, even from your nearest and dearest. Don't even expect a 'thank you'. No! And don't expect people to remember the good you have done them.

Still, we are human beings, so we do have expectations. That's why we cry. A mother-in-law expects comforting words from her daughter-in-law and the daughter-in-law, in return, has expectations she places on the mother-in-law to behave in a certain way, too. And it's their expectations that inevitably cause them both to cry. So, if we want to be happy, we cannot have any expectations.

And who can serve as our role model? Whom can we look to as an example? Mother Nature! She has no expectations. Langkawi, with her picturesque sea view, expects no thanks from you. When we witness and receive the beauty created by the morning sunlight falling upon the sea, the sun expects nothing in return from you. And the wonderful mountain range, filled with lovely trees and flowers, expects nothing in return for the beauty it shares.

The most precious things come without expectations. We humans, however, come with all sorts of expectations.

For example, having given much of myself to bringing up my son, I now have high expectations regarding his career.

God Wants You To Be Happy

On the other hand, the One, Who has given us all our positions in life, the One Who blesses us with plenty and prosperity, the One Who is taking care of every one of us, is Bhagawan Sri Sathya Sai Baba and He often tells students, "I don't expect anything from you. I'm happy, if you are happy." God wants you to be happy!

He also tells students: "Earn a good name for your family and country. That's the only thing I want." Therefore, brothers and sisters, be a good son or daughter, an ideal student, and a patriot. That's all Baba wants for you.

I have seen Baba talking to poor people one minute and then, receiving the President of India the next moment. The love He shows toward the President is the same love He extends to the poorest people. He doesn't show twenty percent, or fifty percent, or even ninety-nine. No! This is not a business. No! **Baba's love is total. It is unconditional. It is beyond time and space. He is not concerned with your nationality, your caste, or your color. He is pure Love. He communicates heart-to-heart.**

So, let us love people equally! Let us consider everyone we meet as equally important. Some people consider themselves V.I.P.'s. But, who could possibly be a V.I.P. to God? God is the only true V.I.P. I know you do not understand Telugu, but I must quote Him and then, provide a translation:

Talli Kante Migula Daivame Daggara
Tandri Kante Sannihitudu Chaala
Atti Daivamunu Maruva Abbunu Paapambu
Satyamaina Maata Ee Sai Maata

Baba says that God is closer to you than your own father and dearer to you than your own mother. To forget such a God is the worst of all sins. So, what Baba wants from you is that you should not forget God.

So, Who is God? And where is He? And how are we to remember Him? What is His address? A simple example: a fellow enters a room lined with ten mirrors and he stands in the centre. And so, the ten mirrors produce ten reflections of him. In the mirrors, there are ten people; but in fact, there is only one man at the centre. That is God!

In one mirror, He is Allah, in another Jehovah, in another Vishnu, and in yet another, Siva, Buddha, and Zoroaster. And yet, there is only one God! Baba wants you to develop this understanding of the unity of faiths. We should honour and celebrate the Muslim festivals of Ramadan and Muharram. We should honour and celebrate Christmas and Buddha Poornima, because all religions are one. Baba wants you to join in the spirit of the unity of religions.

What Does Baba Expect From You?

When Baba looks at a person, He can see what that persons needs. If someone needs clothes, He will provide clothes. If they need food, He will provide it. If shelter is needed, He will provide that too. Giving somebody what he needs is true service. Giving what is needed is service and this is what Baba expects from you. Serve the poor people.

He has given us two hands, so earn with one hand and give with the other. He has also given us two eyes, so see the beauty of nature with one and watch the suffering of the poor with the other. And He has given us two ears, so listen to sweet music with one ear and to the difficulties of the poor with the other. And with the two legs He has given, we should take a step forward toward the good and a step back from any wrong. But, He has given us only one tongue, namely to speak the Truth! Truth is God. God is Truth. So, speak the truth. Speak only the truth.

Baba's Expectation Is That We Should Serve Everybody

Baba's expectation is that we should serve. He wants us to serve everybody. He wants us to give them what they need. So, do for them what He would do. In other words, be His helping hands. Using our hands to pray is not enough. Service is true prayer and this is what Bhagawan Baba expects of His devotees.

Swami knows when you render genuine service to someone. Speaking once with a young engineer, Swami told him, "I know you work late into the night, but I don't want you to sleep in your office. Go to bed earlier." Swami saying that to this man was doing him a good service. It made the engineer very happy.

A few years ago, Swami was speaking to citizens of Mumbai and He asked the crowd, "When there are hungry people outside your house, how can you sleep at night?

You live in high-rise buildings, but right outside, there are people with no homes."

Baba then commanded the people to provide food and shelter to the poor. That is what Baba expects from us. He wants us to demonstrate exemplary character. Just as a businessman should act professionally and demonstrate the required skills and expertise for the job at hand, devotees should serve as soldiers of world peace.

Let us not limit ourselves to India and Malaysia! We belong to the community of humanity. We should not only preach the brotherhood of man and fatherhood of God, but should also embrace and serve all of our brothers and sisters.

Baba Expects Us To Limit Our Desires

We also need to put a ceiling on our desires. Let me provide a simple example. A poor man was strolling along and saw a yogi sitting under a tree. He immediately fell at the feet of the yogi and said, "Swami, help me!"

The yogi replied, "Don't worry boy, I will give you a helper, who will do whatever you ask of him. However, when you stop asking, the helper will swallow you whole!"

The poor man thought, 'Well, I have many desires,' so he went on asking and the helper dutifully went on providing. "I want a good house." The house appeared. "I want excellent furniture." And there it was! "I want very good food." It was provided. "I want a wonderful bed." And there it was. "I wish my wife was here." And so, she appeared.

And then, this fellow thought, 'How can my wife be here? Maybe she has been transformed into a devil!' And so, he began to run away. And he ran and he ran and he ran, but that devil kept on following him, until finally, this poor man came across the same yogi under the very same tree and he said to him, "Swami, the devil is following me! Please save me now!"

And so, the *guru* replied, "Place an electric pole here and ask the devil to climb up and down it, until further notice." And thus, this chap was saved.

Similarly, our endless desires will swallow us whole one day, if we allow them to. If we repeat, "Sai Ram, Sai Ram, Sai Ram," however, life becomes more manageable. Putting a ceiling on our desires, attaining a level of detachment from our worldly desires is something Swami expects from all of us. We need to turn inward. Most of the time, we are focused outwardly, concerned with the world and its *maya*. Turning inward is called meditation. Baba expects us to develop control of our senses and to regulate our minds.

Baba Is In You

If any should ask you where Baba is, tell them that He is in you! People may say that Baba has left us, but has He? If He has left, then where has He gone? If people ask you this, tell them, "He has gone nowhere. Nowhere! Now here!"

Chaavu Puttuku Leni Shasvatundu
Adi Madhyantharahitudu Anadhivaadu
Taanu Puttaka Chaavaka Champabadaka

Sarva Saakshiyai Anthata Alaruchundu
Unna Maata Telupuchunna Maata

Baba has neither beginning, nor end. He has neither birth, nor death. He is omnipresent. He can never leave His devotees and you cannot leave Him! Please hold on to His lotus feet forever. There may be people now claiming to be Baba and some people may want to go and see such men, but a genuine coin is different from a counterfeit. Don't believe such people.

I am proud of Malaysia. You are leading the way regarding the unity of faiths. You are showing the world the way in this regard. And I am proud of Malaysia for the excellent books on Sai philosophy that have been published here by brother Jagadeesan and have gained such international popularity. I especially recommend the book Unity of Religions as a very good reading experience.

This morning, I attended the Chinese bhajan session. The singing was of such a high standard! It transported me to another world! Therefore, Sai brothers and sisters, I will finish today by encouraging you in Malaysia, to continue to maintain your high standards and to strengthen your faith. Continue to spread the Sai message! Please continue to live for Sai!

> Please repeat after me, "Live for Sai!"
> Live for Sai! (Audience)
> Love Sai!
> Love Sai! (Audience)
> Love Sai!
> Love Sai! (Audience)
> Let this be our slogan until our final breath!

Ideal Parenting

(Talk Given by Anil Kumar and Brother J. Jagadeesan of
Malaysia, Langkawi, Malaysia, Nov 28th, 2011)

Anil Kumar: Now, we call upon brother Jagadeesan.

Jagadeesan: For the first time in the history of the Sai
Organisation, Mr. Anil Kumar sang in the Chinese Orchestra.
I learnt a little bit of Chinese, but I am trying to improve it
by watching Chinese movies.

All of us know Mr. Anil Kumar of Puttaparthi. Now, I
would like to introduce Anil Kumar of Malaysia! Anil has
sung so many songs. Okay! So, I, too, would like to sing
one small song in Chinese. This song I learnt when I was in
university. In fact, I composed this song while reading a
Chinese newspaper. In those days, I used to sing this song
to someone else — now, I sing this song to Baba. It goes like
this: It says, "I love you, you love me. But, if you stop loving
me, I am going to fall sick."

Brothers and sisters, what an incredible occasion this
is! Actually, I have been spending a great deal of time
travelling around the world and have got a chance to meet
many Sai families. I am very, very thankful to the Sai
Organisation for inviting me here, today. I will go back to
Kuala Lumpur, Malaysia on Sunday to listen to the Anil
Kumar Sunday Talk and then, on Monday, I fly to Africa.
But now, I would like to expand upon two points from the
brilliant presentation that brother Anil made.

The first thing he emphasised was 'xiao' or filial piety.

Baba Was The Best Role Model

Baba was the perfect role model for filial piety. His mother wanted a small school in Puttaparthi; Baba built huge universities and provided free education to everyone. His mother wanted a small medical clinic in Puttaparthi; Baba built super speciality hospitals, providing free medical service to the poor.

In the village of Puttaparthi, people had to go quite far to get water for their daily needs. Mother Easwaramma asked Baba to build a well in Puttaparthi; Baba built huge water tanks with thousands of miles of pipes full of water, to serve the poor.

So, what did Baba do?

He exceeded His parents' expectations. In today's world, youngsters are falling short of their parents' expectations. Today, thousands of parents are crying, because their children are causing them pain.

Government Intervenes
As Dharma Declines

In Singapore, where eighty percent of the population is Chinese, the Government passed a law, saying that parents can sue their children for not looking after them. Initially, parents said that it was nonsense to think that parents would sue their own children. I was following the story ten years ago.

When that government office opened on the first day of the new law, six elderly Chinese couples came to the office. My heart cried, when I saw them. I wept, because of what one mother was saying. She said, "My daughter prefers to feed the dogs, rather than look after me." Can you imagine the heart of the mother, who was crying like that? And for the Chinese, xiao – filial piety is the foundation of their civilisation. In China, filial piety is the religion of those, who don't even believe in God. This is the greatness of the Chinese civilisation.

Today, this civilisation is already shifting its focus. Some time ago, the Indians thought they were better than the Chinese — that the Chinese were bad, while the Indians were good. The Indians, as well as Anil Kumar, used to think of the Indians as being superior. However, the Indian government passed a law, which allows the government to sue children for abandoning their parents. So, what are the children doing to cause the government to pass such a law?

They take their parents to a big religious festival, where there will be a million people or more and say, "Ah ha! Papa and Mama, come, come and see!" and then, the child will disappear from their sight. The father and mother are left alone and the child is nowhere to be found.

Think of this: India and China are the two most ancient civilisations in the world. Parents, who are the most important people in all of our lives, living in these countries, are crying. Dear brothers and sisters, we should never allow this to happen in Malaysia!

I appeal to the Sathya Sai Council and to the Sai Chinese Affairs to launch massive programmes in Malaysia, to revive filial piety. Every son and daughter must feel proud to look after their parents. Every son and daughter must feel shame, if they make their parents cry. This challenge I present in front of Anil Kumar, to all our Sai Chinese Affairs – in fact, not only to Sai Chinese Affairs, but to the entire Sathya Sai Central Council of Malaysia.

Why am I telling you these things and talking to you like this? All of us talk about God. Okay! Not only do Sai devotees talk about God, but everybody talks about God. You know what the Indians say. They say that, if you cannot worship the God that you can see — your father and mother — then, how can you worship the God that you cannot see? I apologise for being so serious today.

Before I go to my next point, I would like to sing one more song — a Chinese song!

Do you want to know whether you happen to be in heaven or hell? Yes? Do you want to know?

Audience: No!

Do you all want to know how to be an *Avatar*?

Audience: Yes!

Do you want to know, or not? I am only going to ask one more time. Do you want to know how to be an *Avatar*?

Audience: Yes!

Very Good!

Dharmic Son And Dharmic Daughter

But, before I tell you, I would like to mention one more point about filial piety or xiao. The programme that I would like you all to consider launching is one called the '*dharmic* son or *dharmic* daughter in India', meaning 'the noble son or daughter'. And who are the noble sons and daughters? Around the world, we see parents prepared to sacrifice themselves for their children. Parents give their lives for their children.

Nowadays, the father and mother look after their children for many years. From the ages of one to ten, they give their children everything that they want — as our Anil says, fulfilling all the expectations of their children. Then, a girl will meet a boy, whom she will know for only six months, and say, "Oh darling, I love you and you love me. Oh, I need you! You need me!" Blah, blah, blah... And then, the child will be prepared to throw the father and mother away.

The father and mother have given twenty years of love to the child, but the child will throw them away after only six months of love.

Mother Saves Her Child

Nowadays, when I address youngsters, I ask them one question in particular. I ask, "If there was a big lake and standing alongside the lake was your father, mother, boyfriend or girlfriend, and in the middle of this big lake you were drowning and crying out for help, who would be the one person, who would give his or her life to save you?" The answer of course is the mother, exactly!

The boyfriend will say, "Oh, my darling is drowning! I do not know how to swim. Somebody help her! Please, help her!" But, the mother, who does not know how to swim, (not the father!) will dive into the lake to save her child. It is the mother, who will give her life.

The father will follow the mother, but he will tie a rope around his waist, because the father knows that he should come back alive as well. However, the mother does not care for herself. This is a mother's love. Why am I saying all of this?

Until I was thirty-two years old, I was an atheist. I didn't believe in anything. For thirty-two years, I did not believe in God. Some of you may wonder whether I had heard of Sai Baba back then. I won't tell you my Baba story for the time being, but for thirty-two years, I did not believe in God. I had only one God in my life. My mother was my God.

I would never do anything to bring tears to her eyes. Whatever I would do, first I would think, 'Will this make my mother happy?' Only then would I do it. This is the consciousness you must help to develop in every son and daughter today. We launched this programme of the noble son and daughter — *dharmic* son and *dharmic* daughter. But, why did we do it? What gave us the idea? It was only one girl, who inspired us.

Daughter Serves Her Dying Mother

Listen to this fantastic story of that one girl. She was the daughter of a Sai devotee in the Malaysian centre. She went to London to study law and after spending three years in London, she returned to Malaysia.

The rule in Malaysia is that one must sit for one year, bi-exam chambering, before attempting the final exam. But, as soon as she came back to Malaysia to sit for that year, her mother was diagnosed with brain cancer. This family is rich enough to employ three Indonesian nurses to look after the mother, but this devoted daughter said, "No. My mother looked after me when I was young, so I will look after my mother now."

And so, after studying law in London for three years, she threw away her career and stayed home every day to look after her mother. As the second and third year passed, the mother's brain slowly began to deteriorate, because of the cancer. The mother became like a vegetable. The daughter bathed her bed-ridden mother and used to clean her mother's feces, just like a nurse.

She did everything for her mother, but not in the manner of a maid. She served her mother like a daughter would do one generation ago. In those days, it was typical for a daughter to do this, whether they be Chinese, Indian or Malaysian; maids would not provide this kind of care. Nowadays, the Indonesian nurse-maid will do that. Three and a half years later, the mother died. At that time, this young woman sat for the exam and now, she is a lawyer. That is where the motivation to launch this programme, *dharmic* son and *dharmic* daughter, came from.

Some of you may even remember that I presented this program in Pahang, in front of two thousand Sai devotees. When I read this citation, the very same girl came forward. Many mothers were crying. I thanked her for bringing an ancient ideal back into modern times. Because of this, I would like to request Sai Chinese Affairs to launch a massive programme like this one, for the fostering of *dharmic* sons and *dharmic* daughters.

I am very proud to say that on the 26th of November, three days after Baba's Birthday, I have been invited to the Simuda centre, where we are going to give awards to *dharmic* sons and *dharmic* daughters. It is my prayer to launch this programme worldwide.

And what should be the legacy of the Sathya Sai *Avatar* for the world, in twenty or thirty years from now? What will the world remember this *Avatar* for? The world must thank this *Avatar* for bringing back, through the world of Sai devotees, the father and mother as the centre of human life. So, it's up to all of you.

Sacred Activity Is Possible
Only Through Sai Organisation

Anil Kumar: Thank you my boy, Jagadeesan.

If any sacred activity at all is to be undertaken at the universal and global level, it is possible only through the Sai Organisation. I really appreciate you and I wish you Godspeed in your endeavour. Godspeed and success in all of His efforts!

I will tell you what Baba has said about the relationship between husband and wife.

In Kodaikanal, as Swami was passing by, He looked at a student and asked him, "What are you going to do next?"

That boy said, "Whatever you tell me, Swami."

"Okay, you do MRS."

The boy asked, "MRS? What is that, Swami?"

"Mrs. Get Married! The girl is waiting for you!" Then, Baba said to everyone, "Array! This boy says, 'Swami, Swami, Swami,' in front of Me, today. Tomorrow, when he gets married, the wife will become his life and later, she will become a knife."

Even at the age of eighty-five, when Baba thought of His mother, His eyes became wet. He started shedding tears, just as if her body was being laid to rest right then.

Baba started Easwaramma High School in memory of His mother. He started a community hall in the name of His father. There are also a number of mobile medical vans working in the name of Mother Easwaramma.

The Greatest Human Value Lies In Taking Care Of One's Parents

Once, one boy said to Swami, "Swami, I want to stay with You. I want to serve You."

Baba said, "*Pakka gas*," meaning 'false'. Then, He said to that boy, "You know your parents. You know what they want. You know what they need and how to make them happy. If you don't serve your parents, whom you know, how can I expect you to serve God, Whom you do not know? How do you know what satisfies God, Whom you do not know? **Serve your parents. That is service to Swami!**"

So, brother Jagadeesan has championed the call, the quintessence of the Sai message. China and India are the most ancient civilisations in the world, but slowly values are dying out. The dog is still behaving like a dog; the donkey is behaving like a donkey. You don't have to tell a dog to be a dog, because it is already a dog; but, you have to tell a human to behave like a human. So, the greatest human value lies in taking care of your parents. God bless you, sir!

The Sathya Sai Organisation takes this suggestion as a priority. May Sai shower His choicest blessings on him, who proceeds to take this important message all over the world – the message of taking care of one's parents. Oh, we love our parents every day. All should love their parents every day.

Jagadeesan: I will speak to you one more time before the closing tomorrow. At that time, I will tell you how to become an *Avatar*. Be patient. You know that I can't tell you today, because everybody will become an *Avatar* and nobody will be in the hall tomorrow!

Anil Kumar: Brother Jagadeesan, thank you very much! You have brought to light what most parents are feeling nowadays. Children are no more the children of yesteryear, so it is high time that the Sai Organisation do something about this.

We live in a time when, even if parents say one word to discipline their children, that is a lot! We are being democratic and trying to be very nice to our children. We don't want to subject them to what we went through.

In the process, children are taking things for granted and values have gone down the drain. T.V. programmes condition families to become what they watch on television everyday. It is sad to see that even though values have declined, children expect everything from their parents without giving anything in return. They feel that it is their birthright to get everything, without giving anything.

We hope that with the blessings of Bhagawan Sri Sathya Sai Baba, the Sai Organisation will help to restore in each home a tradition of loving Sai families, where parents are loved, respected, and honoured.

About SAI BABA

(Talk by Prof.Anil Kumar, excerpts from
THE NATIONAL NEWSPAPER, Thailand)

FOR MILLIONS OF DEVOTEES OF SATHYA SAI BABA, 2011 WAS THE CATACLYSMIC YEAR, IN WHICH THE INDIA-BASED SPIRITUAL GURU PASSED AWAY, UNEXPECTEDLY, AT 85.

Sai Baba had prophesied that he would live till 96.

His rise from a backward hamlet in Southern India to preside over an empire, whose net worth is estimated at some US$8 billion (Bt253.8 billion), with followers in more than 100 countries, is the stuff of epics.

Even his baiters acknowledged the enormous humanitarian services provided by his organization - encompassing free schooling, free treatment at two state-of-the-art super-speciality hospitals, and an innovative water project.

Professor Anil Kumar, a former Professor of Botany, who translated Sai Baba's speeches for almost four decades and had close access to him, was in Bangkok last week. Here, he addresses the oft-repeated questions of skeptics and critics.

Q: A lot has been said and written over the years about the 'miracles' he performed - producing ash and trinkets, gold chains, rings, and watches, etc. His devotees loved it, critics hated it, skeptics were unconvinced. Scientists and para-

psychologists did studies on them. Some dismissed them as sleight of hand, others were unable to explain them. For someone, who saw them at close proximity, how do you look at it?

A: I'll quote Him. He called it His visiting card. Once you give a visiting card to someone, you don't have to introduce yourself again. He steps into your life as a visitor, sending a visiting card through a miracle in your life. That, which you think is impossible, is made possible through a miracle and makes you believe in something transcendental, extra-sensory. The miracle is a bait to draw a person closer to God. He gives an example: to make a child go to school, what do you do sometimes? Give a chocolate. But, it's the schooling that is important, not the chocolate. Similarly, a miracle happens in your life, so you will turn your mind towards the divine or spiritual life.

Q: But, magicians say even they can perform some of these 'miracles' and you don't need any divine powers...

A: Magicians do it as a profession. But, in Sai Baba's case, miracles are not performed, they happen. The happening of a miracle is different from doing it. One is spiritual, the other is physical.

Q: Can you expand on that?

A: A magician can perform under certain conditions. But, Sai Baba, anytime, anywhere, could materialise something for you. A magician will not be able to do that. He needs special conditions to perform. But, Baba, by His will, could make things happen. Sai Baba's miracles have a higher purpose; a magician is only aiming for attraction with commercial value.

A leading Indian scientist, S Bhagvantham, who was the vice-chancellor of a university and even the director of India's defense research organization, stayed with him and studied the miracles and became totally convinced that miracles happened in Sai Baba's presence, at His will. One Italian doctor, who attended an international meeting of thoracic surgeons in Puttaparthi, said that though his reputation might be at risk, he would like to state that only Sai Baba could run such a sophisticated super-speciality hospital free of charge.

Q: A lot has been said and written about his reported clairvoyance. Apparently, in 1998, he told his inner circle that the world was headed for many natural disasters and that the earth's axis might even shift. We now know that during the Japanese earthquake/tsunami, the earth's axis did shift. Are you aware of any predictions he made, which came true?

A: He said long ago that Muslim nations will go through turmoil and terrorism. We've seen that in Afghanistan and Iraq; He predicted the unification of Germany and long, long ago, He said the Soviet Union will collapse. Then, He also predicted the decline of the US economy and the dotcom bust.

Q: Talking about clairvoyance, he said more than once that he'd live to 96, but actually passed away at 85. How do you explain that?

A: Some Hindu scholars believe that, as per the lunar calendar, He did live to 96. According to the lunar calendar, a year has 324 days. Sai Baba never said He'd live to 96 according to the solar calendar.

Two years ago, He pointed to a spot and told me, "This is going to be My Samadhi [resting place]." When I told Him, "Please don't say that," He said, "Why are you afraid? It's inevitable for anybody. Death is the dress of life."

Q: Since he encouraged everyone to practise their own religion, what kind of role did he envisage for himself?

A: He saw Himself more as a catalyst; as a unifying factor; He wanted synthesis, not antithesis.

Q: He has left an enormous legacy of free schools, educational institutions, free hospitals, social service organisations. His presence obviously helped raise funds all these years. But now, will these institutions be financially sustainable?

A: Right now, we're in a state of shock. But, He has left us with principles to follow and enough money. The interest accrued on the principal amount will be enough for the [Organization's] maintenance. There will be no shortage of funds.

Q: If you had to sum up his message in a few words, what would it be?

A: Love all, serve all; the hands that serve are holier than the lips that pray.

Christmas Eve 2011
Part 1

(Sunday Talk by Prof. Anil Kumar, December 11th, 2011)

Sathya Sai Devotees Celebrate Christmas

On this eve of Christmas, we will have two talks — one this week and one next week. Sathya Sai devotees all over the world celebrate Christmas. So, let us make an attempt to know what Christmas means to us.

Firstly, Christmas is a celebration for all devotees of all religions! That is the unique and wonderful contribution of Bhagawan Sri Sathya Sai Baba to this world. All religions observe Christmas. Yes, this is really an unbelievable phenomenon!

Humanity Has Been Influenced By *Jesus*

Secondly, our Christmas celebration is not merely one of festivity, gaiety, dancing, and dinners. The celebration at Prasanthi Nilayam, and by Sai devotees all over the world, is about the meaning and significance of Christmas. The study of Lord Jesus Christ as an incarnation and ideal man is central to this spiritual celebration. Jesus Christ is a diamond with so many facets to His personality.

One fourth (or even more) of the world is influenced by Him… a baby born in a manger in the little hamlet of Bethlehem. Jesus bore the torch of wisdom and lit the flame, which spread out to a vast humanity. Likewise, the Christian mission is spreading day by day all over the world. *Lakhs* (hundreds of thousands) of people have renounced the world to become Christian nuns and monks. And that is not an easy thing to do!

The Beautiful Churches Of Mexico City

Baba blessed me with an opportunity to visit the great Mexico City. Mexico is full of Catholic churches, all of which are big, beautiful, and wonderful. The moment you step into one of these churches, you feel the spiritual vibrations and atmosphere. You feel the presence of Christ!

The experience has left such an impact upon me that I will happily cherish my visit and memories for several years to come. In one of the churches, I saw a huge raised dais, where at least fifty Catholic priests can sit and offer prayers. Then, there is another church, where prayers are said continually, with the fathers working in shifts, day and night. Also, Pope John Paul visited Mexico City thrice, so there is a statue of him there.

The Huge Statue Of Jesus Christ
At Rio De Janeiro

I also happily recall my visit to Rio de Janeiro in Brazil. I really appreciate and thank God for making this visit possible, to see the huge statue of Jesus Christ on the mountain top there. It is something like our Tirupati temple, where Lord Venkateswara is on the seventh hill.

There is no temple; instead, there is a forty-foot statue of Jesus, with both His arms widely outstretched. "Oh Lord, You are waiting for us!" It is like a grandfather calling you to come close to him. I had the same vibrations there as I had in Shirdi and the feeling was the same as when Bhagawan Baba waits for us on Christmas Day. Unbelievable!

The Inspiring Influence
Of The Christian College

In the past, I was a student of a Christian college (where I also served for twenty-six years). In other words, I spent thirty years of my life in a Christian college in the prime of my youth — not a small thing! If I have, in the least, any missionary spirit of sacrifice, dedication, and commitment, the credit should go to that Christian college, my *Alma Mater*. The speeches of the Father there were wonderful, inspiring, and fantastic.

It Is Important For People
To Enjoy Spiritual Talks

Of late, you might have seen a difference in the churches' presentations by their ministry. I am very fond of watching a lady on television, Joyce Meyer, as she addresses a gathering of at least fifty thousand people. She walks about freely on the dais and makes presentations, using the latest technologies, with huge screens on all sides.

Her talks are not fanatical or dogmatic. No, instead, she speaks about relationships — for instance, those that should exist between parents and children, or between the boss and his subordinates, or among friends. It is religion applied to daily life. That's why she attracts a huge audience. I never miss her sermons!

It is very important for people to enjoy religious talks. Sometimes, we see people with long faces after they have listened to religious or spiritual discourses. That is because, the talks go above our heads and have no application or relevance to our daily life and to our problems. They are not inspirational or motivational. That's why many spiritual meetings are attended by people, who have nothing else to do! But, of late, I find a paradigm shift in the presentation of these Christian missionaries. It is very, very nice!

Sathya Sai Baba, Master Of All Topics Under The Sun

Now, coming to my point, I am sure all of you would agree with me here: **if there is a spiritual Master, who spoke on all topics under the sun, be it to village school children, college students, casual labourers, bank directors, scientists, doctors, or Parliament, it is only Bhagawan Sri Sathya Sai Baba! If there is anyone, who could speak to all classes from all countries and totally convince them of His authority on any subject, it is only Bhagawan Sri Sathya Sai Baba! No one else!**

Sathya Sai Baba, World Teacher

We can all read books and prepare speeches; we can make PowerPoint presentations. But, there is no power in our presentation, nor is there any point to speak of! Yes, we can only do it, because the PowerPoint does the talking and people will look at it, being spared looking upon our face! So, after six months' preparation, you can give a presentation, but nobody will appreciate it.

But, here is Sathya Sai Baba, Who thrilled and excited doctors by His knowledge and wisdom. Famous international doctors quote Him freely in their presentations. Once, a doctor from the United States had prepared his keynote address, but after listening to Swami, he put his keynote address aside. His PowerPoint totally packed up! He spoke instead on points from Swami's inaugural address and said, "I gained knowledge and now know more!" That is Sathya Sai Baba!

When Swami gives interviews to space scientists, astronauts, and cosmonauts, He talks to them about space, the galaxy, and the lunar and solar systems. They all begin to wonder, "Who else can speak of this creation other than the Creator, Bhagawan Sri Sathya Sai Baba Himself?"

Nobody else can speak like that of things unknown. He is wisdom personified; He is knowledge (Truth) on two feet, full of understanding and awareness. His presentations are practical too, having relevance to our daily lives. He enchants, captivates, thrills, and excites all, from a child in primary school to the greatest scholar of our times, by His presentations. For that reason, Sathya Sai Baba is a world teacher.

The Most Popular Man Is Bhagawan Sri Sathya Sai Baba

He is the most popular man in the world. Why is He popular? A few years ago, a magazine conducted a survey on, "Who is the world's most popular man?" Their survey studied all the Godmen and *gurus* (including top film stars!) The most popular Man was Bhagawan Sri Sathya Sai Baba!

No spiritual *guru* was ever this popular. The reason is that other *gurus* speak of do's and don'ts. They speak of hell and heaven. As we are sure to go there some day or other, we are not so interested in knowing about those places! Why advance our trip? Not necessary!

Meanwhile, we don't have any first-hand description of heaven or hell. Nobody has said, "Mr. Anil Kumar, heaven is so nice. You are welcome. Please come!" And nobody has said, "Hell is dangerous, fearful, and frightening, so please avoid it!"

We speak of things we know nothing about and of which there is no first-hand information. However, Baba never speaks of heaven or hell. He never speaks of things that are above our head.

Publicity Of Swami's Miracles Makes Us Egoistical

Then, there is another example — when we speak of things we don't know about. I had not even had my first cup of morning coffee, when I got a phone call. "Mr. Anil Kumar, *vibhuti* (sacred ash) is falling from my picture! Why don't you come and see it?"

I could reply to this person, saying, "Why should I come, when *vibhuti* is falling from the picture at your house? Whether it is a blessing or a manifestation of God's presence at your house, why tell me?"

"It is something like asking me to come to your house at lunch time, to see you eat! Why should I see you eat? It is your lunch and I cannot simply sit and clap as you are

eating. I cannot do that! Similarly, when *vibhuti* is falling at your residence, please enjoy it yourself."

By sharing these things, we may become egoistical, trying to impress people of our devotion. But, are there any degrees for devotion? 'B.A. in Devotion', 'M.A. in Devotion', or perhaps a 'Ph.D in Devotion'?

I am not underestimating or denying these happenings. **All I am saying is don't publicise them, don't publicise! Why? Because we become egoistical due to all that publicity.**

Another person, after seeing that picture on display, has an inner talk with Swami. 'Swami, I have a big picture at home, bigger than that one! Why is there no *vibhuti* on it? What's wrong with You? Swami, are You on a holiday or are You annoyed with me? I have plenty of *vibhuti* for You to use, so I give You one week to have it fall from my picture!'

And a week later, with a little 'help' (perhaps by sticking it on the picture themselves), "Yes, *vibhuti* is falling!" So, this is the situation. By publicising the appearance of *vibhuti*, you are making other people jealous. They then concoct, manipulate, manage, or create their own *vibhuti* on Swami's picture in an unhealthy rivalry, thus making a mockery of a miracle.

So today, we don't know what a miracle is, because everybody boasts about a miracle at their place. I don't deny that it is so — but, we should not market it. We should not indulge in cheap publicity tactics. No!

Silent Spiritual Revolution — The Greatest Miracle Of Swami

Baba's real miracle is the silent, spiritual revolution that He has brought about in contemporary society. Baba is known for this miracle of miracles, the greatest miracle! Many atheists are theists today; many, who had never been to a temple in their lives, have started visiting temples. Many people freely quote from scriptures and even more people think of God. Many non-vegetarians have become vegetarians. We see alcoholics becoming teetotallers and self-centred people starting to lead a life of selfless service.

This kind of spiritual revolution, this silent transformation among millions of people, is done only by Bhagawan Sri Sathya Sai Baba, nobody else! He does not just call people and rub their heads saying, "Now, you are changed!" No, no!

An example of the transformations taking place throughout the world can be seen here, this Christmas. This year, the Christmas decorations were donated by devotees from Croatia and Swami has never even been to Croatia! Until I came to Puttaparthi, I had not ever heard of that country and could not even show it on a world map! Now, today, here are a large number of Croatians, who are in charge of the decorations in Prasanthi Nilayam!

This silent revolution, this silent transformation, this theistic tendency — taking people towards charity, kindness, and consideration — is because of Bhagawan Sri Sathya Sai Baba. That is His greatest and highest contribution.

God Cannot Be Used For Selfish Reasons

And above all else are His Divine messages! Those of us, who are here, don't find time to read them all, because the mind is always engaged, if not the body! Why is the mind engaged? Well, perhaps I go to *bhajans* (devotional singing), not merely to attend, but to see how many are there or not — policing duty! And after the *bhajans*, we spend time gossiping with people. As a result, we are so busy that we have no time to know or read His message.

Those, who are far away, are busy in their own way. They think of Him, when He is necessary to them. When is He necessary? When we fall sick, when we go bankrupt, when children are very disobedient, or when we have a court case! So, He has become an emergency standby!

Serious and urgent cases are admitted to the emergency department of hospitals. Our temples have become casualty wards or emergency centres. But, it should not be like that! God is not need-based, nor is God desire-oriented. And most of all, God cannot be used for selfish reasons.

Swami Engages Us, So Our Lifestyle Becomes Totally Spiritual

Faith in God should be reflected in our daily life, behaviour, and relationships. It should be reflected in our temperament and daily interactions, so that our whole life is spiritualised. Faith should not be incidental and occasional — something like a professional practice or a political platform.

If anyone can spiritualise your life, it is only
Bhagawan Sri Sathya Sai Baba! Nobody else, nobody else!
How? He has created so many education, service, and
spiritual programs. There are study circles for you to attend
and opportunities for all types of service every week. He
engages you in such a way that your lifestyle becomes totally
spiritualised.

Let Us Speak About His Message

I am interested in speaking about the message of Baba.
I am not interested in hearing you say, "Swami appeared in
my dream. He wanted me to meet you today!"

Then, I have to reply, "Swami appeared in my dream
to tell me to avoid you today!"

Dreams and counter-dreams! Why not? You cannot say
that Swami appeared in your dream and wanted me to give
you Rs.1 *lakh* (one hundred thousand Indian rupees). Then,
I would say that He appeared in my dream to collect Rs.10
lakhs from you, because I, too, can dream! Why not? If life is
not a merry-land, let it be a dream-land, at least! But, it is
not like that.

**If at all we have to speak of Baba in public, if we
have to speak about Him to our neighbours, friends, or
newcomers, let us speak about His message and His
philosophy. We may still be interested in these individual
experiences, but let us realise the message behind them.**

Miracles Have A Message Behind Them

Miracles don't just happen without a reason; they also
carry a message. For example, Jesus restored sight to blind

people and He brought dead people back to life. The message there is the expression of Divinity: there is nothing impossible for the Divine! That is the message behind it.

Miracles should not make us proud or egoistic. A miracle should make us more humble and service-oriented. We should become more knowledgeable and aware. Miracles should make us more kind, bringing us closer to other devotees. In other words, we function with more constant integrated awareness.

Presentations Should Reflect Contemporary Expectations

You may take me to be a crazy man, I don't mind! I want to be crazier! I am afraid we have not realised or understood contemporary society. We do not understand what people expect from us and, in particular, their spiritual needs.

Our presentations should run parallel to contemporary expectations. If I speak of *Atma* (Self), *Paramatma* (universal soul), and *Parabrahman* (universal Absolute) to my students, they are helplessly lost! What to do? Education is free and their marks are in my hands. So, there is no protest from them.

They have also learned another technique — to sleep with their eyes open! Yes! The 'eye-tech' is more than the *samadhi* state (a deep state of meditative absorption) of *rishis* (sages). *Rishis* close their eyes and attain *samadhi*. But, some of our devotees and most of our students are more than *rishis*, because they can sleep with their eyes opened! It is their version of *nirvikalpa samadhi* (oneness with God in deep meditation)!

So, what do students need to hear? They should hear about His teachings and message, and what He expects of them. The youth of this country need to know about Sai ideals, goals, and way of life. I should speak on those topics, not on *Brahman, Paramatma,* and so on. We shouldn't do that!

Religion Is To Enjoy Life

Both children and adults need to experience religion as enjoying life by being natural and spontaneous. Religion is there in order to make everybody happy. It should create laughter, releasing tension and stress, not add extra doses of burden! We are already medicated by life; so, why take an extra microgram of gloom? That is not necessary! Sathya Sai Baba, in His lifetime, was very, very successful in making life really enjoyable.

Baba Takes Us Beyond Time And Space

While in Prasanthi Nilayam, you lose track of what day it is and what time it is. You ask, "Is it Sunday or Monday? What time is it — 3 o' clock or 4 o' clock?" "6 o' clock!"

"Six? I thought it was 4'o clock!"

So, Baba was very successful in taking us beyond time and space. Nobody else could do that! Try waiting anywhere else, at a bus stand or a railway station. Easily you can become very irritated, because you have to wait for four hours! But here, time flows easily. That is the charisma and magnetism of Bhagawan Sri Sathya Sai Baba. Here, we outgrow the limitations of day, date, and time. We are never bored, because He always engages our attention throughout the day in every way.

Happiness Is An Interval
Between Two Pains

At every crucial point in our lives, we get something from Him. When we suffer from a heavy loss, we immediately get Swami's message from within: "Don't worry! Everything is like a passing cloud; no cloud is permanent. Happiness is an interval between two pains."

You don't need any *upadesa* (spiritual instructions), nor do you have to get up at 4 o'clock to do some special penance. When you have a problem, you immediately get an answer from within! That is Bhagawan Sri Sathya Sai Baba.

'Zero' Has No Value Without '1' Beside It

When you feel proud of your achievements, you get a message from within immediately: "'Zero' has no value without a '1' beside it. If that '1' has value, any number of zeroes will have value. '1' is the action hero, God. You are all zeroes, so don't feel proud of yourselves."

This message brings you back down to Earth. It is landing time — crash landing time!

Religion Is A Journey From 'I' To 'We'

Whenever you feel the 'I' taking over like, "This is *my* group, this is *my* plot of land, etc.," we hear the message from within, "Boy, are you a fool or what? Did I not tell you that religion is a journey from 'I' to 'We'? Instead of 'my' place, you should have the feeling of 'we', the community. 'We' is religion!"

An eighty-six year old man once told me, "This place (location in the hall) is allotted to me; so, I sit here every day!"

I said, "Very good, sir. But, before you started coming here, it was allotted to somebody else. And after you leave, many other people will sit here." So, we have come here to find a place in the heart of Sai, not a physical position on various slabs or stones.

Seek Out Your Own Faults And Others' Merits

Another message will come, when we criticise others. Perhaps, we find fault with their devotional practice: "Do you attend *nagarsankirtan* (singing of sacred songs at dawn)?"

"No, sir."

"You don't?"

"No, so what?"

"Well, I attend!"

"Go ahead and attend! I didn't ask you to go or not go. Why are you bothered about my attendance?"

When we criticise others, the message from within is, "Seek out your own faults and others' merits."

That is the call from Bhagawan! How wonderful and practical are His teachings! Each one is a diamond, useful for the problem or situation in that moment. That is why Bhagawan Sri Sathya Sai Baba could attract the whole world.

Bhagawan Is The Champion For Unity Of All Religions And Faiths

The teachings of Jesus also contained certain principles very similar to the messages of Bhagawan Sri Sathya Sai Baba. I am always interested in the comparative study of faiths and congregational worship, and the process of synthesis. Bhagawan is the only Champion, Who stood for the unity of all religions and faiths. No one else was like that, take it from me!

Imitation Is Human, Creation Is Divine

One fellow said, "Swami, I want to change my name!"

Baba replied, "Oh, I see! What name do you want?"

"Sathya Sai!"

"Don't change your name! Be Sai!"

What's in a name? You be Sai, not the name of Sai! The name is not that important.

One person said, "I wear ochre robes, the same as Swami!" Or someone else wears a red gown and has hair similar to that of Sai. But, life is not a dress-up drama. Wearing those clothes or having His hair, you still cannot be Sathya Sai Baba. Impossible!

I have a friend from a neighbouring district, who comes here often. He has long hair parted in the centre like that of Abdul Kalam (a former President of India). I said to him,

"You are not Abdul Kalam, you are *gulam* (meaning, a 'servant')!" Impossible!

Appearances are not deceptive. There is another person, who is very lean and dresses like Mahatma Gandhi. He is "white Gandhi" with white paint all over!

People saw him and stared. "Anil Kumar, Gandhi, Gandhi!"

I said, "Gandhi never stood like that at a crossroads, spreading his towel to collect coins. He is not Mahatma Gandhi. He is BG — Beggar Gandhi!"

By imitating, we don't get anywhere. When I want to imitate you, immediately Swami tells me from within: "Imitation is human, creation is Divine!"

These thoughts come automatically on the screen of our mind. So, whenever there is some 'wrong turn' in our behaviour, we get a message from within.

Somebody asked, "What if I wear the same dress as Swami, but in this colour? How would I look?"

Swami, known for His humour, said, "Does wearing the dress of a woman make you a woman?"

Impossible! It is all only dramatisation. There is nothing great about these appearances, clothes, or make-up. No! It's only our nature, spontaneity, natural quality, and commitment that matter.

"Blessed Are Those With A Pure Heart, For They Shall See God"

There are certain very famous quotes from the *Holy Bible*. The *Holy Bible* says, "Blessed are the poor. Blessed are the pure in heart, for they shall see God!"

How am I to know that I have a pure heart? Many people (themselves sufficiently impure) speak of a pure heart. A pure heart cannot see an impure heart.

A Pure Heart Is Desireless

A pure heart is desireless. A pure heart is one of surrender: "Oh God, I accept. Thy will be done on Earth as it is in heaven. Let Your will prevail. I have no option, preference, or choice. You decide and guide my life the way You want. I allow all."

This is surrender! So, the quality of a pure heart is desirelessness, with a spirit of acceptance or surrender to God's will. A pure heart is more than a heart that beats. It is something much more than that!

A Pure Heart Prays
For The Welfare Of The Whole World

A pure heart is one that prays for the welfare of the whole world:

Lokah Samastah Sukhino Bhavantu,
Sarve Janah Sukhino Bhavantu!

Let all the worlds be happy.
Let all people be happy!

An impure heart is one that prays, 'Let only me be happy; let only me be rich.' That is a highly polluted, dirty, useless heart! It should stop functioning for the betterment of society. It is a useless heart! A pure heart is one that prays for the world. That's what Baba says!

A Pure Heart Wishes To Help People

A pure heart wishes to help people. One way of helping is to see that your words do not make them feel unhappy. Don't bore them with worldly talk or self-glorification. It is a help, if you can make them happy by what you say.

We think to help means cleaning the roads or temples.

Once, a *seva dal* convener (service volunteer organiser) brought me a form with details, accounting for the activity and the number of people benefited by it: 'Eye Camp — 50 people benefited', 'Polio Camp — 150 benefited', '*Narayana Seva* (feeding poor people) — 500 people benefited', 'Cremation Ground cleaned'.

I asked, "How many are benefited by cleaning a cemetery?"

It's not this! To make another person happy (or not to make others unhappy) is the greatest service. **So, let's not go by the numbers of people, who receive *seva*, or by the numbers of different activities. Let's go by the spirit behind it!**

A Pure Heart Will Bring A Glow To Our Face

Baba says, "A pure heart will bring a glow to your face." Such a face will have the sunshine of joy, a glow or kind of radiance. It has a magnetic attraction!

When the heart is impure, people avoid us. Some people ask me, "Why don't they talk to me?"

I say, "They don't talk to you, because of how you talk to them. You need to change and stop blaming people!"

Therefore, an indication of a pure heart is the joyful glow on our face, because we spread the sunshine of joy.

"Blessed are those with a pure heart, for they shall see God!" That's what the *Holy Bible* says.

"Oh God, Lead Me To Thy Self!"

What should be our prayer? It should not be any of these: "Swami, that land seems valuable; let me have some of it." "I want a promotion, so help me make the boss pleased with me." "I pray for at least five houses in Bombay or else to buy Connaught Place in Delhi!"

No, let's not ask for money or positions. What should be our prayer? The *Holy Bible* says, "Oh God, lead me to Thy Self!"

The meaning is very simple: you have two paths before you. One leads to the world or creation, while the other leads to the Creator! Are you going to choose the creation or the Creator? Would you rather have some gold jewels or the gold mine? The gold mine is the Creator, while the gold jewels constitute the creation.

Our prayer should, therefore, not be for worldly, sensual, momentary pleasures, but instead for truth: **"Oh God, lead me to Thy Self and Your contemplation! Lead me to Your service! Lead me to that paradise, to that state of singing Your glory continuously!"**

Satatam Yoginah
Sarvada Sarva Kaleshu Sarvatra Hari Chintanam

Everywhere, all the time, every moment, contemplate and sing the glory of God!

"Lead me to Thy Self!" That should be our prayer!

Pray To God Within

How should I pray to God? Shall I announce to you, "Tomorrow, at 7 o'clock, I am going to pray"?

"I see, so you won't pray before then and you have not prayed over the past days, either!" Nonsense!

The *Holy Bible* says (and Baba refers to this verse): "When you pray, close the door and pray to your Father, Who sees what is done in secret."

Do Acts Of Charity Without Publicity

Somebody said, "I constructed that free hostel, do you know?"

"Oh, I see!"

"That hostel bears my name!"

"Oh, good!"

But, when this man went to heaven, those in heaven said, "Sorry, you are out! Go to hell!"

"Why are you transferring me? Why?"

"We brought you here, because you constructed the hostel. But, you named the hostel after yourself, so that people will recognise you. You named your acts of charity after yourself for publicity! So therefore, you have no place in heaven. You are not worthy to be here."

Swami Gives Selflessly

Do you know how Baba helps people? I know, because Swami once asked me to write a cheque for ten *lakhs*! I was stuck, counting all the zeroes.

He asked, "What kind of a professor are you? Don't you know how many zeros are in ten *lakhs*?"

I was not upset with Swami's remark. I was bothered about the others in the interview room. They, too, might ask me, "What kind of a teacher are you?!"

I said, "Swami, I am just a teacher. I have never ever seen ten *lakhs*! I have never given cheques for ten *lakh rupees*; my cheques are only for hundreds! So, how am I to know the number of zeroes in ten *lakhs*? It takes time to work it out!"

Then, He laughed and said, "What a ruckus! Come on, put down so many *(He told me how many)* zeroes."

The point is that the cheque was to be given to a boy seeking admission into a medical college, and Sai quietly put it into his pocket! You and I would not do so silently. If we offer someone a cup of coffee today, we expect regular thanks from him, until he leaves this planet! Baba has no such expectations at all! His help is freely given.

Another example: some poor villagers came here.

"Swami . . ."

"What?"

"We are constructing a temple, but it has only come to this level."

"Is everybody participating?"

"Yes Swami, all are participating."

"What is the rough estimate in *lakhs* to finish the building?"

"Swami, about 20 *lakhs*."

"*Arre* boy, come here!" And He immediately gave them a cheque.

Nobody knows! **God gives silently, whereas man wants to do it publicly. God does many deeds selflessly, but man does a few and immediately expects name and fame. God does it as duty, while man does it as a favour. That is the difference! That's why we are not able to experience God in spite of our many donations and acts of charity.**

Therefore, "Close the door and pray." That's the spirit behind those words.

Endurance Helps Us Grow
In The Glory Of God

All of us are bothered by small disturbances. Simple things disturb us. When I don't find my paper on the table, I become very disturbed. I have a number of other papers I can use, but I keep searching, because this lost paper is more important than the other papers. We become disturbed when we don't find a spoon, even though there are ten other spoons!

If just one person doesn't greet me with, "Sai Ram," I think, "Why didn't he say 'Sai Ram?' Has anyone said anything against me to that man? Is he saying something scandalous about me to others? Is he trying to usurp my position?"

But, the explanation could be that he has health problems, due to high blood pressure and blood sugar levels. So, how can he say, "Sai Ram," when he is ready to meet Sai Ram, the Lord (implying, ready to leave this planet)?

We need not be so easily disturbed like that! The *Bible* says, "To bear and endure is ever a mark of him, who would grow in the glory of God." To bear and endure — that's what *saburi* (patience and perseverance) means! That is *shraddha* (faith).

We should be able to bear and endure in order to grow in the glory of God. Therefore, the quality of endurance to bear all the problems of life and all negative forces will help us grow in the glory of God.

Jesus First, Others Next, You Last

The *Bible* clearly states, "Love for God should be your first priority." That's what Baba always says: 'Jesus' first, 'others' next, and 'you' last — JOY!

You get joy, when you give preference to others. Therefore, first is God, others are next, and you are last. So, when you put Baba first, others next, and yourself last, that is true spiritual life. Who else but Baba could give an interpretation of that kind?

Paradise Is Gained When 'I'-ness Is Given Up

Man has gone into the fathomless depths of the ocean and climbed the mountain peaks. He has made all kinds of flights, with jet fighters or bombers that go at terrific speeds! Ask any pilot, "Oh, you flew up high and all around the world! So, where is paradise?"

He will say, "I don't know where paradise is! You should be in a mental hospital!"

So, where is paradise? Baba clearly states: **"Paradise is where and when you give up your 'I'-ness. The moment you give up your 'I'-ness, God rewards, and paradise is gained! That is the very heaven,"** Baba says.

Love And Longing For God
Are The Best Of All Things

"What is the most noble and pure thing we can do? What is the best of all, the most blessed?" Perhaps, it is going on a pilgrimage, or fasting, or observing vigil throughout the night? No!

The *Bible* answers this question: "Love and longing for God are the purest, noblest, and best of all things!" What is love? What is longing? I may love, but not be longing for . . . or I may long for, but not love.

Here is a simple explanation. When I am waiting for my boss, I am longing for him to come; but I don't have any love for him! You may love your relatives, but you don't long for their visit, because cooking for them is extra work! So, there may be love without longing, or there may be longing without love.

But, love and longing for God come together. "The purest, noblest, and best of all things are loving and longing for God." So says the *Holy Bible*.

Christ Represents The Ananda Principle

Baba is unique and special in every respect. What does He say about Christ? He doesn't speak of Christ as a personality or as a human being. He doesn't refer to Christ as a normal man. No!

Baba gives the meaning of Jesus Christ in His own way. There is no parallel to it! He says, "Christ represents the *ananda* principle — the blissful state." This is not the state of happiness or joyfulness that we experience at the physical and worldly level. It is a blissful, non-dual spiritual experience.

I said, "Swami, nobody else has given that meaning!"

You know His reply? "Who knows about these things? Who can tell you? There is no chance for you to know from anybody else, because no one else knows!"

So, only Swami has given us the implication of Jesus Christ's name!

Imitation Of Christ

"Swami, what shall we do, now that You have told us Christ represents *ananda,* the blissful state?" How does this help us?

Our duty now is to meditate on Him and on His love. This will help us meditate on Bhagawan Sri Sathya Sai Baba, to love Him more and more! This is what is meant by the 'imitation of Christ'.

Christmas Eve 2011
Part II

(Sunday Talk by Prof. Anil Kumar, December 18th, 2011)

Jesus' Light Of Love
Exceeds That Of A Shining Star

Usually, during Christmas celebrations, we find that many Christians put a big star on top of their residences and churches. A special star was seen at the time of the birth of Jesus Christ. There are different interpretations of that event.

What did Baba say about the star appearing at the time of the birth of Jesus? Baba said the star shines, but the brilliance, radiance, and glory of Jesus were much greater than the star. The star is just material, a physical body. But, the life and light of Jesus is one of love and that naturally exceeds the light of any star.

Jesus Symbolises The Non-dual Blissful State

Swami spoke of Jesus Christ as ideal in the sense that Jesus had no attachment to the self at all! If we go through His life, we see Jesus spending time at different places — seven years at one place, twelve years at another. He was in deep penance at one place, but wandered in the woods at another. He was not attached to any group or place. He experienced no pain or sorrow at any moment of time. So, Jesus symbolises the non-dual experience, the experience of a blissful state! That's how Swami represents Him.

Jesus Stands For Brotherhood And Love

Bhagawan always refers to Jesus Christ as the One, Who had a heart that responded to the anguish, grief, and suffering of the poor. He responded to every cry for peace and brotherhood. Jesus taught about brotherhood and love and responded to the poor, suffering, and needy people. Therefore, Christmas celebrations call for every one of us to respond to the needs of such people, giving them our support and help.

The Mission Of Baba
Is The Same As That Of Jesus Christ

Bhagawan also said that Jesus spent all His life preaching the principle of love. He added that in this most recent *Avatar's* incarnation, He did the same. Jesus preached love throughout His lifetime and that is what this *Avatar* has done also. This establishes a parallel between the two *Avatars*, between two saintly, noble, super-human, and transcendental Divinities, Who both worked till their last breath to spread love, friendship, and brotherhood.

Christ, Isa, And Baba Are One

We love Baba for another reason as well: He brought to our attention certain things that we were not familiar with. Even though I spent three decades in a Christian college, I had not heard certain things that Baba said.

What did He say? In Tibetan scripts, it is clearly written that Jesus was in Tibet and was addressed there as Isa! So, Isa was Jesus!

Swami expressed it this way: "Isa — repeat that word — Isa, Isa, Isa… Sai, Sai, Sai! That is this Sai!" Further, He added, "Isa, Eesha, Sai, and Eswara — all mean the same! Isa, Sai, Eesha, Sarvesha, and Saishwara are all the same."

He added further, "It was Jesus, Who addressed His Father in heaven as 'Aba, Aba, Aba'!" *Aba* means 'Father'! Repeat that word: *Abababababa…* It is Baba!"

In other words, Jesus was trying to tell us that Baba is the second coming of Christ! Baba is the cosmic Christ and His mission is the same as the mission of Jesus Christ! This is very clear. I had not heard any of this, until Baba said it.

All Are One, So Be Alike To Everyone

Swami's interpretation is quite novel. It may not be new to any of you. Yet, it is absolutely necessary to remind ourselves time and again that it is an original interpretation, unique in His style!

Swami also speaks of the Last Supper. What did Jesus do then? He washed and wiped the feet of His disciples and dined with them. At the dining table, Jesus said, "The bread you are eating now is My flesh and the wine you are drinking now is My blood."

"The wine is My blood and the bread is My flesh!" On its face value, how can bread be His flesh? How can wine be His blood? Having heard this, can the disciples still partake of it? Do they dare drink the wine (blood) of their *guru*? No!

Swami explains the meaning of this as follows: "Anyone, any person, any individual with flesh and blood should be respected, loved, and cared for with all concern.

The love, adoration, and worship you have towards Me should be extended to every individual with flesh and blood. All are one, My dear son. Be alike to everyone!"

Then, He added, "*Sarva Deva Namaskaram Kesavam Pradi Gacchati*," which means, "Whenever you salute, do *namaskara*, or respect anyone, you are respecting God. It is equal to worshipping God. It is the same as adoration of God."

That's also what Jesus said! If we care to go deeper into the subject, we find many parallels and many similarities between the two Divine incarnations.

Christmas Is Everyone's Birthday

We all know that Christmas is a global celebration of the birth of Jesus Christ. We are grateful that this wonderful event has taken place on this Earth planet. We are really happy for the gift of the life of Jesus Christ, a gift to all humanity.

What did Baba say about this? Beautifully, Swami said that Christmas is not merely about the birth of Jesus Christ. "It is everyone's birthday!" He said.

How is that possible? How can the birth of Jesus be equated with my birthday?

Baba said, "You celebrate this event, because you are very lucky to have been born as a human being! You celebrate the birth of a human being. Had you been born as a bird, or a beast, or a tree, you would not have experienced Jesus. You would not have had an occasion to listen to His message or participate in His mission. Since you are born as a human being, you have every chance of enjoying Him and you have every chance of being with Him. You are given a chance to imitate Jesus Christ." So, Christmas is a celebration of the birth of every one of us as human beings, having the opportunity to recognise Jesus' Divine personality.

Christ As The Messenger Of God

Swami takes us to new heights of spiritual awareness. His information is first-hand information, because these are the words from the cosmic Christ, the second coming of Christ Himself! Even many of my Christian brethren, whom I have known intimately for years, do not know this. Until Swami's remarks, all that has been talked about, written about, and read about Jesus is second-hand information.

Baba talking to us is like Jesus talking to us! It is necessary that we listen to God. It is necessary that we hear His message. What is it that He wants to teach us? We need to be patient, inquisitive, and have the spirit of inquiry while listening to His talks with rapt attention. We can lose ourselves in ecstasy while listening to His melodious voice, His brilliant presentations and orations, as He conveys His message. So, let us continue to listen.

So, as a listener, first we look at Jesus as the 'Messenger of God'. The Lord's message was conveyed to us by His only begotten Son, Jesus Christ. Jesus, the only Son of God, conveyed the message of the Lord or Jehovah. As He conveyed the Lord's message, Jesus played the role of 'Messenger of God'.

"You Are Also A Messenger Of God"

Baba adds one more thought: "You are also a messenger of God." I think everyone of us present must have felt the shock of surprise, excitement, and novelty at the uniqueness of Baba's presentations and interpretations. It is not enough to say, "Christ is the Messenger of God." Swami wants every one of us to be a messenger of God, too!

So, how can you be a messenger of God? When you are devoted to God, dedicating your life to Him, and committing to His gospel or teachings, then naturally you are all a messenger of God. That's the reason Jesus set an example for all of us, showing us the first step of spiritual evolution, the first level of awareness. The consciousness should be awakened. So, the awakening of the consciousness is that first step.

Christ As The Son Of God

The next step is to develop as much love towards God as Jesus had for God, Whom He called His Father. As the only begotten Son, He loved His Father. The unconditional love that Jesus felt towards His Father marks the second stage of His evolution. During the first stage, Jesus was disseminating, spreading, and preaching the message of His Father in His capacity as a messenger of God.

In spreading the message of love, Jesus became very popular. He loved God and nothing else. All the rest was secondary! He didn't mind worldly pain or suffering, scandal or gossip, or rumours spread against Him. He continued to love even His enemies. He forgave those, who harmed Him, forgetting all their sins. Jesus loved everybody. Why? To Him, everyone was seen as a reflection of God, the Father. When everyone was viewed as the image of God, it was quite possible for Him to love all and serve all.

Thus, Jesus had ascended to the advanced stage of unconditional love, seeing God in everyone. That is the state called 'Son of God'. This 'Messenger of God' had become the 'Son of God' by seeing God's reflection in everyone. This was the second stage of spiritual evolution for Jesus and it should be the second stage for us also, on our spiritual path.

Everyone Is A Reflection Of God

It is not enough to just speak of loving God. It is more important to love Him more than anything else, to love Him unconditionally. And it is most essential that we see Him in everyone that we meet.

Isha Vasyam Idam Sarvam,
Yatkimcha Jagatyam Jagat
Tena Tyaktenabhunjitha Ma Gridhah Kasya Swid Dhanam.

There are two phrases that describe this second step, what is called the 'Son of God': *Vasudeva Sarvam,* meaning 'everyone is the reflection of God', and *Eswara Sarva Bhootanam,* which means 'He is present in all beings'.

Every one of us has an equal claim. Yes! I am the son of God. You are also the son of God.

Ekovasi Sarva Bhuta Antaratma
Mamai vamso Jeeva Loke
Jeeva Bhuta Sanatanah!

'Mamai Vamso' means that you are a spark of the Divine. Yes, He accepts you. We are in Him and He is within us.

Therefore, this kind of closeness, this sort of intimacy, this intense, infinite, and unconditional love for God and others are qualities, which are naturally apparent in the second stage of the awakening of consciousness, which is called the 'Son of God'. Thus, the 'Messenger of God' evolved into being the 'Son of God'.

"I And My Father In Heaven Are One"

Then, there is the third state of consciousness, the climax. What is this state? It is the state, in which the love is so intense that nothing appears separate from Him. No one appears separate from God. The devotee finds unity in diversity, seeing God in everyone. And the devotee realises that there is no separation from Him, Who is omniscient, omnipresent, and omnipotent. There is nothing in this world that is separate from God. "I am not separate from my God, nor is He separate from me. I am God." Yes! The third state then is the final state of bliss, the climax of the awakening of consciousness. At this stage, the devotee declares, "I and My Father in heaven are one!"

Dualtiy, Qualified Non-duality, And Non-duality

Swami describes this in another way. The first state, the 'Messenger of God' phase, is the state of duality or *Dvaita*. The second state, the 'Son of God' phase, is the state of qualified non-duality. And the third state, the 'I and my

Father are One' phase, is the state of total identity with Him, the state of non-duality, *Advaita*.

In other words, the devotee evolves from *Dvaita* to *Visishtadvaita* and then, from *Visishtadvaita* to *Advaita*; from duality to qualified non-duality and then, to non-duality. Therefore, there are three levels of consciousness: 'Messenger of God', 'Son of God', and 'I and My Father in heaven are One'.

Baba Finds Essential Unity At Every Stage

Notice that the approach in Bhagawan's Divine discourses is one of synthesis! His approach does not condemn any other school of philosophy. It does not develop any separate school either. He finds the essential unity at every stage, thus helping us understand that it's all one and the same.

He has said, "*Eko Ham Bahusyam*," which means, "I am only One in different forms." He drives that point home time and again.

Why Has Jesus Come In Human Form?

Why should Jesus be in a human form? Why not in the form of an angel? Why not in any other form? Why should He be an ordinary human being? Why?

There have been many occasions, when Swami directly said, "I am so-and-so!" (i.e. "I am Jesus.") There were many other occasions, when He conveyed Who He was indirectly.

Why had Jesus come in human form? Swami answers: "To talk to you, to speak to you, to give you the joy of His proximity, so that all could enjoy nearness and dearness with the Lord!"

Is not the same true with Swami as well? Had He been in a different form, we would not have dared to approach Him. If He had four hands, or four heads, would we not be afraid to see Him? No, we wouldn't want to see such a figure with four heads, ten heads, and twenty-five feet. We wouldn't want it, because we cannot bear that! Better not! Because then, He might start appearing that way even in our sleep!

We want Swami to be one among us, to be available to us. We want to talk to Him and have Him talk to us. Similarly, Jesus was the only begotten Son of God, Who appeared in a human form, so that we could have access to Him and He could speak to us.

All Are A Spark Of The Divine

However, neither Swami, nor Jesus was interested in merely establishing contact and talking with us. There was a greater purpose behind it, which was to make our lives spiritual, to elevate the standard of our spiritual lives, and to help all of us turn Godward.

We have each been leading the life of a human, until now. Hereafter, let's try to tread the Divine path. We have been considering ourselves to be too little, too tiny, as negligible as a particle in the dust. But, Jesus said, "You are the son of God! You are not ordinary!"

Srunvantu Viswe Amritasya Putrah

This means that you are the son of eternity, you are the son of immortality! You are the spark of the Divine! Why do you consider yourself to be a speck of dust? No, no! Do not entertain the thought that you are tiny or negligible. These are words said out of ignorance.

For example, a man may have plenty of money in the bank, but not know it. He could be begging in the streets, because he does not know that there are hundreds of thousands of *rupees* in his account in the bank. He doesn't know — that's all! Similarly, we may each consider ourselves to be a little speck. No! Such thoughts show ignorance! They do not speak of humility. They merely speak of ignorance.

What more do you want than to be the son of God? What more do you want than to be the spark of God? What more do you expect than to be part of God? What more is there than being God? What else is there? There is nothing else! That's what both Bhagawan and Jesus say.

Accept Responsibility For Your Sins

Jesus was a reformer. What does that mean? He did not allow spiritual practices and rituals to be followed in a traditional, meaningless style. Rather, He wanted the observance of rituals and practices to be conducted with full awareness and understanding, not simply with rote rituals. No, not art for art's sake, nor ritual for ritual's sake. Both need heart! Therefore, we should celebrate any festival and observe any ritual with this full awareness.

In fact, Jesus condemned temples being transformed into street bazaars. At that time, if you paid some money, your sins were supposedly forgiven and a berth granted to you in heaven! Temples had not only become commercial, like a bazaar, but some of them had become slaughter houses, even killing animals!

At that time, Jesus stepped into the temples and said, "Nothing doing! Stop it! A priest on the pavement cannot forgive your sins on payment. No! You have to repent for your sins. You have to repent!"

Sathya Sai Baba said, "You should even punish yourself!" Sins are forgiven not because of payment, but because of total repentance. Accept responsibility for your own sins before the Cross: accept, regret, and repent.

"Thy sins are forgiven! Sin no more!" said the Lord.

Similarly, Baba says, "The only atonement for our sins is to admit them and repent."

Proper Worship Includes Service To Man

Jesus, the reformer, also said that the Sabbath day is not simply a holiday. It is a holy day. In those days, in the name of properly observing the Sabbath day, people would not serve the poor and needy on the Sabbath. Jesus asked them to stop this and to help the poor by feeding them, quenching their thirst, and attending to their needs even on the Sabbath day, because service to man is service to God. So, He brought about a spiritual revolution, but it was not accepted at that time.

The priests turned against Him, leading a mass campaign against Him. Unfortunately, their efforts led to a great shame on humanity — the crucifixion of Jesus Christ.

That Christ was crucified on the Cross shows the utter ignorance of man, his total foolishness. It is a shameful blot in the history of mankind!

Jesus was put on a cross, because He fought against rigid, meaningless tradition and He fought against the lifestyle of the priesthood. He was opposed to priests collecting money and temples becoming centres of fun and frolic.

Every Thought Is An Offering, Every Act A Yagna

What did Bhagawan say about this kind of thing? He spoke about proper worship, when he spoke about *yagna*. **He said, "*Yagna* is not a ritual. It is not a traditional value. It is not a routine affair. No! Every act is *yagna*. Every thought is an offering to that *yagna* and the place of *yagna* is your mind. The sacrificial fire is your mind. Your every thought must be an offering and every act a *yagna*."**

What a wonderful interpretation! It can even apply in this age of computers! Any man of space sciences and any man of computer sciences will have to accept the logical, rational, scientific approach of Bhagawan Sri Sathya Sai Baba! Such an interpretation is really great!

Baba's Message Is Universal

Many people ask me, "Why did you go to Baba? What is it that attracts you?"

I tell them, "His message! His message attracts me, because that message is universal. His message is applicable to every individual the world over — every age group, profession, nation, and nationality." So, the universality, the catholicity, and the applicability in practical life of His teachings are the main features that you find highlighted in Bhagawan's Divine discourses.

What Is A True Christmas Celebration?

Having explained the Divine mission of Jesus, describing what Christ stands for and how the evolution of Jesus created a spiritual evolution from dualism to non-dualism, Swami tells us what Christmas should mean to every one of us.

What is a true Christmas celebration? What are we supposed to do? First, during this time we should resolve to serve the poor and the needy. Second, we should let Christmas help us cultivate certain values like tolerance, forbearance, charity, and magnanimity. Let us cultivate these noble qualities this Christmas eve. The Lord calls for patience and Jesus calls for personal sacrifice.

On Love

Jesus is another name for love. Why does the Lord love us so much? Why does He shower love on all of us? The answer is simple!

Jesus said, "I love you, because My Father loves Me! My God loves Me, therefore I love you!"

This is an indirect message to all of us that we should love everyone. "Love thy neighbour as thyself!" That's what is conveyed in the dictum, "Love all, serve all."

Let us love everybody, because Swami loves us. My love towards you is a reflection of Baba's love towards me. If I don't love you, it only means that I have not tasted a drop of Bhagawan Sri Sathya Sai Baba's love.

Cultivate The Quality Of Tolerance

Swami also said, "On this day, cultivate the quality of tolerance. Be tolerant to everybody."

But, we are not! Why? We are annoyed, when someone differs from us. We get disturbed, when someone attacks us. However, Jesus was tolerant, the very personification of tolerance. He tolerated all that was said against Him. He tolerated all that was done against Him. We have to cultivate that quality.

Follow His Message

Bhagawan also says, "The Christmas celebration is not an occasion of festivity, gaiety, pomp, and show. Instead, adhere to and follow Jesus' teachings, especially in our observance of Christmas."

Lord Jesus said, "Follow Me!" And Bhagawan Sri Sathya Sai Baba says, "Follow the Master!"

This does not mean running after His car wherever He goes! It's not that! It means follow His teachings.

"My Life is My Message," He says. Following His message is truly following Him, not just following Him in a hired car. The lifeless car has followed, but we have not!

Let us celebrate Christmas by following His teachings in our day-to-day life, as Baba has asked us to do.

Dance In Bliss

Swami once said, in a sarcastic way, that at midnight on Christmas day, people begin to dance hysterically! They dance while intoxicated! They dance into forgetfulness! Is that what He wants? No! That kind of dancing is physical, cheap, and sensual.

What kind of dance does Baba want us to do? He wants us to dance in bliss! You dance in bliss like Lord Siva danced, when He danced the *Siva Tandava*. Or dance like Lord Krishna did, when He danced in the *Rasa Leela*. But, the dance of Krishna and the dance of Siva are not the dances that you witness on Christmas. I have seen quite a number of dances, which are nice to look at, but very difficult to imitate. That is not the kind of dance Baba expects us to do on Christmas Eve.

Let us dance in bliss; let us dance in non-dual bliss. Sri Ramakrishna Paramahamsa danced in bliss and He did not even know that He was dancing! Lord Chaitanya danced, but he also did not know he was dancing.

If you know that you are dancing, you are a dancer. Don't be a dancer. Be the dance, not a dunce. So, be the dance, but not a dancer. Be lost in the process of dancing. The dance remains, while the dancer is lost.

"I and My Father in Heaven are one!" That is *Rasa Leela*! That is *Siva Tandava*! That is the celestial dance! So, dance is religion. But, unfortunately, we think being stiff-necked is religion. No! Perhaps, you are stiff-necked, because of neck pain. Perhaps, you are stiff-necked, because of spondylitis. No!

Sacred dance is religion, creating a state of transcendental forgetfulness. Then, the dance happens! You don't decide to dance — it just happens! Yes, Swami wants us to dance in bliss, but not in the ordinary way we see everywhere.

A Pure Heart Is The Temple Of God

Bhagawan also says, "On this day of Christmas, let's make our hearts pure with holy thoughts, with feelings that are beneficial to the whole community, with helpful, profitable feelings towards your brethren! A pure heart is the temple of God!"

That's what is also said in the *Gita: "Iswara Hrdaye Arjuna Tishtati,"* which means, "God installs Himself in the altar of a pure heart."

So, this Christmas, let us each have a pure heart with good will toward all, ill will toward none, and where all our thoughts are beneficial and profitable for the entire community.

Dont Criticise, Blame, Or Judge Others

On this Christmas day, let us resolve not to criticise anybody from now on, as Baba has exhorted us to do.

Too often, we find happiness in criticising others and are very happy blaming others. If at all I am to blame anyone, let me blame myself. If I am to criticise anybody, let me criticise myself for not being up to the mark. So, let me not blame or criticise others.

As Jesus said, "Judge ye not, lest thou shalt be judged!"

And as Bhagawan Baba says: "Seek out your own faults and others' merits! Know how good others are. Find out your own mistakes! Do not criticise."

Paramahamsa said, "Criticism is the worst sin you can ever commit!"

Bhagawan Baba has expressed this in an even simpler way: "When you point at others' mistakes, are you aware that three fingers are directly pointing at you? Therefore, you are three times more wrong!"

Spend Time In Satsang

Swami also wants us to spend time talking about God and working for Him, rather than gossiping and spreading rumours. Life is like a candle burning — the fire may get extinguished at any moment. When the oil is exhausted, the wick will not give light any longer. Life is also like ice that is melting away day-by-day. A moment gone by shall never come back. Life is getting shorter and shorter. Yes!

'Why should I spend time in gossip and useless talk?' I ask myself. 'Can't I hear something Divine, something religious, something spiritual, perhaps a noble talk, or a spiritual discourse, or a *satsang*? If I am not able to appreciate *satsang*, it only means that there is something wrong with me.'

Spiritual topics and spiritual discourses should be of immense interest to every one of us.

Promote Understanding
Rather Than TradItion

The teachings of the *Bible* are applicable to you and me at this moment, right now! Swami's discourses are necessary right now!

Swami said, "There are two faces here: the 'upholders of tradition' and the 'promoters of deeper understanding'." The upholders of tradition want tradition to be continued.

Some apologetically ask, "Mr. Anil Kumar, we are not able to chant the Vedas. What should we do? We don't know Sanskrit. What should we do?"

My regular answer to them is this: "God knows English also! Don't bother to pray in Sanskrit; He knows other languages also."

So, you don't have to struggle to learn Sanskrit. It is good that some know Sanskrit and we compliment them; but, we don't have to be breathless, feeling suffocated or guilty if we don't know Sanskrit. I can talk to Baba and you can talk to Baba. A mother can talk to her child and the child talks to the mother in her own style. The child doesn't need to know Sanskrit in order to talk to the mother!

Yet, the foolish upholders of tradition are the type to uphold tradition for the sake of tradition. For example, some may say, "Pray between 4 o'clock and 5 o'clock." I see! So, the rest of the day, what should we do? Play cards? Pray from 4 to 5 and then, play the rest of the time? Nothing doing! We should not be mere upholders of tradition. Rather, we should be the promoters of understanding and of awareness. That's what Baba says.

Therefore, celebrate the silent night of the arrival of Jesus on Earth, the baby of Bethlehem, Who bore the torch of light and wisdom. He carried the torch of love for the entire humanity.

Jesus And Baba Carry
The Torch Of Wisdom For Humanity

Will Baba succeed in His attempt to spiritualise our lifestyle?

In the epilogue of the second volume of his book *Avatar,* Howard Murphet answered this question in a beautiful way: "Why not?" he asked. "When the infant Jesus, born in a manger in Bethlehem, could carry the torch of light and wisdom for the entire humanity, why shouldn't a baby in Puttaparthi, Prasanthi Nilayam, be able to do the same? Why do you doubt it?"

Therefore, we are fortunate to be alive at this moment. We are doubly fortunate to have been exposed to a message that offers us new heights of understanding about the unity of religions, providing an awareness that is without any contradiction, conflict, disagreement, or difference. It is not a message of anti-thesis; rather, it is a message of synthesis.

Miracle in Puttaparthi

(Special Talk by Prof. Anil Kumar, December 21st, 2011)

Our Faith Should Be Unshakeable

Before Swami left His physical form, He created many miracles all over the world; but, there were very, very few miracles created here in Puttaparthi. When He was here, He did not create miracles within Prasanthi Nilayam. But now, His miracles are taking place here and they are within the walls of the *ashram*! Why?

There may be two reasons for this. First, devotees outside (away from) Prasanthi Nilayam have always known that Baba was with them and they continue to have no doubt about this. Their faith and devotion are deeply rooted and so, they have no need for such special experiences now. They are already strong. They already know that He is with them.

However, maybe in Prasanthi Nilayam, devotees' faith has been shaken by His physical departure, by His leaving the body, by His quitting the form that they took so for granted and with which they were so familiar. Foreign devotees abroad are accustomed to communicating with Swami without the presence of His form, whereas here, we are not. So, perhaps we need these miracles, His miracles, as medicine to restore our faith.

The second reason that Baba may be creating miracles here could be to encourage devotees to continue making the pilgrimage here, to have His *darshan*. Therefore, continue to make the journey here to this holy place. Continue to come here for His *darshan*.

Swami's Samadhi Is The Source Of Divine Energy

Just touch the Samadhi with your forehead and then, tell me what you experience. You need to experience it. The energy is incredible! Experience the Samadhi, experience it for yourself, and you will see! It is a source of pure Divine energy, from Him to you!

The Samadhi is a place that bestows peace on everybody. Baba's Samadhi is a centre that rewards and confers boons on everybody. The Samadhi cures and heals ailments. His Samadhi gives us answers to all our questions and solutions to all our problems. So, Bhagawan's Samadhi is multi-dimensional. Therefore, I am so happy that so many of you from South Africa have come here for the *darshan* of Sai's Samadhi. To be here right now is greater than it was before. So, I congratulate you!

When Bhagawan was still here in His body, we came to Him, because He wanted us to be here. But now, you are here, because you prayed to be here. A devotee, who has prayed to be here, has a far greater experience than one simply invited by God to be here. God is now giving priority to His devotees! Every father hopes that his son will follow him. I am sure that Bhagawan Baba's heart jumps with joy, looking at all of you here in this moment. I pray that Bhagawan bestows His choicest blessings upon each and every one of you!

Bhagawan Speaks From The Samadhi

It was Shirdi Bhagawan, Who said, "From this Samadhi, I answer all of your prayers. Though I am not here in a physical body, I do respond to your prayers." He also promised that whoever surrendered to Him shall have their prayers answered. The same is true at Sathya Sai's Samadhi, today. He waits here to grant us boons, to reward us, and to confer peace upon us. He waits here to encourage, cajole, console, and support us. Bhagawan is very much here!

True Christmas Is The Birth Of Divinity In Us

Christmas does not merely represent the birth of Christ. No. Christmas is also about the birth of Divinity in our hearts. Christmas is not merely a blessing on Christian families. It is a universal celebration! It applies to every individual.

There are many Christians, who have seen Christ in Bhagawan. There are many Christians, who believe He was the Christ, that He was the second coming of the Christ. To conclude, Sai is here, Sai is acting silently. Sai is prompting us silently. Sai, the eternal witness, is guiding us every second in our lives!

Interview For Sai Wisdom

(Interview with Professor Anil Kumar,
Prasanthi Nilayam, December 28th, 2011)

We are grateful for the grace of our beloved Bhagawan Sathya Sai Baba and thank Him for giving us this exclusive interview with Prof. Anil Kumar. And we welcome all of you to visit the website, which publishes his talks: www.saiwisdom.com.

Prof. Anil Kumar, Sai Ram. We welcome you to this question and answer session. Our questions are from all over the world, especially from Italy. We shall begin, inviting your comments to each question asked. May I proceed?

Thank you. Yes.

Q: *Being so close to Him, did Swami ever give you any indication about His departure?*

A: Well, not to my knowledge. He has not given any last message or any indication as such. No. We knew that His health was deteriorating, but He did not comment about it.

Q: *In Italy, there were some talks about different types of Samadhis. Some thought Swami would leave His body by walking into the Chitravathi River. No one expected that Swami would take this medical course! Can you comment on this?*

A: Well, they are simply expressing their imagination, expectations, hallucinations, or idiosyncrasies! There are three meanings to the word '*Samadhi*'. First, *Samadhi* is a place, where the body of a holy saint is laid to rest. The second meaning indicates that He starts functioning from there, just as Shirdi Sai operates from Shirdi. The third meaning is that *samadhi* is a balanced state of mind, the non-dualistic mind; the mind that does not get tossed, baffled, or confused. It is a balanced state of mind that is not reactive to the bumps and jumps of life. That, too, is *samadhi*.

Q: For many devotees, Baba appeared to be very ill. Was there any message in the fact that Swami had such a difficult ending?

A: It may seem difficult to you, but may not have been so for Him. It may look painful to you and to me, but it may not have been painful to Him, because He is beyond the body! When He is beyond the body, no ailment can ever affect Him.

Q: There are a lot of questions about Prema Sai Baba. Now that Sathya Sai Baba has left His physical form, some people believe that He will be born as Prema in eight months, while others talk about eight years. What do you think?

A: How ridiculous we are! We make fools of ourselves! Some people have even gone beyond that. Some have started raising funds for the construction of a temple for Prema Sai, Who has yet to be born! They want to get a temple ready now for an unseen Baba, for Prema Sai, and are raising funds for that purpose.

However, Swami has not given any time frame for Prema Sai. On the other hand, He repeatedly said, "Enjoy the present Sai." The present Sai has as much of a message to convey to you as the coming Sai. So, concentrate on the present, live in the moment. God is here now! He is the existential reality.

Q: Prof. Anil Kumar, what kind of advice would you give to the people, who are mourning, because they could not see Swami for 'a last time' — people, who could not make it to the 2010 pilgrimage and who didn't see Swami just before He left?

A: There are three categories of people, who fit that description. The first set is those, who have never met Swami at all. The second set is those, who had seen Swami, but could not see Him in the year 2010. The third set is those, who were very intimate with Him for decades. So, we have these categories of people, grouped according to their exposure to the Divine. But, I think it is not the duration of exposure that matters. Unlike the workplace, it is not the seniority that counts.

What matters is the intensity of your feeling, the profundity and depth of your love for God, not the number of years you spent in His proximity. Here's a simple example: We have not met Lord Rama. Have you ever met Lord Rama? I don't think so. But, we do love Him and worship Him. We have not met Krishna either, but we worship His picture. We love and worship both Lord Venkateswara and Shirdi Bhagawan, though we have not met them either. So, it is the intensity of the feeling of love, respect, devotion, and adoration of the Lord that counts, not merely the years spent with Him.

Q: Can you give any words of solace for the people, who have never seen Swami, and for those, who have seen Him, but didn't get to see Him at the end?

A: Those, who have seen Him, should live up to His expectations! Even for those, who were with Him for a long time, if they don't live up to His expectations, their time with Him is just meaningless! Divine investment wasted! If those, who have seen Him and met Him for a long time, don't carry the values He stands for, it will not speak well of them. Those, who have come to know of Him later, who never saw Him, but have read His biography or seen His pictures — they are 'fresh stock'. They will begin with new dimensions of experience and new awareness of consciousness — very fresh!

Q: I love your words: 'Divine investment' and 'fresh stock'. They give a lovely descriptive feeling. The Italian community, as well as the world community, wants to know how to cope with this feeling of being 'orphaned'? This is the word I have picked up from many of the questions received. They feel as if they have been orphaned. What words can you share with them?

A: Becoming an orphan only happens at the family level. 'I lost my father' or 'I lost my mother'. But, gradually, one confronts that negative feeling and overcomes it. After a period of time, the orphaned person decides to be a worthy son in the community: "I want to bring a good name to my family and to my parents."

So, similarly, instead of mourning, crying, or feeling that you are an orphan, you can try to live as worthy devotees of Baba, so that the whole society will look at you and say: "Here are the marvelous devotees of Baba! What an impact Baba had on their lives!" That should be the situation.

Q: Thank you for those beautiful words of advice. Let's move on now to philosophy. Can we use your wisdom and your knowledge of philosophy to clarify whether we are in the Kali Yuga or the Golden Age? When will the Golden Age come? Will it come with a bang or calmly? What is your opinion, knowledge, or experience with Swami on this topic?

A: Good question! One thing is sure: We are not going to live, until the time of a total withdrawal of the universe (*pralaya*)! And we will not see the whole planet get drowned! We are not going to live that long, so we can be free from imaginary thoughts of catastrophic or chaotic situations.

The Golden Age you are referring to is not material. The Golden Age is psychological; it is intuitive, temperamental, and behavioral. The Golden Age refers to the attitudes of people. For example, a balanced state of mind is the quality of a person, who belongs to the Golden Age. He need not be a millionaire. A millionaire belongs to the golden age of the material world.

So, the man, who has a balanced state of mind, belongs to the Golden Age of the spiritual world. The material golden age is different from the spiritual one. Swami refers to the spiritual Golden Age.

What are the characteristics of the citizens of the Golden Age? The citizens of the spiritual Golden Age that Swami refers to are detached, non-possessive, egoless, selfless, peaceful, blissful, truthful, righteous, friendly, and loving. They possess the spirit of sacrifice and promote universality, catholicity, and the unity of all religions, while experiencing the Divinity within.

Q: In your opinion, are you seeing this transformation now?

A: Yes! The very fact that Prasanthi Nilayam and Puttaparthi attract devotees from all over the world is enough proof of the current Golden Age. How else can you explain why people from Latin America or South America still come to Prasanthi Nilayam? How do you explain why people from Saudi Arabia, Oman, Muscat, Iran, Iraq — all Muslim countries — come to this place? So, the very fact that Muslims, who are alien to Hinduism, and Christians, who are from a different school of philosophy altogether, could think of being here is a sign of the Golden Age.

Today, young children, who are in *Bal Vikas* (spiritual education for children), and young students, who are in *Seva Dal* (volunteer program), speak of contentment, satisfaction, peace, and love. Even adults take to service activities. It is very strange in this competitive world, where only the sounds of coins seem to matter, to see how Sai devotees care for their neighbours! They give respect to God, they have deep faith in Him, and they love service activities! These are all signs of the Golden Age.

Q: So, there will not be any 'big bang'?

A: No big bang! You can bang, if you so wish, in a big way, but there cannot be a big bang.

Q: Professor, we feel very fortunate to have been in Puttaparthi for the past few days and to hear you speak about Christmas. For the viewers of www.saiwisdom.com, will you share some views on what you think is the true spirit and meaning of Christmas?

A: I do remember giving talks on Christianity. They are available on www.saiwisdom.com. That does not mean that I am going to escape from my responsibility of sharing one or two ideas now! Spirituality is fathomless, like an endless ocean, or infinite like the vast sky, without a beginning or end. So, I can collect one or two gems from my memory and share them with you now.

Christianity, according to Baba, does not centre solely on a person named Jesus Christ. It does not focus solely on Christ. Swami's way of presenting Christ is to talk of Him as a spiritual seeker, or a spiritual aspirant. A spiritual seeker or aspirant starts with a dual state, a feeling that 'God and I are separate'. Then, slowly, he gets to the state of 'qualified non-dualism', where he feels nearness, dearness, and closeness to God. When he totally identifies himself with God, he reaches the non-dualistic state.

So, Christ represents these three steps of consciousness or three levels of awareness — three rungs on the spiritual ladder of self-realisation. It is not Christ, but Christhood that matters. Christhood is an attainment, while Jesus Christ was an individual. Christhood is realisation, whereas Jesus Christ was a person. Christhood is spiritual evolution and such a Christ is one among many, and the best of all.

So, Christhood should be the aim of every religious man. Christhood should be the goal of every meditative or contemplative mind. So, Swami's presentation of Christ reflects a state of evolution, a state of conscious awareness.

With this sort of an idea, Christianity is acceptable to all religions. If you want a Hindu to accept Christ, it is very tough. But, if you tell him that Christ means Christhood (self-realisation), reflecting the values that He lived, it would be easier. So, we have to represent Christ from the values He taught and the values that He lived for. That would be marvellous!

Q:Swami has been very explicit in affirming faith in His devotees. He said that, He is here to make a Muslim a better Muslim, a Christian a better Christian, and a Hindu a better Hindu. There are some questions about this. How can we accept this, knowing that there are conflicting beliefs? For example, Christians believe that the soul reaches a place, where it awaits judgment. Other religions believe in reincarnation. Why do we have these conflicting beliefs? What should we do?

A: Now, there is a trend toward unity in modern philosophy. If you go through some of the books written by Christians, if you listen to some of the sermons of missionaries, or if you just listen to some of the modern philosophers, you will find an underlying unity, although their presentation is different.

They may not say 'rebirth'; they may not say 'reincarnation'. But, all agree on one point: Everything revolves around the three R's: reaction, reflection, and resound. Having done good now, you will have a good life. Having done something bad now, naturally the consequences will be equally bad. Therefore, the principle of reaction, reflection, and resound is accepted by everybody. However, one may or may not call this 'reincarnation'.

So, the presentation of religion today is more universal. You can follow anybody now — anybody! None is as dogmatic today as before. Many are trying to present things in a more acceptable way, an approach that offers a synthesis of religions, a unity of religions. They don't portray religions as having conflicting views or contradictory opinions.

Baba puts it this way: "Don't worry about all these things. What is today? Today is the foundation for tomorrow. What is today? Today is the result of yesterday. Yesterday was the foundation for today and today is the foundation for tomorrow. Yesterday and tomorrow are connected to today, so take care of today. So, the present is not simply the present. It is also the omnipresent, carrying with it all the three periods of time.

Q: On a different subject, some devotees have asked for your opinion on organ transplants. Is there a preferable time, considering the time a soul takes to leave the body? And will it affect re-birth?

A: *Sanathana dharma,* the ancient and eternal philosophy, clearly indicates that you are not the body. You are not the body, you are not the mind, and you are not the intellect. The body is like a water bubble and the mind is like a mad monkey.

Who are you, if you are neither the body, nor the mind? You are consciousness. That consciousness is unpolluted, blemishless, immortal, and nectareous. It is not affected by the body at all. So, organ transplantation has nothing to with consciousness.

Q: We are going to move on now from philosophy to guidance in life, starting with questions about dharma. It is said that, we all have to follow our own dharma and that dharma can be different for different people, depending upon their mission. In modern society, it is difficult to live a dharmic life. Some devotees have cited examples such as this one: We are asked to accept a promotion to a very good job and we know this would be good for our families. Yet, we also know that the higher we go in the corporate level, the more adharmic behaviour we may be exposed to. What is the dharmic thing to do? What do you think?

A: Good! There is a little bit of confusion about this. Career prospects, career advancement, professionalism, expertise are all one thing and are different than values. However, *dharma* depends on, or is related to, values. What you are referring to is the quality of life of a personality. If you have eligibility, if you have the ability, capacity, skill, and talent to tackle situations, either corporate or otherwise, that is your personality, your personal abilities.

Then, there is the other side of it: individuality. Individuality is based on values that we live, while the personality keeps changing. Twenty-five years ago, I was quite presentable and handsome. That was just 25 years ago − that's not much! Even combs used to break, when I combed my hair! And now I don't need a comb at all!

So, personality changes with age. But, the principles for which I stand − my upbringing and community orientation and the educational institutions, where I studied − have all made my individuality value-based. So, this personality and individuality support each other. They are not contradictory.

One can strive to be successful in life, join corporate offices, and earn money. There is nothing wrong with earning money; but, you should have some values. Earn money in a righteous way. Pick-pocketing is not righteous. That is not earning, so it is wrong. When you earn money in a righteous way, it is okay. But, if you earn by putting your values aside, it is not a righteous way. So, you can be an expert, be skilled and talented, and have your own career advance! Why not?

Always listen to your conscience or inner voice. Here are some possible examples: If I want to go to a casino, my conscience tells me, 'No, nothing doing. There is a service activity, go there.' If I want to go to a club for some merry-making or dancing, my conscience tells me, 'No, there is a study circle over there.' If I want to bluff my father, my conscience tells me, 'Don't do it!' If I want to cheat somebody, my conscience would tell me, 'You are cheating yourself, don't do it!' So, we don't need to draw any bottom line, or benchmarks for such things. The conscience tells us to follow the Master, so follow the conscience. This inner guidance will take us in the correct direction.

Q: The scientist will say that conscience is just your higher mental activity. Did you say that conscience is God?

A: The conscience is the Divine prompting, the Divine's reflection. Take a balloon, for example. There is air in it and air all around it. The air in the balloon and the air all around it are the same in quality, right? But, the air in the balloon is limited, while the air around it is unlimited. Similarly, the Divinity all around is consciousness and the Divinity in the individual is conscience.

So, universal Divinity is consciousness and conscience is the Divinity at the level of the individual. Both are of the same quality. If I hold water from the ocean in my palm, the water will have the same taste as the ocean. Similarly, conscience and consciousness are the same. One is at the individual level, while the other is at the universal level.

Q: But, I am not letting you go on the question of dharma. How about adharmic duty? Many countries are engaged in wars and people, who don't believe in wars, are asked to represent their country to fight as soldiers. What should one do in such a situation?

A: A war or a fight on selfish grounds is unethical, immoral, irreligious, and non-spiritual. But, when people fight to defend the whole community, where it involves the prestige of the nation, where it involves the independence and sovereignty of the nation, they are patriots. When I fight for my job or for an increase in my salary, it is not patriotism; it is greed. So, we should differentiate between interests that are good in the long run and selfish interests of the moment.

Q: Many countries, especially the European countries, are going through an economic crisis. Many devotees feel this has affected their spiritual upliftment. Can you tell them how to deal with this difficult time?

A: Actually, in the more affluent societies, we find the maximum violence, Himalayan selfishness, and infinite ego! Where money accumulates, evil collects. When a person has just enough money, or when a person lives hand-to-mouth, he is more likely to cultivate some values, some consideration for others, and willingness to sacrifice. Middle-class families cultivate sacrifice, friendliness, concern, and consideration. All such values develop there.

When we circumambulate Goddess Lakshmi, we pray: "Oh Goddess, please bless me with some money, so that I will have enough for myself and to sacrifice for others." We want to do some charity to help others. So, Lakshmi manages a 'joint property'. You may have money in your bank account, but all the money is not yours. There are people, who have contributed to it.

Take this house, for example: Is it your house? It may be in your name, but masons built it, carpenters made it, and electricians completed the fittings. So, it is a collective effort, though you may be the owner, isn't it? Similarly, we should understand that everything is the result of a collective effort. Nothing is done by any one individual.

Q: Many devotees from different countries are concerned about the youth. They are concerned that it is difficult to motivate the youth. Do you have any advice for them?

A: Who are the people, who are most valued in India, today? They are people like Mahatma Gandhi, who was a man of sacrifice. He gave up everything, as did Buddha and Christ. So, who is valued in the long run? Certainly not the rich people.

Society needs to have good values, human values, such as *sathya, dharma, santhi, prema,* and *ahimsa* (truth, right conduct, peace, love, and non-violence). When these attributes are respected, then naturally youngsters will get inspired.

So, parents, teachers, and society should understand that every child is God's gift. A child today may become a leader tomorrow. He can become a nation-builder, a national emancipator! He can bring a good name to the family and to the nation! That should be our concept.

Instead, too often, we neglect our children. It is irresponsible to think that the teacher will take care of them at school, or some nanny will take care of them at home, or that they will have some other children in the neighborhood to play with, while we make little or no time for them. When you don't have time for your children, it is better not to have children. Tomorrow, the child may ask, "Daddy, you don't have time for me? What have you been doing instead?" Then, how will you answer?

Therefore, parents have got to be more responsible. When I talk like this, don't think that I am an ideal parent. Certainly not! I was a most irresponsible parent! I had no time to think of my children, as I was busy in the service activities of Sri Sathya Sai Seva Organisation. Swami played my role at home, always guiding them, so they all had a professional education. They have all studied and come up very well on their own, under the Divine guidance of Baba. But, as a parent, I cannot claim anything for their success. No! As I did Baba's work, He did my work. That's all.

Q: As we conclude this lovely interview, I would like you to tell the devotees and the thousands, who will watch this video on saiwisdom.com, about one special experience that you have had with Swami — maybe something beautiful that will stay with you forever.

A: The special experience that I can share is that Swami's presence is felt more now, than ever before! People are thinking of Him more than ever before. They used to think of Baba occasionally, but now they are thinking of Him all the time! So, concentration and focused attention have increased. See how things are happening here! Festivals are taking place as usual, institutions are running as usual. All festivals are attended by a maximum number of devotees. This is all proof that His Divinity guides, monitors, shapes, and decides the destiny of the organisation.

Thank you very much Professor, from the devotees in Puttaparthi and the world over, for this lovely time and flowing wisdom. We have been very blessed.

Thank you.

www.ingramcontent.com/pod-product-compliance
Lightning Source LLC
Chambersburg PA
CBHW022002090426

4274 1CB00007B/853